THE
TRANSFORMATIONAL
LEADER

THE
TRANSFORMATIONAL
LEADER

NOEL M. TICHY

MARY ANNE DEVANNA

JOHN WILEY & SONS

New York · Chichester · Brisbane · Toronto · Singapore

We dedicate this book to our children

*Michelle, Nicole and Danielle Tichy and
Eva Marie, Nicole and Joseph Devanna*

*with the hope that the world they inherit
will be filled with opportunity,
challenge, and the joy of achievement.*

Library of Congress Cataloging in Publication Data:

Tichy, Noel M.
   The transformational leader.

   Bibliography: p.
   Includes index.
   1. Organizational change.   2. Leadership.
I. Devanna, Mary Anne.   II. Title.
HD58.8.T52   1986   658.4'092   86-4043
ISBN 0-471-82259-0
ISBN 0-471-62334-2 (pbk)

Printed in the United States of America

90 91 10 9 8 7 6 5 4 3 2 1

PREFACE UPDATE

When *The Transformational Leader* was published in 1986, we talked about the accelerating pace of change. But in looking back on the past four years, we admit that change took place far more rapidly than even we would have predicted.

Looking first at the American marketplace, we find that 40 percent of the companies that appeared on the *Fortune 500* list a decade ago are no longer there! Mergers and acquisitions, leveraged buyouts, and other financial sleights of hand resulted in a massive redistribution of wealth but did little to produce world class competitive organizations.

If we turn our attention to the global arena, the changes are even more dramatic. No American money center bank is still ranked among the top ten in the world, and among the largest 1000 companies in the world one-third are American and one-third are Japanese, with the balance spread across the rest of the world.

The competitive battles have been fierce. Companies like Canon, Honda, and Kamatsu—ignored in competitive analyses conducted by industry leaders Xerox, General Motors, and Caterpillar as recently as 20 years ago because they lacked the technology and resources to be taken seriously—now set the standards for innovation, productivity, and quality in the marketplace. Looking at these companies, we realize that many of them are Japanese, but the notion that their country of origin was the basis of their success has been largely ignored by serious students of organizations.

Their success more likely lies in their ability to exploit the weaknesses of scale. They discovered the Achilles heel of companies blessed with large amounts of capital and well-entrenched positions in major markets. These weaknesses included

- an indifference to customer needs born of a lack of serious competition
- organizational structures and processes that made it difficult to react swiftly to nontraditional competitive threats
- a set of beliefs about organizational trade-offs that served to blind them to the possibilities of continuous improvement

The new competitors discovered a new source of competitive advantage—the managerial process. They structured themselves to seize the advantage through speed by reducing cycle times, through knowledge creation by learning from both success and failure, and by erasing the hierarchical and functional impediments to information flows. Consequently they were able to respond to customers' requirements more quickly through the introduction of new products, continual improvements in existing products, and greater attention to service. For established, traditionally organized and managed firms, these requirements are difficult to meet without fundamental changes in the design and management of the organization, and that has proved to be a truly daunting task.

More than ever the key to global competitiveness will be the widespread capability of institutions around the world to continously transform. The transformational leadership capabilities of creatively destroying and remaking institutions are of greater import in the 1990s than when we first tackled the topic in the 1980s. Our own thinking has developed since we first considered the phenomenon.

On the one hand, we see a greater applicability of our three-act transformational leader framework at the macro level as we see the challenges of Mikhail Gorbachev attempting to transform the USSR, Salinas in Mexico, Bhutto in Pakistan, the Solidarity-lead government in Poland, and the need for a U.S. transformation. The leadership challenges are clear; whether we have the global macro transformational leaders is a serious question.

On the other hand, we see a much clearer need for transformational leadership at all levels of the organization. Since writing the book, we have worked with thousands of middle managers using the framework. It helps them. It works as guide and framework for leadership throughout an organization. At GE, it has been used to help thousands of new college hires understand the macro GE transformation being led by Chairman Jack Welch, as well as to understand their immediate workplace and their own personal challenges.

If we examine the companies and the leaders we identified four years ago, we see that the struggle for organizational transformation has had mixed results in the group. It has taken a significant toll among the protagonists we identified. Jeffrey Campbell's hopes of revitalizing Burger King ended when Grand Metropolitan succeeded in acquiring Pillsbury, Burger King's parent; Fred Hammer's plans for Meritor were dashed on the rocks of inaccurate interest rate forecasts.

Two leaders in computer company turnarounds, Jim Renier at Honeywell and Michael Blumenthal, also face deteriorating competitive conditions. In 1986 Blumenthal succeeded in pooling the resources of Burroughs Corporation and Sperry to form the world's third largest computer maker and financial analysts, and industry experts were impressed with the progress he made, increasing the company's size to $10 billion by 1989 and continuing to move Unisys from a mainframe company to a UNIX firm. By year-end, however, Unisys was struggling once again as execution of an applauded strategy continued to elude Blumenthal.

Honeywell has yet to enjoy the respite that Blumenthal earned for Unisys, and the last four years find Renier, who acquired the Sperry aerospace business from Unisys Corporation in late 1986, attempting to stem Honeywell's continued performance problems. In 1988 Honeywell sold all but 20 percent of its computer operations with the result that its aerospace business now accounts for almost half of its sales. This is not good news as defense contractors face the reality of reduced budgets for military hardware.

Automakers face the specter of significant overcapacity on a worldwide basis, and American carmakers, lagging in product innovation, quality, and productivity, enter the 1990s without any marked gains on foreign competitors. Indeed, with Iacocca's approaching retirement, Chrysler finds itself in the unenviable position of slipping behind Honda in domestic auto sales and wondering if the long-awaited replacement of the K-car platform in 1992 will come too late to help eroding market share.

Robert Stempel became the 17th president of General Motors in 1987, and it is expected he will succeed Roger Smith when Smith retires as chairman. Although General Motors's position is less perilous than Chrysler's, the last four years have not been easy for GM. Attempts to gain needed concessions from labor and to forge new, cooperative working relationships between management and organized labor have not been totally successful. Moreover, GM's massive investment in automation has not resulted in hoped for productivity gains.

Dave Whitwam succeeded Jack Sparks as president and chief executive officer of Whirlpool Corporation. While Sparks held the position, Whirlpool grew from $2.3 billion in net sales to over $4 billion and net earnings increased almost 50 percent. Sparks initiated a $1 billion capital expenditure program with the hope of increasing volume-enhancing efficiency. Although the company incurred a short-term penalty, Sparks believed these investments were critical to Whirlpool's future growth. In 1988 Whirlpool entered into a strategic alliance with Dutch giant Philips N. V. that created the world's largest major appliance business. Sparks's legacy has been to successfully position Whirlpool to take advantage of markets outside the United States.

John Harvey-Jones stepped down from the chairmanship at ICI in 1987. His legacy was also impressive. He brought about changes that affected the company's size, its product base, and its markets. To reinforce its global strategy, he added a German, a Japanese, and an American to ICI's board while cutting the size of the board from 12 to 9. His successor, Denys Henderson, will face substantial challenges as will most of the chemical industry from the powerful environmental lobbies in Europe and those emerging in other industrialized countries as well.

Don MacKinnon retired from Ciba Geigy and the Swiss giant continues to prosper, but like ICI its chemical businesses face increasing pressure from environmental groups in Europe and in the United States. The role of the North American subsidiary will grow in importance, however, as CIBA wrestles with the consequences of being housed in a country that has chosen to go it alone as Europe moves toward 1992.

Mary Ann Lawlor is back in the thick of things at Drake Business Schools. Personal decisions by senior operating personnel find her spending more rather than less time directing Drake's future, which looks relatively bright in an industry beset by problems such as reduced government spending in areas like education. And although she expressed a desire to move on to other challenges, she correctly predicted that if she had to lead the organization through another renewal, she felt up to the challenge. The major issue she faces is identifying the next generation of Drake leadership willing to take responsibility for an organization whose survival depends totally on the quality of its people and their commitment to a population in need of skills to manage their future.

Our final protagonist, Jack Welch, announced his leadership agenda for the 1990s and it is corporatewide cultural change. Having emerged from the decade of the 1980s with a portfolio of stronger businesses, GE stands as a model of successful restructuring. While many CEOs would be content with this legacy, Welch continues the drive to become more competitive. He is concerned with GE's productivity record and believes the answer lies in eliminating bureaucracy and developing a workforce who understand that their own dreams and ambitions can be fulfilled in the GE he is trying to build.

The 1990s promise to be in many ways a more interesting decade than the 1980s for those who prefer to watch competitive battles fought by managers heavily invested in securing the future of their businesses than those fought by dealmakers whose interest and investment in an organization frequently lasts for fewer than six months and who are never requried to visit a factory or have a conversation with an employee.

If we look beyond the scope of the companies we considered in 1986, we find some interesting examples of companies that have made a recovery and that bear watching to see if they can sustain a transformation over time. These include U.S. examples like Motorola and Xerox as well as European giants like Siemens and ASEA & Brown Boveri.

Their recovery and drive for excellence show their recognition of the need for total employee involvement and the role that training and development play in achieving results that a decade ago would have been considered unreasonable. For example, Motorola refused to lay off large numbers of employees and close U.S. plants. Instead, starting in 1982 their chairman said that 1.5 percent of every manager's budget must go to training. In 1989 they spent $50 million on training everyone from Robert Galvin down to the factory floor. Almost half of that training focused on skills needed to improve quality. Galvin's goal is to make all Motorola departments—not just those involved in manufacturing—capable of achieving

Six Sigma quality by 1992. This means that they expect to have no more than 3.4 defects per million parts or transactions!

The focus on quality has gone hand in hand with an effort to speed products to the marketplace. It used to take Motorola three to five years to bring a new electronic product to market. It now takes 18 months. Engineering excellence has enabled Motorola to manufacture cellular phones with 70 percent fewer parts, and this has reduced assembly time to 4 hours from 40.

Using similar programs, Xerox, which had seen its share of the small copier market shrink to 8 percent, has more than doubled its market share and now commands a 17 percent share.

These organizations see their accomplishments and current goals not as final destinations but as milestones in a process of continuous improvement. They present a formidable challenge to competitors whose goal is to catch up, because they represent a moving target determined to push the frontiers of excellence in both the product and process arenas.

In reflecting on the last four years, we see the pace of change accelerating at a faster rate than we predicted; as a consequence the window of opportunity that represents the organization's ability not simply to survive but also to prosper continues to narrow. Organizational growth increasingly depends on taking market share from competitors in markets that are not growing instead of maintaining share in an expanding market. This forces companies to learn to compete instead of looking for pristine marketplaces not yet bloodied by the competitive struggle for excellence. And increasingly, excellence is the condition not just for dominance but for survival.

In 1986 we talked about companies whose competitive environment had changed gradually enough to make them unaware of the need to change. We used the metaphor of the boiled frog to describe these victims of increased competition. Today the water heats up more rapidly, and if the frog is not always prepared to jump it may still become a casualty.

Many people also took an unintended message from the book. They believed that organizational transformations simply require a transformational leader at the top. We did not believe this in 1986, and our belief in the importance of gaining commitment from all levels of the organization to continuous improvement remains strong.

Personally, we continue to grapple with understanding the dynamics of successful transformations and the process and structural rquirements for self-renewal in large, complex organizations. The last four years have been both enlightening and humbling. We have a much better understanding of what organizations must be if they wish to be competitive, and we can cite examples of organizations that are able to achieve these conditions at least temporarily.

The transformational leaders of the 1990s are the ones who will determine the quality of life inside and outside of the workplace in the 21st century. We continue to admire those with the strength and will to take on these challenges. We continue our journey to understand the phenomenon and hopefully to add to our collective abilities to productively lead continuous transformations.

NOEL M. TICHY
MARY ANNE DEVANNA

PREFACE

This book is about corporate leadership, America's scarcest natural resource. At a time when our economy, as well as that of the entire industrialized world, is in the midst of major upheaval and transformation, a new type of leadership at the middle and senior levels of our corporations is desperately needed. It's now a well-known story that the "emperor's clothes" from the end of World War II until the first shocks of the Organization of Petroleum Exporting Countries were provided by rapidly growing domestic markets and a less than tough network of foreign competitors. Since that time the American position in the world economic structure has changed. From undisputed leadership we have at best become *primus inter pares*. Many are concerned that we may fall further behind. The Japanese have certainly led the way in product excellence and the South Koreans and other former third world nations are trying hard. A resurgent Western Europe is gaining fast.

This fall from supremacy has been painful. Many people are clearly angry and looking for scapegoats. The Japanese have been a frequent target. Theodore S. White, writing in a recent issue of *The New York Times Magazine*, warned them:

The superlative execution of their trade tactics may provide an incalculable reaction, as the Japanese might well remember of the course that ran from Pearl Harbor to the deck of the U.S.S. Missouri in Tokyo Bay just 40 years ago.

Our government may respond to building pressure from special interest groups to address the real or perceived advantages of the Japanese and other nations in international markets. But any action along these lines will be a short-term solution to a problem that has been germinating for many years: the increasing inability of many companies and industries to be effective competitors in international markets. Anger and putting the blame on others for our problems will, in the long run, only hasten our decline.

The time has come to talk about how corporations, our wealth-producing institutions, can develop the type of leadership with the courage and imagination to change our corporate lifestyles. What's needed, in historian James MacGregor Burns's terms, is not the old style transactional leadership but a new *transformational* leadership. Transactional leaders were fine for the earlier era of expanding markets and nonexistent competition. In return for compliance they issued rewards. For all intents and purposes these managers changed little. They managed what they found and left things pretty much as they found them when they moved on.

Transformational leadership is about change, innovation, and entrepreneurship. We agree with Peter Drucker that these are not the provinces of lonely, half-mad individuals with flashes of genius. Rather, this brand of leadership is a behavioral process capable of being learned and managed. It's a leadership process that is systematic, consisting of purposeful and organized search for changes, systematic analysis, and the capacity to move resources from areas of lesser to greater productivity. This strategic transformation of organizations is not something that occurs solely through the idiosyncratic behavior of charismatic geniuses. It is a discipline with a set of predictable steps. Transforming an organization to make it strategically competitive is a complex task. However, the evidence we've accumulated and present in this book shows that transformation can be thought about and acted on within a framework that's easy to understand. We see corporate transformation as a drama that can be thought about in terms of a three act play:

Act I: Revitalization—Recognizing the need for change

Act II: Creating a new vision

Act III: Institutionalizing change

Within the context of our framework, we use examples of real leaders involved in the tough, grueling, gut-wrenching challenge of trying to transform companies, save employee jobs, and strengthen the fabric of society. Many of the people we profile are in a race against time and it's not entirely clear if all will be successful. Whatever the outcome, it's clear that the old style of leadership was inappropriate for the situations in which they found their companies. The ultimate purpose of this book is not for other managers to imitate the actions taken by the people in this book. Rather, it's to spread a new way of thinking about corporate transformation, to make *true* leadership an everyday way of acting rather than a talent limited to a few select individuals. Transformation can be accomplished and the new leadership style can be learned. Rather than a scarce resource we hope that it will soon be found in abundance.

Our thinking was affected by the earlier work of Abraham Zaleznik, who contrasted leaders and managers in a 1977 *Harvard Business Review* article. Managers were characterized as individuals who maintain the balance of operations in an organization, relate to others according to their role, are detached, impersonal, seek solutions acceptable as a compromise among conflicting values, and identify totally with the organization. The leaders on the other hand were characterized as individuals out to create new approaches and imagine new areas to explore; they relate to people in more intuitive and empathetic ways, seek risk where opportunity and reward are high, and project ideas into images to excite people.

An encouraging sign in the United States is the growing intellectual and executive interest in the whole topic of leadership. We are happy to join our colleagues who are trying to map out this important terrain. The number of thoughtful treatises on the topic is increasing. They include Levinson and Rosenthal's *CEO;* Bass's *Leadership and Performance Beyond Expectations;* and Bennis and Nanus's *Leaders.* These books as well as the popularity of Iacocca's autobiography reveal a yearning to understand the phenomenon of leadership.

Michael Maccoby's book *The Leaders* specifically shifted our attention to the important bridge between Burns's work on transforming leadership and industrial settings. Maccoby, who made the "Gamesman" popular in the 1970s, argued in the 1980s:

> The gamesman's daring, the willingness to innovate and take risks are still needed. Companies that rely on conservative company men in finance to run technically based organizations lose the competitive edge. But unless their [the gamesmen's] negative traits are transformed or controlled even gifted gamesmen become liabilities as leaders in a new economic reality, a period of limited resources cutbacks, when the team can no longer always be controlled by promises of more, and one person's gain may be another's loss. Leadership with values of caring and trust that no one will be penalized for cooperation and that sacrifice as well as rewards will be equitable.

Even though most of what is written about transformational leadership focuses at the top of the organization, we feel that the challenge is for transformational leadership at all levels in an organization. Rosabeth Kanter's *Change Masters* focused our attention on such leaders in the middle of the organization. She provided new insights into the role of middle level leaders in transforming organizations.

Finally, we want this book to be a challenge to our academic colleagues interested in leadership and change. We have taken positions in this book that are really hypotheses. We do not have a large systematic sample that we have followed over a long period of time with data from multiple sources; instead we have a small number of clinical cases based on individual interviews with limited data from others in their organizations. Our hypotheses therefore need to be tested empirically, they need to be tightened and strengthened conceptually or challenged and discarded. Our belief that it is time for action with reflection has led us to be more prescriptive than strict science would justify. We hope you will join the growing number of academics and practitioners who are struggling for solutions to difficult problems.

NOEL M. TICHY
MARY ANNE DEVANNA

CONTENTS

THE
TRANSFORMATIONAL
LEADER

PROLOGUE

THE THEMES, THE PROTAGONISTS, THE TRANSFORMATIONAL DRAMA

1

Either senior managers don't know what is going on or they don't want to tell us. Whenever someone asks a question, the response is, we don't know yet. If they don't know, then what the hell are they doing disrupting everyone's life?

The uncertainty surrounding job performance and job security is unnerving, and in my opinion, no one gives a damn.

I do not think that we are being told what we need to know to plan our lives and our future.

MIDDLE MANAGERS IN
ORGANIZATIONS UNDERGOING CHANGE

Competitive pressures are forcing companies to reassess the explicit and implicit employment contracts they have struck with employees over the last three decades. The opinions and feelings voiced by middle managers and others caught up in organizational change are part of a growing chorus of anger, confusion and dismay. The change they are being asked to make is not marginal; it is fundamental. It demands the commitment of the many not the few. Its nature is revolutionary not evolutionary. It cries out for leaders, not managers, to effect the transformations required by most organizations.

And across the industrial landscape, we are seeing the emergence of a new breed of leader to meet this challenge—the transformational leader. These people take on the responsibility for revitalizing an organization. They define the need for change, create new visions, mobilize commitment to those visions, and ultimately transform an organization.

Transforming an organization is a human drama that involves both joys and sorrows. Winning—beating the competition—is exhilarating, but it's painful to lay off workers, sell off businesses, and disrupt traditions. These phenomena are often part of a renewal, for what worked in the past may have become the cause of failure in the present.

Transforming an organization also requires new vision, new frames for thinking about strategy, structure, and people. While some entrepreneurs can start with a clean slate, transformational leaders must begin with what is already in place. They are like architects who must redesign outmoded factories for a new use.

The traditional managerial skills, such as financial acumen, manufacturing expertise, and marketing prowess, are important ingredients in most organizational success stories but not sufficient for organizational transformation. We focus on the most critical element—leadership—as organizations are challenged by an increasingly competitive environment. Systems can be designed to create operating efficiency, but it is leadership that enables an organization to maintain a dominant position in its industry. Organizations must be revitalized because continued dominance requires adaptation to changing market conditions. This need for transformation is not limited to smokestack America. It includes many of the relatively new high-tech companies in Silicon Valley and along Route 128.

The middle managers we quoted at the beginning of this chapter were caught up in the maelstrom of change. From a psychological viewpoint, their feelings are predictable. The human desire to balance the search for variety and adventure with the need for constancy and security has been documented by philosophers and poets alike. To the extent that change involves uncertainty, most people have difficulty facing it. *Hamlet,* one of the most compelling dramas written in the English language, centers on his fatal flaw—a reluctance to act.

As organizations try to change, they must learn to deal fairly with the anxieties and criticisms of both managers and employees who will have to adapt to change. Ironically, still healthy organizations sometimes encounter greater resistance to change than organizations in the midst of crisis. For example, seeing the prospect of bankruptcy made change an immediate and acceptable priority at Chrysler.

THE TRANSFORMATIONAL THEMES

Transformational dramas develop around three themes. As we watch organizations struggle with the need to change, the developmental sequence bears remarkable similarity to a three act play. We've chosen to use this theatrical metaphor throughout the book, since it provides an easy way to remember and use the framework for understanding a complex phenomenon.

Act 1. *Recognizing the Need for Revitalization.* The first act of the drama centers on the challenges the leader encounters when he or she attempts to alert the organization to growing threats from the environment.

Act 2. *Creating a New Vision.* The second act of the drama involves the leader's struggle to focus the organization's attention on a vision of the future that is exciting and positive.

Act 3. *Institutionalizing Change.* In the third and final act of the drama the leader seeks to institutionalize the transformation so that it will survive his or her tenure in a given position.

THE PROTAGONISTS AND THEIR CHALLENGES

Drama must, of course, have protagonists, and as you might guess our protagonists are the transformational leaders. And just as the program you receive when you attend a play lists the *dramatis personae,* we will do the same. Our protagonists are chosen from dramas that we have had the opportunity to observe. Some have received a great deal of attention while others have played to smaller houses. Most were senior level managers when their plays begin, but the lessons to be learned are applicable and useful for middle managers as well as policy makers. Indeed, we have selected these transformational leaders because they have exhibited transformational leadership at different levels of the organization and throughout much of their careers.

Our protagonists are not part of a representative sample of business leaders. Our academic colleagues hopefully will help us carry out expanded research to determine how generalizable our findings are. The leaders in this book are individuals that we had personal knowledge of who fit the following criteria: they were involved in a major overhaul or transformation of an existing organization; they were self-acknowledged change agents who defined themselves and their criteria for success in terms of fundamental change of their organizations; and their organizations were accessible to us to conduct interviews and assemble case material. With the exception of Lee Iacocca, we conducted in-depth interviews of several hours to a full day duration with each of our protagonists. In the case of Iacocca we relied on secondary sources and people who know him, some still at Ford and others at Chrysler. The complete story of these protagonists and their organizational transformations requires both longitudinal study and more in-depth data from within their organizations. It will take several years to amass these data and while we share our observations and insights now, we will continue to track these transformational dramas.

Since we draw heavily on the interviews we conducted with these transformational leaders, the following summaries of their organizations' plight and change agenda will provide a context for their remarks.

In introducing our protagonists we also look ahead. We do not know whether they will ultimately win; thus we want readers to be aware of the challenges they still face as we examine their leadership actions. These dramas will continue right into the 1990s before we can judge the degree of their success.

MICHAEL BLUMENTHAL, BURROUGHS CORPORATION, DETROIT, MICHIGAN

After serving as Secretary of the Treasury during the Carter Administration, Blumenthal had to evaluate his options. As the former CEO of Bendix, he felt he was qualified to run a large company. He also realized that healthy companies rarely look to the outside when they pick a new CEO. The probability that he would be offered such a position was slim. So when Burroughs approached him he considered himself lucky, since the company had an excellent record. He describes his response:

> I must confess that I did not do my homework in sufficient detail to be able to sense any kind of problem. Burroughs had an excel-

lent reputation. It hadn't had a down quarter in 11 years. It had the reputation of having some kind of secret formula in the computer business that made it as successful as IBM—which it had been.

Not until he had been at Burroughs for a couple of months did he realize that he was faced with a serious need for revitalization. He could see that old problems were about to produce the first red ink on the company's books.

Blumenthal accepted the implications and is now in the second act of the transformational drama, creating a new vision for Burroughs and mobilizing commitment to it.

We no longer have a philosophy of one product, one plant. We no longer look for volume for the sake of volume; we look for return on investment. We no longer look for accounting profits, we look for cash. We don't worry about getting shipments out by the end of the quarter if we are not sure they are 100 percent OK. To hell with the end of the quarter! We'll lose more business six months from now if we ship out lousy stuff. In the *new* Burroughs we take pride and only ship out what works.

Blumenthal's Remaining Challenges

By early 1986 Blumenthal had increased Burroughs's sales from $3.6 billion to $4.9 billion, restructured management, pared operations, consolidated engineering, opened up new markets in China, and stayed ahead of many of the competitors. The tough decisions include initiating a series of layoffs in mid-1985, delaying the groundbreaking for the $40 million expansion of a corporate headquarters for a year, and trouble-shooting the technological problems Burroughs ran into with the Memorex disk drive.

In the summer of 1985, Blumenthal commented on the long-term challenges Burroughs faces:

I would be very surprised if, in the course of the next five years, we don't have at least one recession, or one period of significant

> slowdown in the computer market . . . you can't always expect things to be going up. That's not the history of our economy . . . .

He views the challenges of the next five years in terms of the continued paradox of consolidating operations while simultaneously managing expansion. He stated:

> I predict over the next five years we will make other acquisitions. We will look for companies that can help us expand our core business. It could be in software. It could be a line of specific business applications . . . . It could be in telecommunications.

Blumenthal made this statement after a failed attempt to take over Sperry Corporation. He was able to take time out from the race and pause, reflect, and put corporate life in perspective when he stated:

> In an industry in which companies come and go at dizzying speed and there are shooting stars that are here today and gone tomorrow, you could say that Burroughs has stood the test of time. I am very proud that I have a chance to play this kind of role in a company that is this well established . . . to be 100 years old, there aren't that many around.

J. JEFFREY CAMPBELL, BURGER KING, MIAMI, FLORIDA

Campbell joined Burger King in 1971 as an advertising manager. He spent time in marketing and operations and three years running the New York region where he had responsibility for real estate, marketing, construction, operations, franchising, and personnel. In 1981, Burger King was having problems and Campbell was asked to come to corporate headquarters as marketing vice president. Ten months later he became President of Burger King U.S.A. Eleven months later he was asked to address himself to a deteriorating situation in Europe and Canada by assuming the responsibilities for Burger King Worldwide.

And when the chairman quit two months later he was given that job as well.

In fact, Pillsbury, Burger King's parent company, had taken a hard look at the acquisition it made in 1967 for less than $20 million. Burger King had provided a great deal of growth, but it was a low return business in the Pillsbury portfolio. Comparisons with other fast food businesses like McDonald's and Wendy's on sales, profits, and relationships with franchisees showed Burger King's performance was below the competition.

When he became president of Burger King U.S.A., Campbell decided that he was not out simply to

> have a good year, make more money, and meet the plan. These traditional measuring sticks had encouraged us to make short-term decisions. We were not going to have them as our ultimate goals. We were going to try to do those things, but basically we were trying to turn the pyramid upside down in the industry and improve ourselves dramatically . . . and . . . transform what Burger King was as a corporation and what it represented in the Pillsbury portfolio.

In his first two years, Campbell dramatically changed Burger King's relative value to Pillsbury by increasing profits 76 percent. Despite significant successes, Campbell feels the transformation of Burger King has a way to go both in improving its relative position in the marketplace and in institutionalizing change within the organization.

Campbell's Future Challenges

Campbell must keep his people emotionally turned on after a period in which they have been pushed very hard. It will be difficult to find the necessary psychological reserves for the next act. Burger King faces new strategic challenges over the next couple of years as Campbell leads the way in a planned diversification of the portfolio into related food businesses.

ALEX CUNNINGHAM, LLOYD REUSS, AND ROBERT STEMPEL, GENERAL MOTORS, DETROIT, MICHIGAN

In January 1984 General Motors announced the largest reorganization since the days of Alfred Sloan. It would affect over 360,000 jobs. GM set up two new car groups, Buick-Olds-Cadillac (B-O-C) and Chevrolet-Pontiac-Canada (C-P-C), and headed up each group with a group executive. This reorganization was a major move intended to get GM closer to the marketplace by decentralizing operations which had become overly bureaucratized and unresponsive to changing consumer demands. General Motors made the move after more than a year of intensive planning.

To run General Motors North American Auto Operation, GM created a transformational team headed by Alex Cunningham, executive vice president, with Bob Stempel and Lloyd Reuss each in charge of one car group. Each member developed his own leadership agenda, but all three are tied together to change the way GM deals with automobile manufacturing, marketing, and sales. Since Stempel and Reuss are major contenders for the GM presidency, there is a mix of cooperative and competitive forces within the team.

Cunningham, Stempel, and Reuss have already redistributed the 75,000 employees of the Fisher Body Division, 90,000 employees from General Motors Assembly Division, and 3500 from the Guide Division across the two car groups. To understand the enormity of this change one must realize that Fisher Body employees strongly tended to identify with Fisher Body first and GM second. The team has instilled a new commitment to GM by means of participative management and market-driven, quick-response decisions. They have had to struggle against years of bureaucratic decisions embedded in a Detroit auto-fortress mentality.

Cunningham's Reuss's, and Stempel's Future Challenges

In February, 1986, General Motors announced that Alex Cunningham would retire at the end of a medical leave he took in the fall of 1985. Stempel became Executive Vice President of the Truck and Bus and Overseas Groups. Reuss became Executive Vice President of the North American Car Groups. Both Stempel and Reuss are now members of The Board of Directors and The Executive Committee.

General Motors is about to face the real test of battle. With the reorganization in its fourth year, the EDS and Hughes acquisitions in place, the GM/Toyota California plant in operation, and the Saturn project underway, the bold stage setting is done. Now expectations have been raised both internally and in the world outside of GM that the bottom line should begin to reflect the success of the strategy. The 1985 results were not as good as the 1984 results. This raised some serious questions.

While the stage was being set, some disquieting issues surfaced. The production cost differential between United States and Japanese automobile manufacturers rose from approximately $2000 in the early 1980s to nearly $2500 by 1985. GM lost several points of market share during this period. The innovative new products are not yet in the marketplace. Consolidation of professional and managerial staff is still required to create the lean and agile organization needed for global competition. Our GM protagonists probably will face an industry-wide cyclical downturn in the next year or two. This will be the true test of the ability to survive tough competitive conditions.

FREDERICK HAMMER, CHASE MANHATTAN BANK, NEW YORK, NEW YORK

In the mid-1970s, Chase Manhattan Bank hit rocky shoals. It was plagued by poor decisions that resulted in an accumulation of bad loans. Criticism escalated to the point where there was talk of asking David Rockefeller, Chase's chairman, to resign. In response Rockefeller made a number of changes in key personnel. He brought Alan Lafley, a former GE executive, into Chase as executive vice president for human resources. Lafley's job was to help Rockefeller and Willard Butcher, the president, restructure the bank leadership. After a careful audit of personnel, Lafley convinced Rockefeller and Butcher to break with tradition and look outside the bank for talent.

They brought in Fred Hammer to head up and revitalize retail operations. Hammer, a Carnegie Mellon Ph.D. in mathematical economics, is charismatic and outspoken. Following the deregulation of the financial services industry, he dramatically reshaped consumer banking at Chase. He recently accepted another transformational assignment when he became chairman of Meritor, formerly Philadelphia Society for Savings.

Chase's Future Challenges Without Fred Hammer

The Chase consumer banking strategy set by Hammer is being tested in the marketplace. Since he is no longer there, we will not know whether the implementation phase would have followed the same script if he had stayed. Hammer's area of responsibility was divided into two businesses when he left Chase—the branches and acquired savings and loan will now be managed by the national banking sector while the nondeposit businesses, such as mortgages and credit cards, remain in the consumer sector. Both businesses continued to flourish through 1985.

Hammer's Future Challenges

In his new job, Hammer has assumed responsibility for a transformation begun by Todd Cooke, the former chairman. Cooke turned the biggest savings bank in the United States into a publicly held company with an aggressive strategy to succeed in the national retail financial services arena. Under Cooke a number of major acquisitions took place that will provide the building blocks for Hammer's new transformational challenge: to make Meritor a major player in the national retail service arena.

JOHN HARVEY-JONES, IMPERIAL CHEMICAL INDUSTRIES, LONDON, ENGLAND

The only European transformational leader in our cast is John Harvey-Jones, chairman of ICI, a $15 billion a year chemical giant. Harvey-Jones is the only chairman of a major corporation that we know of to have been elected by his peers. (At ICI, the internal board of directors elects a chairman from its membership for a five year term, with mandatory retirement at the end of the term.)

Harvey-Jones is distinctive. He wears bright ties, appears on British talk shows, is quick with his wit, and claims that laughter has become an important part of directors' meetings. He is, however, deadly serious about transforming ICI. He describes his election:

> I could have gotten odds of 8 to 1 against my election. The odds were so long, nobody even mentioned them to me. I wouldn't have risked a lot of money on my being elected . . . . My colleagues knew that I believed in a smaller board and they knew that I didn't believe in deputies and that's one of the reasons that the board paid a price in electing me. They knew that half of them would be on the line if they voted for me. They knew that I had very strong views on change in business style . . . I don't think they bought a pig in a poke. I went to a lot of trouble so that they would not. I wasn't campaigning for the job. In fact, I not only was not campaigning but I had planned to leave the company at this stage.

In the first three years of his term, Harvey-Jones has taken ICI from its first quarterly loss into a revitalization that will take a decade to complete.

Harvey-Jones's Future Challenges

The mandatory retirement of the internally elected chairman at ICI after five years makes executive succession an important issue for Harvey-Jones. He keeps the broader challenges for the company in clear focus as he talks about what is left to be done.

> Limitless. There are always more things to be done. I'm not sure that we're making the most of the research that we're doing. I'm concerned that the more we delegate—the more we let the flowers bloom—the more we need a strong corporate culture to hold us together. At the moment, people are quite willing to give up some part of their freedom to help out the corporation because they have just come out of the valley of the shadow of death and our troubles are still a pretty conscious memory. I worry about whether they will be willing to help when they are up running and feeling their oats. How are we going to move the ownership of the corporation as well as the individual units further down the line? And how do we persuade them that the rewards come from helping to build a great institution?

Harvey-Jones will not resolve this dilemma before he retires, but his obsession with creating the appropriate corporate culture for ICI will be the foundation for the long term.

LEE IACOCCA, CHRYSLER CORPORATION, HIGHLAND PARK, MICHIGAN

After being fired by Henry Ford from his position as president of Ford Motor Company, Iacocca spent a very painful and difficult summer thinking about what to do. He decided that he wanted to stay in business. Since he loved the automobile industry and Chrysler was the only show in town, he accepted Riccardo's offer to join the Chrysler Corporation in 1979.

Like Blumenthal, Iacocca was coming off a bad experience and approached the Chrysler offer without knowing the extent of the automobile maker's difficulties. He knew there were problems at Chrysler but he did not realize that the company was on the brink of bankruptcy. He managed to assemble a new top management team at Chrysler and mobilized the organization to fight its way through one of the most well known turnarounds in American history. In the process Iacocca became the best known business leader in America and assumed the status of a national folk hero.

Our analysis of him aims at a systematic appraisal of his transformational leadership activities and the organizational dynamics which took place at Chrysler.

Iacocca's Future Challenges

Like Harvey-Jones, Iacocca must prepare Chrysler for the time when he retires. This transition will be important to Chrysler's future and complicated by the strong identification the turnaround has had with Iacocca's role. Can the company successfully develop effective leadership in the shadow of Iacocca?

Chrysler will face significant challenges in the marketplace in the next few years. It lacks the financial resources of a General Motors or a Ford, and the 1985 UAW contract eliminated the labor cost advantage that Chrysler enjoyed over these domestic competitors. The Japanese continue to be relentless as they seek world dominance in the automobile industry. Chrysler's decentralization in November 1985 is meant to help it meet these competitive threats. The remainder of the 1980s will provide the real test of long term viability.

MARY ANN LAWLOR, DRAKE BUSINESS SCHOOLS, NEW YORK, NEW YORK

Lawlor credits a Catholic education with instilling the idea that you must not only do well in this world but you must also do good, and she thanks her parents for her determination to succeed. In 1970, she took over a proprietary business school with antiquated equipment, lacking state certification, and with not enough money in the bank to meet the current payroll. She covered the shortfall with her own funds and set out to turn Drake around. She says that the challenge required "more courage than brains since anyone could look around and see what had to be done. The real question was whether sane people would want to attempt to do it."

Lawlor put together a management team of bright young women, who were to become Drake's officers, shareholders, and directors. Asked if she had deliberately set out to create an organization run by women, she says, "No, they were willing to work for less than equally qualified men. So I hired them. We are now compensated according to our value in the marketplace, but in the beginning everyone here accepted the opportunity they probably would have been denied in a successful organization as part of their compensation package." Four of the original management team of five women remain with the school today. Lawlor is now Chairwoman and CEO; Diane Scappatticci became President and COO in 1980; Cheryl Pagnozzi, formerly Drake's treasurer, formed her own company which now provides financial and accounting services to the school; Faye Joyce provides consulting services; and Gemma Brophy, who "retired" 10 years ago, remains a good friend.

In the past 15 years, Lawlor has increased Drake's enrollment from 50 part time to more than 1500 full time students. The schools draw from a predominantly female and poor population. Lawlor describes a typical Drake student as 24 years old, single, with two children ages three and seven. The school tries to help this student break the cycle of poverty by learning business skills that will make her independent. Thus Lawlor believes she is in the transformation business, and she pushes excellence so that the population Drake serves can experience the pride of accomplishment.

Lawlor projects boundless energy. Her commitment to Drake's students extends beyond the learning environment to political issues that affect their ability to succeed: adequate child care, voter awareness, and tax reform. She sees a serious threat from cutbacks in aid for postsecondary school education for the disadvantaged. She plans to expand the pool of potential applicants by opening satellite schools and offering programs to attract more male students as well as students seeking careers outside the office.

Lawlor's Future Challenges

The most obvious challenge will be to sufficiently diversify the school to meet the challenges of a world where secretarial work will never be the same. Computer and telecommunication technology are still way ahead of most work settings, but when you are in the business of educating it is important to be educating for the settings of the future. Much of Drake's curriculum, student market, and employment market is undergoing a transformation. This is coming at a time when federal support for postsecondary education is being reduced. Lawlor recognizes the need for growth if the school is to remain vital. Her challenge is to mobilize the key members of the organization to accept this new challenge and embark again on the transformational drama.

DON MACKINNON, CIBA-GEIGY CORP. ARDSLEY, NEW YORK

MacKinnon joined CIBA-GEIGY in 1967 and became president and COO of the American subsidiary in 1980. The Swiss chemical and pharmaceutical company needed to restructure its large American subsidiary to meet a more globally competitive environment. MacKinnon has dedicated the last five years to transforming the management strategy of CIBA-GEIGY. Among our protagonists, his drama is unique because he must lead a subsidiary operating in a culture different in many ways from the culture of the parent company. The tensions between the highly centralized Swiss corporation and its increasingly decentralized American subsidiary grow out of the need to rapidly transform an organization within a company with 200 years of history and a conservative mind-set.

CIBA-GEIGY's Future Challenges

In a company which is several hundred years old, time is measured differently than in most companies. MacKinnon led CIBA-GEIGY's U.S. operations through what would be characterized as revolutionary change for CIBA-GEIGY. Yet the change is tenuous. To borrow a phrase from Harvey-Jones, "What is left to be done is limitless."

Even though MacKinnon speaks of changing the culture through new programs, the culture has not yet changed. It is beginning to change. It is fragile. MacKinnon understands that his successor will play a key role in determining the success of the change effort. There are still pockets of resistance among both the Swiss company managers and the American managers, who may see MacKinnon's retirement on April 1, 1986, as an opportunity to regress to the good old days. The choice of Charles O'Brien to succeed him, however, is a positive sign that the changes MacKinnon began will continue.

JAMES RENIER, HONEYWELL, MINNEAPOLIS, MINNESOTA

As the 1980s began, Honeywell (like Burroughs) was at the end of an era in computer development. IBM, free at last of the government's antitrust suit, came out swinging. It was clear that Big Blue was going to chew up its competitors unless they were able to reposition themselves out of the direct line of fire. Honeywell's Information Systems accounted for almost one third of the company's revenues, and it was in trouble. Leadership was lacking, layoffs were necessary, and there was no viable long-term strategy. Steve Jerretts, president at the time, resigned. Renier, a Ph.D. in physical chemistry, then president of the Control Systems side of Honeywell, was moved over to deal with the problems at Information Systems. In 1985, Honeywell made him vice chairman.

Renier had to confront low morale, a lack of teamwork at the top, declining market share, lack of new products, and the potential for large scale layoffs. He spent three years repositioning the business and setting the stage for integrating the computer side of Honeywell with the control side.

Renier had a vision, took bold moves, and made unpopular decisions. He has turned over the day to day operations to a new leader, Bill Wray, while Renier tries to direct and institutionalize change.

As Renier shares his entry into the Information System business and some of his ideas on change, note how his background at Honeywell has influenced his leadership philosophy:

> I had the benefit of being in the computer business from 1968 to 1974 and I had developed some convictions about the business, about the markets, about what was happening. This was an advantage because I knew immediately where I could take some action without a lot of thinking and analysis. I've always been a very strong believer in empirical results. My scientific training gave me respect for analytical thinking and the development of theory, but I've always approached a business problem by saying let's look at the observables. I think there are too many variables and too many interdependencies for the theoreticians or the staff people to be able to describe it in all its horrendous detail. No one is that smart. Incidentally, calling it what it is is the most important part of solving a problem. You have to look at a problem and call it a problem instead of denying there is something wrong.

Renier's Future Challenges

Another 100 year old company is left with tremendous challenges in the information business. As vice chairman without operational control of Information Systems, Renier must watch from a distance as others attempt to complete what he started. Yet he is faced with bigger challenges. Can Honeywell actually implement its espoused strategy of gaining synergy among its parts by finding a way for its information systems business, its controls business, and its aerospace business to work together to provide major systems solutions in the factories of the future?

Taking the historically decentralized and self-contained pieces of Honeywell and weaving some parts together is the challenge. Renier has the background. He has managed all the parts. He has a career, both technically and managerially, that fits the task, and he has demonstrated the leadership drive. However, the challenge is complicated by succession issues at the top of Honeywell, namely who will succeed Edson Spencer and when that will occur. With no anointed crown prince, there remains sufficient political uncertainty at the top to make the exercise of leadership by any one key player a delicate art.

JACK SPARKS, WHIRLPOOL CORPORATION, BENTON HARBOR, MICHIGAN

Sparks deserves the Horatio Alger Award for personal success. At 16 Sparks began his career at Whirlpool as a laborer. In 1941 he joined the Army Air Force, serving as a pilot and rising to captain before his discharge in 1946. He returned to Whirlpool to a position in personnel and eventually worked his way through sales and marketing to become CEO. Sparks has several more years as CEO and is dead set on positioning Whirlpool for long-term results in the increasingly competitive world where the Japanese have turned their attention to the major appliance business.

Like many transformational leaders, Sparks felt that he had been mentally preparing himself for years.

> I wasn't in line to be the CEO. I was a surprise entry. . . . Two things in my life kept me current. One, I've always read everything I can find on subjects that interest me. Two, I kept outside contacts. I went to Conference Boards. I went to marketing seminars. I went . . . where I thought I could meet people and learn. As a consequence, I built up a wide acquaintance in not only the

business world but the academic world. I was doing that for marketing reasons because I recognized that marketing was changing and the old Willy Loman syndrome was going by us in a hurry. An early introduction to the computer made me aware of its potential. That came about through some work we were doing with A.D. Little on forecasting and I got my first exposure to progressive type analyses. We were doing this in the 1950s and we got kicked off the computer because they needed to track Sputnik. Can you imagine?

I spent two weeks at Aspen Institute, humanistic studies, understanding that I had no formal higher education but I exposed myself to the reading. We had to read 80 to 100 publications before we got there. Then all of a sudden it occurred to me that there was more to this whole business and my life than what is going to happen tomorrow or next week. What is important is what has happened in the past and what is going to happen in the future. . . . These things changed my perspective and I started to watch our business differently. . . . Once I got the reins I knew what I was going to do . . . I'd been through it a thousand times in my head.

Sparks's Future Challenges

Succession is the top issue at Whirlpool. There are two vice chairmen in place and Sparks will retire in December 1987. He has repositioned Whirlpool by changing internal managerial processes, acquiring Kitchen Aid, and consolidating the organization. He must position Whirlpool for global competition by getting his managers to think about global markets and global competitors.

EDWARD THOMPSON, SCHNEIDER TRANSPORT, GREEN BAY, WISCONSIN

In the late 1970s, Thompson left a successful management career at Procter & Gamble to become president of Schneider

Trucking Company, a $100 million company providing trucking
and distribution service to most of the Fortune 500. He took his
job in the late 1970s because it gave him a chance to run a total
business. In his first two years at Schneider, Thompson had
begun instituting some major managerial changes when the
federal government deregulated the trucking industry with the
Motor Carrier Act of 1980. Thompson found he had to drasti-
cally revise his job description. No longer was it enough to be a
competent, professional manager. Now he had to assume the
role of a transformational leader.

Deregulation changed the rules of the game. Under regulation a trucking company's ICC-issued operating authority effectively served as a barrier to entry. The grants of authority, much
like in the airline industry, prescribed operating territory, route
network, and the type of goods that could be distributed.

Thompson and his colleagues at Schneider looked at deregulation as a significant intervention that, when well managed,
would be a major springboard for positioning their company as
the industry leader in their marketplace segment, which is full
truckload distribution. Thompson provided the leadership to
deal with the very difficult realignment of operating costs of the
existing unionized portion of the Schneider operation as well as
the development of a new vision for his company. The vision
had as its foundation the deep involvement and empowerment
of drivers and mechanics in the running of the business. Further, the vision called for rapid, 25 to 30 percent, nationwide
sales growth through the establishment of nonunion operations
in the West, South, and East.

The test for Thompson and his colleagues has been severe. A
goal of the deregulators was ease of entry and free market pric-
ing. In the first two years literally thousands of new companies
entered the field. This flood of entrepreneurial enthusiasm,
coupled with the recessions of the early 1980s, created 30 to 40
percent over capacity in the industry and rapid price erosion. In
1985, the full truckload industry was operating at absolute price
levels lower than those in 1979. Many trucking companies

viewed these changes as a threat and chose to fight the rearguard action rather than create new visions and provide innovative leadership. Hundreds have left the industry in the wake of the postderegulation shakeout.

The transformation at Schneider is not complete. Although the company is well positioned as a respected, cost-effective nationwide carrier with a 1985 bluechip revenue base of $500 million, the environment continues to demand more and more responsiveness from drivers all the way up through senior management.

As Thompson describes it, he was a bit surprised by the magnitude of the challenge:

> I didn't realize that the leadership challenge would require the initiation of such massive change so fast. I see the opportunity as one of having a broader and more significant impact on a smaller company—smaller than Procter & Gamble. I had known several managers at Schneider. They were bright, had a good track record in place and some aggressive goals in mind. Deregulation appeared to be an opportunity. It sounded like fun and I knew my background would be valuable. The surprise came in the need for such an accelerated time frame for change. I was simultaneously developing our vision, teaching classes on the basic stuff like key fact management, dealing with critical labor negotiations, putting a nationwide sales force in place, and initiating the building of an entirely new type of relationship with our customers. A benefit of the fast pace was the sorting out and selection of the managers who would lead the transformation.

This was the start for Thompson. The need for quantum change was introduced in 1980 by a major change in the industry.

Thompson's Future Challenges

Thompson wants to see Schneider grow. He believes that much of this expansion will come through acquisition. The transformation of the company's culture is now in its third act. Like transformational leaders before him, it is important for Thompson to institutionalize his efforts so that they will survive his stewardship.

JACK WELCH, GENERAL ELECTRIC, FAIRFIELD, CONNECTICUT

With the appointment of Jack Welch as chairman in 1981, General Electric embarked on revitalization. An article in *The Wall Street Journal* describes Welsh's leadership agenda.

Mr. Jones and Mr. Welch, the new CEO, agree that GE either must keep gaining or risk being trampled by the foreign competition that can produce higher quality goods, faster and cheaper. Many of GE's old line manufacturing businesses, such as consumer appliances, electronics and industrial equipment have been buffeted by foreign competition and by the recession . . . . Mr. Welch blames the foreign threat to GE and other American companies on many of the management principles that GE itself helped to shape in the 1960s and 1970s, a time, he says, when companies were managed not led. He fears that managing assets as if they were investment portfolios, seeking short term profits at the sacrifice of long term gains, and stressing conservatism over innovation may have permanently crippled many of America's major industries.

GE's change of heart comes at a time when its profits are rising more comfortably than those of many other American industrial companies. GE is trying to instill a sense of urgency when there is no emergency. It is profitable now and has options . . . . Getting the competitive message down through the hierarchy isn't going to be easy . . . there is a built-in arrogance that comes with being the biggest factor in so many businesses. GE managers tend to believe there is a GE way and there is a wrong way . . . .

Welch's first five years as chairman of GE have resulted in dramatic changes. The portfolio of businesses is significantly different with the divestiture of the housewares business and Utah Mining, to name the most notable. In addition, the workforce was reduced by 85,000 people. The financial performance of GE outpaced the rest of the Standard & Poor's companies. This was a difficult, wrenching time of change for many in GE. Welch described his challenge in the following terms:

> A big company that fancies itself as world competitive today is likely to use words like "entrepreneurial, lean, and agile." What these really mean is the ability of an institution to take the rigidity out of its bureaucracy—to move at a faster rate than the world around it . . . . Most bureaucracies—and ours is no exception— unfortunately still think in incremental terms rather than in terms of fundamental change. They think incrementally primarily because they think internally . . . . Changing the culture— opening it up to quantum change—means constantly asking, not how fast am I going, how well am I doing versus how well I did a year or two years before, but rather how fast and how well am I doing versus the outside world? . . . Why do newly made heroes so quickly fall back into incrementalism? People want to come out for the second bow when the world is waiting for the second act.

Welch's Future Challenges

At the beginning of 1985, people were wondering what Welch would do to increase revenues at GE. The early stages of revitalization were marked by divestiture and cost cutting that resulted in a leaner and more agile organization, but no growth strategy had been announced. Then, in December 1985, Welch embarked on the second act of GE's revitalization drama by initiating the $6.28 billion acquisition of RCA. The acquisition makes GE a $40 billion plus company with over 400,000 employees. The integration of two giants will be a complex and difficult task. The task will be made more difficult because of the relentless global competition these businesses will face while they work to put their internal house in order.

Some of the specific challenges are to implement a culture

that encourages GE's business leaders to "own your business." The move to decentralization means that managers will have to design their own management processes, human resource systems, and subcultures. The paradoxical challenge will be to continue to address the "What is GE?" questions. Will the acquisition exacerbate the issues already troubling GE? How far should decentralization go? Will GE simply become a financial holding company? Will the only common cultural experience be the management education experience conducted at its Crotonville educational facility? The next phase for Welch will also be an important test of people management. Before the announcement of the acquisition there were pockets of resistance to the change in GE's culture. The additional problem of integrating another organizational giant presents Welch with one of the major cultural leadership challenges of our time.

THE DRAMA: LEADERSHIP AND PARADOX

Leaders must deal with the tensions expressed by the middle manager whose organization was about to embark on a major transformation.

I yearn for the good old days. We seem to be turning everything upside down without any clear sense of where we want to go. Until we straighten that out and are sure that we will be better off than we are, we should leave well enough alone. Who said "nothing succeeds like success?" We've been pretty successful. We shouldn't try to change that.

Leaders deal with these feelings by creating organizations that embrace paradox. The organizations are characterized by the ability to manage uncertainty in their environment. The paradoxes create the dramatic tensions in our transformational drama. They include:

1. *A Struggle Between the Forces of Stability and the Forces of Change.* Successful organizations must find ways to

balance the need for adaptation with the need for stability. Organizations that cling too tightly to tradition present us with dramas of eventual decline while organizations that fail to regain their equilibrium after embarking on a change spin out of control and eventually destroy themselves.

2. *Dramatic Tension Between Denial and Acceptance of Reality.* Potential revitalization dramas become tragedies when key protagonists attempt to deny reality and hide from its implications. Many of our protagonists wrestled with this problem in their organization in Act I of their own drama.

3. *A Struggle Between Fear and Hope.* Organizations, like the legendary phoenix, are capable of regenerating themselves. The process, however, demands that the aging and increasingly impotent form must be destroyed before the new form can emerge to again dominate its environment. This leap of faith that destruction will result in rebirth is tied to the tension between stability and change and countered by the denial that change is necessary.

4. *A Struggle Between the Manager and the Leader.* Managers are dedicated to the maintenance of the existing organization, whereas leaders are often committed to its change. The philosophical difference between doing things right and doing the right things creates tension in organizations that are being pressured to change.

The transformation drama is played out at both the organizational and individual level pictured in Figure 1.1. Leaders must pull the organization into the future by creating a positive view of what the organization can become and simultaneously provide emotional support for individuals during the transition process. There are three distinct stages to each of these dramas.

The Organization During Act I

Trigger Events. The need for change is triggered by environmental pressures. But not all organizations respond to signals

Transformational Leadership: A Three-Act Drama

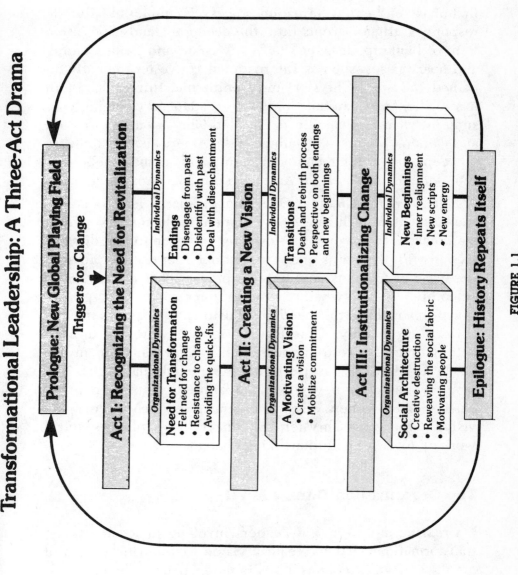

FIGURE 1.1

from the environment indicating change. The external trigger event must be perceived and responded to by leaders in the first phase of the transformation process. Examples of failure to respond to trigger events litter the economic landscape in the form of bankruptcies, such as W. T. Grant and Penn Central, and near misses, such as International Harvester (recently renamed Navistar), Chrysler, and Continental Illinois. The failure of the American auto industry to adapt to changing consumer demand for small cars crippled Chrysler and hurt Ford and General Motors. The failure of the American steel industry to keep pace with technological innovation may well have sounded a death knell for American dominance in steel.

Felt Need for Change. Once organizational leaders accept the fact that their business environment is changing, key decision makers in the organization must be made to feel dissatisfaction with the status quo. The felt need for change provides the impetus for transition, but this process does not always go smoothly. A key to whether resistant forces deter the organization from making the needed adjustments to environmental shifts is the quality of the leadership that is brought to bear. International Harvester appears to have had management that chose a defensive posture to environmental challenges. The result was a lack of new vision and failure to mobilize employees to behave in new ways. In contrast, Lee Iacocca created a vision of the "new Chrysler," mobilized the employees, and is working toward institutionalizing change.

The Organization During Act II

Creating a Vision. The leaders involved in organizational transformation need to create a vision that a critical mass of employees will accept as a desirable change for the organization. Each leader must develop a vision and communicate it in a way that is congruent with the leader's philosophy and style. At

General Motors the vision emerged from several years of detailed committee work and staff analysis, while at Chrysler Lee Iacocca relied on his intuitive and directive leadership philosophy and style. Both General Motors and Chrysler ended up with a new vision because transformational leaders shaped a new organization mission proactively. The long-term challenge to organizational revitalization is less "how" the visions are created and more the extent to which the visions correctly respond to environmental pressures and create transitions within the organization.

Mobilizing Commitment. The organization, or at least some critical mass within the organization, accepts the new mission and vision and makes it happen. It is in this stage of the transformational process that leaders must tap into a deeper sense of meaning for their followers.

The Organization During Act III

Institutionalizing Change. Revitalization is just empty talk until the new vision becomes reality. The new way of thinking becomes day-to-day practice. New realities, actions, and practices must be shared so that changes become institutionalized. At a deeper level this requires shaping and reinforcing a new culture that fits with the revitalized organization. How people are selected for jobs, appraised and rewarded on their performance, and developed for future responsibility are of overwhelming importance.

What happens at the organizational level is by itself not sufficient to create and implement change. Major transitions unleash powerful conflicting forces in people, and individual psychodynamics of change must be understood and managed. Change invokes simultaneous personal feelings of fear and hope, anxiety and relief, pressure and stimulation, threats to self-esteem and challenges to master new situations. The task of transformational leaders is to recognize these mixed feelings, act to help people move from negative to positive emotions, and mobilize the energy needed for individual renewal.

The Individual During Act I

William Bridges, in *Transitions: Making Sense of Life's Changes,* outlines a three phase process of individual change involving endings, transition states, and new beginnings. During each of these phases a set of psychological tasks can be identified. Individuals must work through these if they are to complete the change process successfully.

Endings. All individual transitions start with endings. Employees who cling to old ways of doing things will be unable to adjust to new demands. They must follow a process that includes disengaging from the past; disidentification with its demands; disenchantment with its implications and disorientation as they learn new behaviors.

Transformational leaders provide people with support by helping replace past glories with future opportunities. This will happen only if they are able to acknowledge individual resistance that is derived from a sense of loss in the transition. Leaders should encourage employees to accept the failures without feeling as if they had failed. It does not help to treat transitions as if the past did not exist. The past will hold the key to understanding what went wrong as well as what worked and can frequently provide a useful map to the future.

The Individual During Act II

Neutral Zones. Employees need the time to work through their feelings of being disconnected with the past and not yet emotionally committed to the future. This phase causes the most trouble in action oriented Western cultures, for it tends to be viewed as nonproductive. Yet the difference between success and failure in organizational transformations can occur during this stage. Passing successfully through the neutral zone requires taking the time and thought to gain perspective on both the ending—what went wrong, why it needs changing, and on what must be overcome to make a new beginning. It is during this phase that the skills of a transformational leader are really put to the test. A timid bureaucrat who revels in the good old days will not provide the needed support to help individuals traverse the neutral zone. A strong dictatorial leader may also fail, by forcing a new beginning before people have worked through their feelings and emotions.

The Individual During Act III

New Beginnings. Once a stage of psychological readiness to deal with a new order of things is reached, employees must be prepared for the frustration that accompanies failure as they replace thoroughly mastered routines with a new act. Adequate rehearsal time will be needed before everyone learns their new lines and masters their new roles so that the play can become again a seamless whole rather than a set of unintegrated scenes.

ACT ONE

RECOGNIZING THE NEED FOR REVITALIZATION

2 THE GATHERING STORM

In arguing that culture must deal with the problem of external survival and internal integration, I am implicitly accepting the notion that the human system cannot tolerate too much overload or too little sensing stimulation, nor can it cope with constantly changing signals. We require a fairly high level of predictability and certainty in order to relax enough to feel comfortable and seek novelty and creativity. From this point of view culture can be seen as a giant cocoon which we have invented for ourselves to be able to survive at all in a hostile environment and a potential human jungle.

EDGAR SCHEIN

The call has gone out for transformational leaders because the environment has become less predictable. It is their responsibility to provide the vision and through example show people that there is no place to hide. To better understand the nature of the drama they embark on, let's visit their world. They live in a world in which resources have become scarcer and changes in technology, political alignments, and the rules of the economic game happen more frequently. Much of the pressure comes from the increasing interdependence of world economies. Global economic interdependence brings with it increasing environmental uncertainty. In the 1970s the industrialized world reeled from the impact of a series of rapid increases in the prices of oil mandated by the Organization of Petroleum Exporting Countries. Today, oil prices are falling, and the threat of economic disorder is being triggered by the inability of less well developed countries to repay loans collateralized by oil.

It is not the price of oil alone that creates instability. There is also the threat that supplies will be disrupted for political reasons. Thus economic problems are exacerbated by tensions in a world where we often seem incapable of resolving either international or intranational differences without resorting to violence.

The result is a declining American economy. Productivity is falling, trade deficits have grown from $69 billion in 1985 to over $150 billion in 1986, and the U.S. standard of living is being supported by an exploding national debt.

Transformational leaders are being asked to address not only economic issues but moral ones as well. Various interest groups put pressure on them about issues as diverse as conducting business in countries such as South Africa to the legitimacy of closing plants in one-company towns. They must also deal with a myriad of demands and regulations from highly diverse constituencies in their country of origin and in every other country where they do business.

Domestic political pressures also complicate the transformational leader's job. In the United States there is a continuing shift in the demographics of the workforce. In 1985 white males became a minority in the workforce, yet they continue to hold virtually all the positions of power in large organizations. Similar pressures are emerging in Japan as women look for a more meaningful role in society. No society is immune to this growing hunger for opportunity and equity. Laws and sanctions to correct inequity are formulated by the government but they are implemented by organizations. And it is in the implementation that the debate about equity begins. The core challenge is to mobilize an increasingly pluralistic workforce where many groups have no significant decision-making role. This tends to set up the dynamic for confrontation rather than collaboration.

Many organizations, faced with the need to be more globally competitive, must resort to cutting back the workforce. This contraction is one of the most difficult change problems that transformational leaders will encounter. It brings to the surface tensions surrounding issues of equity and justice that often go unnoticed in times of organizational growth. American companies have traditionally handled cyclical business contractions by laying off blue-collar workers, usually on the basis of seniority. Some companies faced the issue of professional and managerial layoffs for the first time in the 1970s. Since 1979, 20 percent of the white-collar labor force at General Motors has been laid off, and at Chrysler, 20,000 white-collar positions and more than 40,000 blue-collar jobs were eliminated in the effort to save the company. Reducing the workforce played an important role in the turnaround strategies of General Electric Lighting and Honeywell Information Systems. For many of the companies, these Draconian measures were necessary to correct questionable managerial decisions that allowed managerial and staff numbers to mushroom over the previous two decades. The solution also caused severe internal disruption, since employees of long standing felt it had been implicitly understood that they had earned the equivalent of academic tenure and could be severed from the organization only for cause. As painful as these layoffs were, the results tended to be positive. Organizations became more productive and efficient since, in most cases, they were provided with an opportunity to eliminate marginal and poor performers.

Transformational leaders continue to face a more difficult challenge. The initial round of cuts did not result in world competitiveness. There is still fat in General Motors, General Electric, Honeywell, Burroughs, and scores of other U.S. corporations. This is not the burden of employees who do not carry their own weight but simply too many good employees relative to the size of the competitors' workforce.

It will be necessary to remove professional and managerial employees whose performance is good but whom the organization can no longer afford to employ. Transformational leaders need to be sensitive to issues of political allocation and the attendant concerns of equity and justice if they wish to operate in global markets, to lead increasingly pluralistic organizations, and to motivate the people involved when they cannot be rewarded by frequent promotions and hefty pay increases.

The success of the American economy from the late 1940s to the late 1960s creates its own set of pressures; it raised expectations that are not easily satisfied. As the tail end of the baby boom generation enters the workforce, we will have to deal with the fact that the majority of this well-educated population will not experience the upward mobility their parents had, yet they will have to work harder simply to maintain their employers' competitive position. To meet this challenge, we must create a broader definition of quality of worklife and examine our traditional concept of organizational success. If we do not change the present value system, we can be reasonably certain that large numbers of well qualified people will be disappointed and unfulfilled in their work. The widely accepted definition of organizational success—upward mobility—must be examined so that we can decide if it will really motivate employees at a time when many good people cannot move up the corporate ladder.

At the present time, quality of worklife and productivity are concepts largely confined to the industrial shop floor, where worker-union-management collaboration has developed programs that lead to greater productivity and higher levels of satisfaction among blue-collar workers. Little experimentation has taken place to enhance the productivity as well as the quality of professional, managerial worklife. Yet in the absence of substantial opportunity for upward mobility, it is important to find ways to make this work intrinsically more rewarding. Dealing with professionals and managers who have reached a plateau remains an important challenge.

The pressures are mounting. Industries that have become complacent over the past several decades, either because they enjoyed the benefits of protective trade barriers or because they had no significant foreign competition, will find the pace of the game is quickening. World class competition demands that organizations that wish to survive learn to measure their progress against the competition rather than against an internally generated standard.

This reality has not been fully accepted. Recent articles, such as the one that appeared in *BusinessWeek* heralding a new era of improved U.S. productivity, continue to focus on productivity gains made against last year's accomplishments rather than against the competition's current performance. Companies cannot hope to maintain, much less regain, their positions of dominance if their gains in productivity do not equal or surpass those of their competitors.

Table 2.1 makes it painfully obvious that it is going to be very difficult for the United States to be world competitive while productivity lags and wages lead those of the more competitive economies of the world. These data underscore the "give me mine while I can still grab some" attitude which permeates the American workforce from the CEO down to the shop floor. This beggar thy neighbor strategy weakens the overall competitive base of the U.S. economy as the standard of living goes down

**TABLE 2.1   MANUFACTURING SECTOR WAGES AND
PRODUCTIVITY IN SELECTED COUNTRIES**

Country	Percent of U.S. Wages	1984 Productivity Gains (Percent)	Change in Hourly Labor Costs (Percent)
United States	100	3.4	+0.1
West Germany	75	4.7	−11.2
Sweden	72	6.8	+2.3
Italy	58	6.3	−10.1
France	56	5.0	−9.5
Japan	50	9.5	−5.7
Great Britain	46	3.9	−8.4

Source: Compiled from U.S. Department of Labor Statistics

for increasing numbers of Americans. We are left with workers
and management fighting over who gets what part of the shrinking pie.

For some time now we have depended on the service sector
to replace the jobs that are disappearing in the manufacturing
sector of the economy. While it is difficult to imagine a first rate
economic power in which the basic manufacturing industries
have withered away, the creation of service-sector jobs helped
to ease the growing malaise among displaced workers. An article that appeared in the *Los Angeles Times* on June 2, 1985
suggests that these gains may soon be under attack.

*Japanese companies have expanded in the service field in the United
States, a field that until recently seemed impervious to foreign competition . . . but now that so many Japanese manufacturing corporations have set up American operations, more Japanese firms in service
fields such as cargo and shipping, construction, finance and banking,
advertising, travel and insurance are following their traditional Japanese corporate clients. . . . Until recently, America had partially offset its mammoth trade deficit in manufactured goods by exporting
services, but its edge in services has been steadily eroding over the
past few years . . . .*

We believe that most U.S. industries are vulnerable and that many will need to undergo quantum change to develop the globally competitive standards needed to survive. Transformational leaders must be prepared to deal with a world in which resources are increasingly scarce and change happens more rapidly.

Thus the organization cocoon enveloping many organizations has produced a mounting threat to the American economy. Lester Thurow described this threat:

America faces a problem that is simply put. The huge technological edge enjoyed by Americans in the 1950s and 1960s has disappeared. Whereas America once had effortless economic superiority, it is now faced with competitors who have matched its economic achievements and may be in the process of moving ahead of it. If present trends continue, America's standard of living will fall relative to those of the world's industrial leaders, and it will become simply another country—Egypt, Greece, Rome, Portugal, Spain, and England—that once led the world economically but no longer does. What is worse, at precisely the moment when America's effortless superiority has vanished, the American economy has been absorbed into a world economy . . . America faces the difficult task of learning how to compete in a new world economy just at a point when America's relative economic strength is weaker than it has been at any time since World War II.

Our protagonists live in the changing world. Every day their organizations hear about and experience the challenges in the world around them. We might expect, therefore, that our drama will be an adventure story in which the transformational leader slays the dragon that threatens the inhabitants of the kingdom. However, this is not entirely accurate. A significant part of this story is a psychological drama involving the will of the inhabitants to safeguard the kingdom. Or as Pogo said, "We have met the enemy and it is us."

ASKING THE BASIC QUESTIONS

Why do transformational leaders, like the Biblical prophets of old, often find themselves crying in the wilderness, trying to get people to change their ways before it is too late?

Because It Is Difficult to Overcome the Boiled Frog Phenomenon. The label comes from a classic physiological response experiment involving two live frogs, a pan filled with water, and a bunsen burner. The first frog is placed in a pan of cold water. The pan is then placed on a bunsen burner and the heat is turned up very gradually. If the change in temperature is gradual enough, the frog will sit in the pan until it boils to death. The creature could have jumped out of the pan at any time, but the change in its environment happened so gradually that no response was triggered in the frog and death ensued. This is a demonstration of the just noticeable difference threshold.

If we take the remaining frog and place it in a pan of water that is already boiling, it will not sit there but will promptly jump out—and survive. We can clearly continue to refine this experiment so that we can discover how great the change has to be in a given time period in order to get the frog to respond, but the analogy is clear. Like the frog, there are organizations that do not respond to trigger events in their environment in time to avoid catastrophic consequences.

Companies become boiled frogs because their threshold of awareness is set too high; they do not read changes in the environment until those changes have disastrous consequences for the organization. One can argue that U.S. industries like steel and automobiles were victims of this phenomenon.

It took a lot to trigger change in General Motors. The giant corporation did not wake up easily. Roger Smith became chairman as General Motors faced its first year of losses since before the Great Depression. He faced a depressed economy, soaring interest rates, increasing market segmentation driven by shifting consumer demand, stiff foreign and domestic competition, intensive technological competition, and high labor costs. These factors resulted in declining sales and profits at a time of increased capital expenditures. Smith's problems were compounded by the flight of executive talent to other industries. There was a reaction: by 1982 GM's investment structure had been rationalized; 23,000 white-collar jobs had been trimmed; 170,000 blue-collar workers had been laid off; obsolete plants had been sold or closed; and the U.S. economy was turning around. Even though the market was returning, GM needed to design new products, settle its differences with the UAW, and convince the U.S. consumer that it offered quality cars that would fulfill their needs. To accomplish these goals, the company had to reverse business practices and habits that evolved over decades.

Even though Ed Thompson went to Schneider Transport as a change agent, he had little idea how rapid and difficult the change would be. The external environment between 1978 and 1983 proved to be different from that of the previous decade as the trucking industry was forced to simultaneously absorb deregulation and the major economic recessions of the early 1980s. The Interstate Commerce Commission began granting greater operating authority to carriers in the late 1970s and the industry was totally deregulated in January 1980, two years after the airline industry. Two of the more significant changes brought about by the move to a free marketplace were rapid price reduction and the opportunity for a significantly different shipper-carrier relationship. Under regulation price was seldom a factor in a shipper's choice. Rate levels were generally controlled by a ponderous bureaucracy. This all changed. Even though this represented a dramatic or quantum shift, Thompson saw it as an opportunity. As he stated:

> **Deregulation certainly provided an exciting chance for us to pull off a major change. Industries transform in major ways but once in 50 to 75 years. Our competitors and the basic carrier-shipper**

relationship had only known regulation. The trucking industry had, by and large, not attracted its share of change oriented managers. We recognized that a rapid move from a relatively internally oriented entrepreneurial setting to an organization form with more customer focus employing more professional management skills would put Schneider National aggressively in the lead. Competitors would be slow to move. This provided the energy and sense of purpose required to forge the new vision and get the organization moving.

The boiled frog phenomenon is something the leadership of General Electric wants to avoid. Jack Welch is reading signs that say GE will cease to be world competitive in many industries by 1990 unless transformation continues. Some GE managers have not detected a change in the temperature of the water, and the success or severe impairment of the transformation will depend on whether Welch can convince a critical mass of these managers to share his sense of urgency.

Thus organizations like people create cultural cocoons. Sometimes these cocoons surround the organization with a false sense of security; changes in the outside environment are not detected in many organizations until the very existence of the enterprise is threatened. In the United States, cultural cocoons kept whole industries like steel, motorcycles, and consumer electronics from sensing the threat in the outside environment, and did the same for specific companies like W. T. Grant and International Harvester.

Some people believe that these events are inevitable—that little can be done to stem the decline and demise of organizations. Their versions of these dramas would put the fate of our protagonists and their organizations in the hands of the gods. We believe that the fate of these organizations rests in the ability of their leadership to deal with the forces of fate and the competition. Leaders, unlike managers, are not focused internally but are constantly surveying the competitive jungle for signs of danger. A colleague of ours, Kirby Warren, related a story illustrative of these different views of the world. The chairman of a major American steel company was participating in a seminar about the problems that the industry was facing back in the early 1960s. He attempted to explain the growing dominance of the West Germans and Japanese in the industry by saying that their plants were more efficient because they had all been built after World War II. "Why," the chairman said, "we would have been better off if our mills had been bombed during the war just as theirs were." An anonymous response emanated from the back of the room, "I dare say, sir, that would be true only if your management had been locked inside."

Do All Transformational Leaders Face the Same Resistance in Organizations? No, the irony is that transformational leaders frequently find the effort they must expend in convincing the organization of the need for change is in inverse proportion to the urgency of the situation. At one end of the spectrum we find Lee Iacocca, who assumed command of Chrysler when the situation was so grave that he had little convincing to do; at the other end we find leaders like John Akers of IBM trying to create a sense of urgency about the company's need to fulfill its potential to become a $185 billion company in the next decade.

One of the most difficult transformational tasks is to create a sense of urgency before there is an emergency. Time sometimes runs out and the transformational leader is forced to take action before he or she has obtained total commitment. Jim Renier talked about the process at Honeywell and the problems he faced when he had to take action before certain people were committed. He was frustrated because key people

> continue to look at the old situation, at the way things were, at what was being done and continually parrot that there was nothing wrong with it. I think those people need counseling, they need help, they're not well. And again, I'm not saying they're nuts, they're stuck. They can't get out of it. They need more than I can give them and I haven't got the time.

Why Can't They See Parallel Situations in Books Like In Search of Excellence *or* A Passion for Excellence? Reading about how Ray Kroc built McDonald's, or how Tom Watson turned IBM into a great organization, or how Procter & Gamble and Johnson & Johnson continue to carry out their founders' entrepreneurial visions does not help much when the problem is revitalization. The difference is that the histories of those companies contain myths and legends that reinforce some important organizational values, whereas the histories of companies in need of revitalization contain myths and legends about bad habits that must be broken. The organizations will have to solve problems and develop systems that are in sync with the current environmental conditions, not those of the past. The entrepreneurial organizations described by Peters and Waterman generate enthusiasm and excitement for the future by building on their past. Leaders who want to revitalize organizations must generate a similar level of energy to face a future that is different from the past.

How Can Leaders Effectively Transform Their Organizations? To lead effectively in turbulent times we must return to basic questions about the nature and purpose of the organization in question. A reexamination of its technical systems undoubtedly will result in a new mission and strategy. It should also result in a major revamping of the financial, marketing, production, and human resource systems as well so that they will drive the organization toward the new goals.

This technical realignment will force a consideration of the political allocation system in most organizations. In many, new criteria will determine who gets ahead, how they get rewarded, and who has the power to make decisions. And, finally, they must look at the values and beliefs they have helped to install in their members and ask if this culture supports the change the organization wishes to make. Because of the dynamic nature of organizations these systems rarely reach a state of equilibrium where they do not require some attention, but the major initial wrenching that is necessary will provide a major challenge to transformational leaders.

The technical, political, and cultural (TPC) framework provides the contextual map to guide this effort and becomes an important conceptual tool for organizing the actions and decisions of transformational leaders. Whereas TPC issues are intertwined in organizations, we have pulled them apart for the purposes of our discussion.

Technical Design Problems. All organizations face technical design problems. People, money, and technical resources must be arranged to help minimize environmental threats and maximize environmental opportunities. Strategic planning, goal setting, organizational design, and the design of management systems are all tools used to solve technical problems in organizations. The quest is for a solution that provides profitability.

Political Allocation Problems. Similarly, all organizations face the problem of allocating power and resources. Questions of who is to be involved in the decision-making process and how rewards and benefits are to be allocated are essentially problems of political allocation. Unlike the technical arena, in which there are formalized tools, such as strategic planning and organization design, the political arena frequently suffers from a lack of formalized, systematic analysis. This is unfortunate, since the greatest leadership challenges tend to lie in the strategic political arena. It is here that the tension between organizational goals and objectives and individual aspirations most often comes into play.

Cultural Value Problems. No organization can write a set of procedures so complete that they specify people's behavior in all situations. Consequently, organizations are held together in part by normative glue. If we consider the excellent organizations discussed by Peters and Waterman, we find that a common thread is their ability to articulate their values to their employees. This helps to inform decisions at all levels of the organization. Whereas it may not be as critical for blue-collar workers to share the value system of the top management team as it is for the top management team to share a common set of beliefs and values, it should be recognized that conflicting values and beliefs within the organization lead to confrontation rather than cooperation.

An important caveat in this discussion is to distinguish between a difference of opinion and a value conflict. All organizations benefit from open and honest debate on important issues and it is vital that they recognize the difference between healthy deviance and destructive heresy on the part of their members.

The Strategic Rope. The TPC issues can be seen as three intertwined strands of a rope. The rope metaphor underscores several points. First, from a distance, individual strands are not distinguishable. Similarly, a casual observer cannot distinguish the TPC systems in organizations. Second, close examination of the rope will reveal that each strand is made up of many substrands, just as close examination of organizations will reveal many TPC systems. Finally, the strength of the rope depends not only on the strength of the strands that make it up but also on their connection. A rope can unravel; an organization begins to come apart when its systems work at cross-purposes.

While the entrepreneurial founder of an organization weaves the rope from scratch, the transformational leader must unravel the old rope and reweave it. The task of the entrepreneur is difficult and the failure rate among new ventures bears testimony to that fact, but it is an essentially different problem from that faced by the transformational leader. People and organizations find this situation difficult, and human nature throws its weight on the side of resistance to change or failure to revitalize.

If we examine the leadership challenges, it will help to reflect on the basically conservative nature of people and organizations. Technically, people approach their work in a way that reduces it as quickly as possible into a standardized routine.

This has been established not just for people working at fairly routinized tasks but with top-level managers as well. Research supports the notion that people try to use their successful solutions even in situations where they are not the best fit. Similarly, people reduce uncertainty in the political arena by instituting fairly stable power relationships in groups. While it takes longer to establish the cultural values in a group, these values become the most stable and the most difficult to change. The rope is not only a metaphor for what exists in organizations but also for what gets woven into people's thinking. Their view of the TPC order of things provides a filter through which they view the world. To preserve the integrity of their world they interpret events in a way that makes them congruent with it. To do otherwise would be disruptive and lead to uncertainty. This explains why there are thousands of people working in the automobile industry who choose to interpret the events of the last five years as a severe business cycle. To do otherwise forces them to raise serious questions about the global competitiveness of the industry and its ability to survive over time.

Environmental Triggers Don't Always Trigger a Response. When we discussed the boiled frog phenomenon or "just noticeable difference threshold" dilemma, we pointed out that one of the principal problems faced by organizations is that they tend to set too high a level for detecting problems. This becomes more understandable when we see people struggling to maintain a coherent view of their world. Transformational leaders must first adjust their own threshold so that they can make more sensitive reading of environmental triggers, and then they must lower the threshold for key members of their organization.

Lowering the threshold is no easy task, as people can go to great lengths to protect their view of the world. The "world is flat" view took many years to change. Transformational leaders frequently face the challenge of shifting existing paradigms. While market analysts in other industries consistently looked to California for early signs of shifts in consumer preferences,

American automobile executives dismissed the signs. It seems almost unbelievable, in retrospect, that during the 1970s the Detroit automobile mentality filtered the California car market data in such a way that the beginning of a national preference for foreign made cars could be dismissed as idiosyncratic. They would not respond to this trend until the early 1980s, after domestic market share had eroded significantly.

Once people become sensitized to triggers for change, the transformational leader must find ways to deal with the plethora of often conflicting signals coming from a variety of stakeholders. This network of customers, suppliers, employees, investors, financial institutions, and governments presents its demands to the organization. Embedded in the messages are the first early warnings of the need for change. For two decades customers of automobile and steel companies were sending signals that the product and price were not meeting their needs. The current crisis in the steel industry and the continuing battle in the automobile industry bear testimony to the fact that the messages were ignored.

Often the organization finds it necessary to signal employees about the need for change by bringing in an outsider to head up a key operation or business. Some of our protagonists were put in their positions to deal with deteriorating situations in the organization. They were Blumenthal at Burroughs, Hammer at Chase Manahattan, and Thompson at Schneider Trucking. All came with a clear mandate to revitalize the organization. Their first challenge was to trigger a felt need for change among key members in the organization. In all cases this turned out to be a difficult task. Bringing in an outsider has both advantages and disadvantages—clearly these individuals do not identify with the past and feel no responsibility or guilt for its shortcomings. On the other hand, they have no informal networks they can depend on or chits they can call in to accomplish their agenda for change.

One could argue that the choice of some of the insiders was also a signal to the organization that change was required. John

Harvey-Jones feels he would not have been the logical choice
for chairman if things had been going well. Clearly, Renier was
promoted to address a deteriorating situation at Honeywell Information Systems, and the appointments of Welch and Campbell to head up General Electric and Burger King, respectively,
at relatively young ages was a signal to the organization that the
old way of doing things had to change.

Visionary insiders experience the greatest difficulty in
sounding the alarm that all is not well. Their presence is usually a sign that things have not reached the critical stage that
would bring an outsider aboard. On the other hand, this lack of
urgency places them in the position of trying to turn up the heat
on colleagues and introduce uncertainty in their lives when
most sense no emergency. This is the challenge that both Jack
Welch at General Electric and Roger Smith at General Motors
face. They must find ways to lower the threshold of awareness
for key organizational members so that the need for change is
felt before the situation becomes critical.

How to Create a Felt Need for Change

One simple way of stirring things up is by forcing managers and
professional employees to become externally focused. Activities that help to keep organizations in the mood for revitalization include:

1. *Challenge the Leader.* One of the greatest failings in
most organizations is that there is no one to tell the emperor
that he has no clothes. Effective transformational leaders must
develop mechanisms that provide dissonant information and
surround decision-makers with people who can operate effectively in the role of devil's advocate.

Our protagonists vary greatly in their ability to provide an
environment where this challenge can take place. Strong leaders must learn to be listening leaders as well. For Lee Iacocca,
Jack Welch, Mike Blumenthal, and Fred Hammer this runs

against the grain. They enjoy a good verbal exchange, almost as if it were a game, and one sometimes senses an underlying belief that if you can't engage in a good volley, you must not have good ideas. A frequent complaint voiced about these leaders is that it is hard to get them to listen patiently. Among the rest of our protagonists, this was less of an issue for Harvey-Jones and Lawlor, who seem to go out of their way to elicit differing opinions from people. This is also true of Campbell, Cunningham, Thompson, and Renier, who create settings where their subordinates let their hair down and speak out on important issues. The point is that strong, dominant leaders often are their own worst enemies when it comes to stirring up challenges to their views, even when they sincerely want such challenges.

2. *Build External Networks.* People pay the most attention to networks that tend to be reinforcing. Listening to colleagues at the Business Round Table, the Conference Board, and trade and professional associations tends to provide redundant views of the world. There is a strength in weak ties, and transformational leaders need to cultivate networks made up of individuals with different views and concerns. Differing views of the world can keep the threshold at a lower setting.

3. *Visits to Other Organizations.* Seeing the way other companies, especially those in Western Europe and Japan, do things can have a profound impact. When General Electric began taking manufacturing people to Japan, the managers had feelings that bordered on terror when they realized that Japanese companies were frequently turning out products with half the number of employees and significantly lower defect rates that competed with their own products. It is not only senior line executives who need to be exposed to the world outside the organization's walls. Middle managers and technical and professional employees need to look outside for the benchmarks of excellence. We frequently talk with senior management teams who are convinced that their company must change, yet further down in the organization an arrogance about past success

causes middle managers to turn a deaf ear to suggestions that all
is not well.

4. *Management Processes.* A powerful vehicle for creating
a felt need for change can be built right into the management
processes. Thus when General Electric changes the budgeting
process from one that measures progress against last year's
results to one that measures progress against a competitor's progress in a given business, the stimulus for change becomes both
more powerful and more relevant.

Intellectually, people may acknowledge the need for change,
but emotionally they may not be ready to deal with it until a
serious event causes them to face up to the changes that occurred. John Harvey-Jones said the clear trigger moment at ICI
was

> **the first time we had turned a loss in one quarter, it was the first
> loss that we had turned since the company was set up. As a result
> we had to cut our dividend.**

Our protagonists varied considerably in terms of the urgency of
their situations. Blumenthal, Harvey-Jones, Lawlor, and Renier
were more clearly grouped at the same end of the spectrum as
Iacocca and Chrysler. Their organizations had reached the
point where the balance sheet clearly testified to the gravity of
the situation. Don MacKinnon felt that CIBA-GEIGY's performance in the United States was sluggish, but the overall health
of the parent company did not create a great sense of urgency.
Thompson was jolted by a significant restructuring of the trucking industry brought about by deregulation. Hammer was
brought into Chase specifically to deal with the implications of
similar deregulation in the banking industry. Campbell, like
Hammer, felt that he had been handed the job of turning the
organization around. Cunningham, Reuss, and Stempel led an
organization that had recently experienced the first loss in its
history, but which commanded considerable assets to address
its problems. Finally, Jack Sparks, like Jack Welch, inherited a
successful, highly profitable company in no immediate danger

and took on the task of convincing the organization that they faced long-term threats from global competition if they did not significantly alter the way they did business. Thus each protagonist's drama began differently, but the difficulties they faced in convincing people that change was necessary and that the state of readiness for change must always be present bore remarkable similarities.

The ideal situation for a leader would be to manage an organization whose transformational challenge is not to avoid disaster but to defend a position of industry dominance through constant vigilance. The task is not easy, but organizations that cannot find the will to respond until the threat is severe are surely playing a game of Russian roulette, and the day will come when the trigger will activate a mortal wound instead of a near miss.

Spreading the News

Information about the environment that the organization faces should be widely disseminated through the organization so that all of its members understand the challenge. In Japan at Canon, the workers see a poster when they come to work each morning. The message is that Canon wants to beat IBM in the telecommunications field by the year 2000. For Americans, this might seem bizarre. Canon is a relatively small company—why focus the workforce on this goal? Canon's management believes that the challenge of taking on a world-class company will keep everyone focused on their long-term objectives. Contrast this approach with the reaction at General Motors to the suggestion made by one executive that Japanese cars should be placed at every GM plant so that the workers would constantly be reminded about the nature of the competition. The idea was shot down. It was seen as rubbing salt in the wounds of the workers, rather than as a way to focus their attention on the real objective.

While most American companies seem to pass on information about the competition on a need to know basis, the Japanese make sure their workers have full information about their competitors' products, manufacturing processes, and strategies. The argument is that everyone must assume a leadership role in helping the organization to meet its goals, and it is exciting to see the energy that gets released when people are able to place their work in a larger context.

An illustration of what can be done occurred at one of the tool and die groups in Packard Electric. The group had about 435 hourly employees, 27 first line supervisors, and about 10 engineers. In the early 1980s the general foreman of the group triggered some change by focusing attention on the external environment. If the tool and die group did not change, it was increasingly likely that General Motors would close the operation down and manufacture the components they made offshore or by outsourcing them.

The general manager and first line supervisors woke up the organization and shifted the mission of the group from one where they made decisions about their products without consulting the users to one where they viewed their role as essentially one of providing service. They stopped viewing themselves as an internal producer safe from competition and started responding to the real situation, which was that they were competing with other possible components manufacturers. Everyone in the unit was aware of the need for change and responded by reducing product costs and improving quality.

The formidable challenge facing transformational leaders can be met only by enlisting everyone in the organization and giving them responsibility for helping to ensure the viability of the company. Transformational leaders, having sounded the warnings to the organization, must now move into the second scene of the first act, where they will come to understand why there is so much resistance to change.

3 OVERCOMING THE RESISTANCE TO CHANGE

A long habit of not thinking a thing wrong gives it the superficial appearance of being right.

THOMAS PAINE

Change, whether at the societal, organizational, or individual level, means dislocation or discomfort. Toynbee observed that a society facing change must go through a period of disintegration before it can reintegrate. During the disintegration there are dislocations, discomfort, and a price paid for change. This process is true for organizations and for people as well.

People in organizations going through quantum change must come to grips with some unpleasant realities. As they change their behavior they must struggle to get some closure on the old way of doing things and learn to establish new routines.

The first scene of Act I dealt with the importance of intellectually recognizing that change is necessary. The second scene, emotional adjustment, is in many ways more difficult. Most of us know first hand how difficult this adjustment can be. We set out to change behavior patterns that we know are not beneficial by promising to quit smoking, lose weight, get more exercise, or manage our time more effectively. It's easy to sabotage these good intentions. We light up the cigarette, order the dessert, or put off the exercise because the weather is not ideal. Therefore, we should not be surprised that when organizations intellectually commit themselves to self-improvement programs to lower defects, increase productivity, or be more innovative, we find that the old way of doing things subtly begins to sabotage the success of the program.

Transformational leaders must understand how people deal with change. Overcoming resistance by people used to the old ways is more complex than merely issuing orders that a new era now exists. People must be given a way to work out the psychodynamics of closing off what has been ("endings"), working through a transition period, and taking up new beginnings.

Lee Iacocca provides us with an interesting example of this process. He had virtually no warning that Henry Ford was going to fire him. Iacocca could have responded with anger but instead he turned his feelings into a positive source of energy. In a television interview Iacocca told Tom Brokaw that he "would never forgive the bastard" for leaking the story of his firing to the press before he had a chance to prepare his family for this trauma. He told his children, "Don't get mad, get even. I did it in the marketplace, it took me five years but I hurt him in the marketplace. You [Brokaw] and a thousand others ask me, is that a vendetta? No! You don't have time to get angry. If I had gotten angry, I wouldn't have had the energy to do what needed doing at Chrysler." Iacocca believes that getting angry just "sucks the energy right out of you." However, he *was* angry. But what he was able to do was channel that anger in ways that were neither self-destructive nor destructive to other people. He didn't end up with a coronary, nor did he end up lashing out at other people. His anger became a source of energy to revitalize and rebuild Chrysler.

It's interesting to reflect on other transformational leaders, such as Tom Watson, Sr., who was fired from NCR and devoted his life to creating an IBM that was bigger and better than NCR. In both cases, these men were able to deal with their disappointments and sense of unfinished business by channeling them into productive, new beginnings. This is a hallmark of a transformational leader.

Another hallmark is understanding human nature, their own and others. Transformational leaders are able to sort out those people who really can change and those who can't. Mike Blumenthal reflects on an individual who couldn't change, his predecessor once removed at Burroughs. He says:

> Like all of us, he, too, was a prisoner of his past experience and tended to want to repeat all of the formulae that he had used successfully when he was 10 to 15 years younger in a different environment. He had grown up in the age of accounting machines and in the early transition from the accounting machine to computer, the intelligent accounting machine. Mainframes were giving way to intelligent desk-top computers, and the requirements of the marketplace were rapidly changing. He didn't see that. He just kept repeating the formulae that had worked in the past.

People have a tendency to play old tapes or to repeat scripts they have learned earlier in life, especially if they've been successful. Not all people have the capacity for adjusting the tapes or rewriting the scripts to meet the new conditions. However, transformational leaders must do their best to provide the conditions for testing whether an individual can unhook from the past.

Thus the first step in dealing with resistance is creating the appropriate climate for people to make use of their abilities. An important challenge is to find ways to get people to let go of the past and to develop innovative new solutions for organizational problems.

INDIVIDUAL DYNAMICS

Our experiences as consultants lead us to the conclusion that the more important part of the change framework rests on individual rather than organizational dynamics. A recent example will help explain our view. A high-tech company facing serious economic problems asked us to develop a workshop for top management. The request had been made by the president, who had been brought in from the outside by the board of directors following a major layoff with the hope that he could turn the company around.

As preparation for the workshop, interviews were conducted with each of the 10 senior managers, all of whom had been with the organization for long periods of time. The shortest tenure was about five years. Five of the 10 managers, at some point in the interview, made the following statement, "Before we go into the workshop next week, I must share something with you in confidence. I am not totally sure I will be here in the long run. As a matter of fact, I currently have some discussions going with headhunters and my resumé is on the street. This absolutely cannot be brought up in the workshop next week since my colleagues are not aware of it."

Caught on the horns of a dilemma, we spent the weekend before the workshop deliberating whether it was an exercise in futility to conduct a meeting focused on creating a vision for the future when half of the senior management team was not committed to staying with the company. Yet ethically, nothing could be said about disclosures made under the promise of confidentiality. Convinced that vision must be forged by people committed to the struggle to turn the organization around, we began to think about the emotional conflict going on in both the managers committed to stay and those who felt it might be best to leave. In all cases, including those who were thinking of leaving, there were strong approach/avoidance feelings. On the one hand they felt that it would be terrible for them to leave because they had invested so much of themselves in the company. At the same time there was a real fear that they would be unable to change the way they did things sufficiently to contribute to a revitalization of the organization.

The similarity between these emotions and the framework identified by William Bridges in *Transitions* suddenly struck. Bridges talks about people going through a difficult life transition, such as the death of someone close to them, the loss of a job, or a difficult geographic move. None of the cases that Bridges talked about focused on organizational transitions, but the possibility of relating his framework to the dynamics in this company's top management team seemed useful.

Bridges's framework is simple and straightforward. There are some predictable psychological processes that occur in life transitions—ones that trigger deep emotions. It is Bridges's contention that unless people successfully work through these psychological processes they can never really get off to a new start. Thus the argument is that the ending of one situation must be successfully worked through before there can be new beginnings and renewal. If these psychological stages are not completed there is a tendency to repeat the same mistakes again or simply to yearn for the past so much that people are unable to make new lives for themselves. We have all seen people who go through one marriage after another, repeating the same dynamics that inevitably lead to failure without ever appearing to learn. Or people who lose a spouse and who focus so completely on the past that their memories prevent them from forming new relationships.

Organizational transitions tend to evoke the same strong feelings in their members. For many of them, their lives and identities, as well as their self-esteem, are tied to their professional identity. Consequently, the dynamics of change are as powerful as those experienced by people dealing with the death of a loved one or a geographic separation from family and friends. It is useful to take a closer look at the basic framework as Bridges applied it to individuals and then relate it to the transformational leadership framework.

THE ENDINGS/TRANSITION/NEW BEGINNINGS FRAMEWORK

Phase One—Endings

Bridges argues that there are four basic processes that need to occur in an ending. The first is *disengagement*. That is the explicit event that triggers the transition: someone dies, someone is fired, someone moves. The second activity associated with endings is more subtle—*disidentification*. When a disengagement occurs, the individual must work through a process in which his or her identity is altered. When a spouse dies or a divorce occurs, the part of an individual's identity that was defined as John's wife or Mary's husband is no longer valid and the individual's identity must be recast to fit the new reality. This does not occur overnight and the more central the change in terms of the individual's identity the more difficult the process of disidentification. When a person is heard saying things such as "Let me tell you about how things were where I used to work," or mentally compares each new relationship with the one that was lost, the process of disidentification is not complete. The third dimension of an ending is *disenchantment*.

This is possibly the most important part of the process of endings. It involves coming to grips with the fact that what was enchanting in the past can no longer be. If this process does not take place, disillusionment sets in and individuals may set out on futile attempts to recapture the past enchantment, to recreate what cannot be, to yearn for the good old days.

An example of disenchantment that many of us share was our belief in Santa Claus. We were once enchanted with the idea of Santa Claus. We wrote notes telling him what we wanted for Christmas. When Christmas Eve arrived we left cookies and milk for Santa, and the following morning our belief was rewarded and reinforced. The cookies and milk were gone and under the tree were the presents that he had left. By the time we were seven, however, we were disenchanted with the idea that Santa Claus actually existed. If you asked one of us if there was a Santa Claus we would have laughed and said, "There's no Santa. Our parents stay up late at night and put the presents under the tree." Bridges would maintain that this disenchantment process is healthy. We would have replaced one reality with another more in keeping with our own development and ability to appreciate that the spirit of giving resided not in Santa Claus but in people who loved us. But the idea of Santa Claus was nice, and if we had younger brothers or sisters we wouldn't spoil it by telling them what we discovered. A successful ending would be appreciating the enchantment we felt in the past for Santa Claus and replacing it with an enchantment for the spirit of giving. If the child, however, feels disillusioned with the notion that there is no Santa Claus and refuses to recognize the worth of the new reality it is difficult to achieve this ending. Coming to grips with this process of disenchantment is a task that many executives face.

To give you a sense of just how powerful this process is, each of us encountered a reaction from employees of AT&T following the divestiture agreement. Tichy attended a dinner with the president of one of the operating companies about four months after the actual divestiture took place. A casual remark prompted a tirade from the president. He shook his finger and said, "You will be sorry for what has happened, it is unfair. There was no reason to break up the best telephone system in the world. Your service will deteriorate and your costs will go up . . . ." What makes this episode important is that thousands of people depended on the president's ability to develop a vision and commit people to that vision so that the organization could be revitalized. However, like most human beings he was struggling with the endings and had not yet worked through the process so that he could begin to plan for the future.

Another example of failure to deal with endings occurred further down in a sister operating company a few weeks later. Devanna tried to have a telephone serviced. It took three telephone calls to try to find out whose responsibility it was to come and look at the telephone. The considered opinion of all concerned was that AT&T should do the job since they leased the telephone. The AT&T repairman arrived and said the problem existed in the wires leading to the house. A NYNEX repairman arrived and announced that the problem was in the AT&T equipment illegally hooked up to their lines. He said there would be a service charge for the call since the problem did not emanate from the NYNEX equipment. Feeling like a victim, Devanna called the service representative to complain about the service charge. For the first time in all of the years of dealing with telephone company service representatives, the response was not one of reason and concern but of anger and belligerence. "We are going to charge you for the call—it is not our fault that your phones are permanently connected and that you can't bring them in to be tested. This is what you wanted and now you've got it." Attempts to interject a light note into the conversation by pointing out that Judge Green had not called for a consultation before making the decision on divestiture did not have the desired effect. When we talked about these incidents we realized that people at many levels of AT&T were struggling with the issue of disenchantment with the past.

The AT&T case makes an interesting point. Many people would agree that telephone service by practically any measure you want to use was better before the divestiture—so the past was clearly better for virtually all the stakeholders except the competitors of AT&T. Perhaps we were better off before the divestiture, but the divestiture is a reality that AT&T employees and customers must deal with. Like telephone service in the predivestiture era, the post-World War II period we discussed in the previous chapter was more comfortable for Americans. Markets that lacked sensitivity to price and quality because they lacked competition were easier to manage. Employees preferred them because their wages could be increased without increases in productivity. Divestiture, like competition, has changed the way we must act if we are to survive.

The final process involved in endings is *disorientation,* and both of the people we encountered at AT&T in the months following the divestiture showed signs of disorientation. The anchors are neither in the past nor in the future. Some of the transformational leaders we interviewed talked of periods of disorientation in their organizations. Blumenthal spoke of the reactions at Burroughs as the realization set in that all was not well:

> Now a tremendous amount of turmoil and dismay, fear and disquiet set in further down in the organization. Here they thought they were working for a company that was forever moving upward. Suddenly they were reading one item of bad news after another about the company in the paper. They had been living with the fact that the machines were not working properly for some time, but now the financial results were bad and two or three levels down people didn't have enough of an overview of the company to put that together. And some of them finally realized what they had suspected all along, that something was wrong with the company and that it badly needed fixing.

John Harvey-Jones described a similar situation at ICI:

> We were in real pain, we were reducing our numbers like hell and I was carrying a lot of responsibility for that. The fall from grace in this country was for us very rude indeed. My company

has for years enjoyed the reputation of being the outstanding British company, and all of our people believed they belonged to a corps d'elite. If you believe that, when you are defeated in battle there is an enormous fall from grace, and indeed there were quite a few people outside the company who took quite a pleasure in our discomfort and more or less ran around saying the company was not that good anyway and it serves them right.

This experience: reducing our numbers, cutting our dividend, and getting hell from the press, left us disoriented. In addition the company had always had a reputation for being paternalistic and we were losing that reputation, too. People were leaving the company who had not actually underperformed but whom we just could not afford to keep on. So a lot of pictures of the company as we were began to be destroyed. There had been little fundamental organizational change for a long time in the company and there was a belief that if guys would just do what they had been doing better all would be well. But, I must think there was great feeling around the company that here we are, Rome is burning and all we're doing is trying to do more of what we were doing before and we needed to do something different. I believe that is why I was elected chairman, in spite of the fact that I was the most radical in English terms of the three possible candidates.

Jim Renier at Honeywell describes the dynamic of individual endings a little differently. He uses a simple categorization scheme that describes the stages people go through when dealing with their problems: denial, anger, negotiation, depression, and finally acceptance. Renier believes it is extremely important for managers to help people to work through these processes:

See my point is that you can't get out from under until you get by the denial stage and the anger stage and convince people there's no point in sitting around trying to negotiate their way out of a mess. You're in it and let's not be depressed for too long. When you get acceptance of the reality, then you can solve the problem . . . . The hardest stage you have to deal with in a troubled organization is denial.

Renier's focus on denial comes from some very personal experiences in his own life from which he has been able to learn and put to use in his role as transformational leader.

> Years ago when my wife was very, very ill, I was having lots of trouble. After she died I had a hell of a time coming out of that, and a priest friend of mine, a very good friend, gave me a very useful little book that pointed out these things . . . . I said to myself, well hell I've been in the business now for all these years, at that time it was about 20 years, and that's all I've been looking at all the time. I'd been engaging in this denial thing myself, not just with my wife, denying she had cancer, but with businesses that I've been involved in that are in trouble. It's very interesting—what I call pyramid effect. The top of the organization comes out of denial last. The bottom comes out first. They see the problem clearly. Perhaps, they have less to lose, personally. The bottom grumbles about why can't they see this up at the top. There was a time when they didn't see it either but they say, why can't management solve the problem. You get an absolute polarization. I don't know if the bottom of this organization knew what they were bitching about in detail but they certainly knew there was trouble. Just like the troops are out there and the guns don't work and the Pentagon is saying, the hell they don't . . . .

Transitions—The Neutral Zone

The critical point for companies trying to figure out their future is the transitional state. This is the time when there is a need to leave the past productively—a process of death and rebirth. This stage is an extremely difficult one in our culture. We tend to think of change as something to be added to the present state, a new frontier, an improvement over the past. Consequently, our approach can be summed up in statements such as "let's get on with it," "forget about the past," "let bygones be bygones." There is an attempt to deny that every change process involves a process of destruction. This approach works best in rapidly growing organizations where the major challenge is to move as rapidly as possible to new frontiers. On the other hand, organizations whose challenge is transformation and revitalization face a process of change similar to that of a phoenix, which must immolate itself so that it can rise from the ashes with renewed vigor.

Bridges calls this time the neutral zone and equates it to standing in the middle of a busy highway with the traffic going in both directions. This is a frightening experience, but psychologically that is what people involved in change must do—simultaneously experience the forces from the past and those pulling us toward the future. During this stage of a transformation we see a great deal of inconsistent behavior. One day a person may be excited about the prospects the future holds and the next day be quite pessimistic that things will not work out. The Bell operating company president who was angry and upset about the scope of the changes in the organization may have been excited about the opportunities for autonomy that the divestiture offered him. It simply takes time to work through the transition.

In our culture we have many customs and ceremonies that implicitly recognize the importance of transition states. Many formal religions conduct funeral services to serve as transitions for both the living and the dead. They are meant to provide both support for the living and a time to come to grips with the loss of a loved one. At the same time many religions see it as a transition for the dead as well, from this life to a life hereafter, and as such, a time for celebration as well as for mourning.

Many organizations implicitly recognize the importance of handling certain transitions well. For example, good outplacement practices start with helping the individual to understand what went wrong—why the ending; help is then provided for the transition state in the form of counseling, severance pay, and office support as they begin to search for a new beginning. Properly handled outplacement leads to a period of revitalization for the individual.

New Beginnings

The final phase is the period of revitalization. At this point the individual has made the necessary adjustment to changing circumstances and is able to release the energy needed to deal with the new situation. People are truly excited about the possibilities. They have managed to unhook themselves from the behaviors, patterns, and attitudes that need to be left behind, and they have started to write new scripts that contain new behaviors and attitudes. Like the phoenix, they are emerging from the ashes of the past to face the future with enthusiasm and energy.

Now let's return to the case of the 10 executives going off to work on the vision for their organization. This was a new beginnings task. The president had no history in this organization and consequently didn't feel the need to unhook from the past. But most of the team he was leading were struggling with the ambivalence that accompanies transitions. This ambivalence was being played out by actions like looking for a new job. They were not ready for a new beginning.

We thought that the group might be struggling through the individual dynamics of change and would benefit from Bridges's framework. Before a vision could be created and before people could be committed to that vision, they needed to work through their own feelings about what was happening to the organization. We presented the Bridges framework on the first day of the workshop. Two days of fairly open discussion about the difficulty of working through this transition followed. These managers were helped because they had a way to frame the problem and a vehicle to use in talking through some of their ambivalent feelings. As a result, most made a decision to stay with the company through the transition. Two left after a very open and candid set of discussions that extended over a period of several months. They realized that the new beginning that the company required was not one that fit with their own goals and objectives, and that opportunities that existed outside the company suited them better. Both sides agreed that the decisions to leave were the right ones. By working through this process, the senior group was able to develop and to commit themselves to a new vision of the organization. They went on to develop a strategy that enabled them to help their subordinates and then the rest of the organization through this transition.

Since people make up organizations, leaders need to be attuned to the psychodynamics of change which Bridges frames for us. It is this understanding that provides the way to deal with resistance. The remainder of this chapter examines resistance at an organizational level.

ORGANIZATIONAL RESISTANCE TO CHANGE

It is important to come to grips with the paradox that many organizations facing environmental pressures do not change and thus collude in their own demise. This happens in organizations where the trigger events demanding change were evident even to outsiders. Yet the change did not take place. This leads us to believe there is something in the nature of organizations and people that makes it difficult for them to change in a fundamental way. The transformational leader must understand these resistant forces and mobilize the energy needed to overcome them in order to transform the organization. The ability to change organizations is hampered in many different ways. Jack Sparks describes some of the responses from subordinates to his plans for transforming Whirlpool.

> The resistance. It was coming back to me through some people, particularly some of the older guys who were near retirement, that I had a lot of people upset, that I was creating new offices, reorganizing, and a lot of people were nervous. What's Sparks trying to do? Well, I was asking for accountability and they were not used to that and it made them nervous.

Mike Blumenthal and John Harvey-Jones faced different problems when they assumed control at Burroughs and ICI, respectively. They were confronted with organizations that were used to being led. Blumenthal describes the situation at Burroughs:

> At the top levels of the organization there was no resistance to me at all because most of them wanted another father figure. Most of them wanted another leader. They had never worked in a company without a father figure and they sort of came in and said "What are your orders, sir?" And, they would loyally carry them out. The problem was that their passivity was a reflection of their ability. I recall asking my predecessor what do people say when you tell them that this strange character is going to become CEO—because I was curious about what the reaction was—and he said, "Well, very good reaction, one guy came to me and said he really thought it was good and necessary for Burroughs that someone like Blumenthal was coming in. He said he realized that he would probably lose his job but that it was good for the company."
>
> I was shocked. I said, "What kind of a statement is that? You must be kidding." He assured me that he was serious. I asked why anyone would say something like that and was told that the guy did not think he would measure up to my standards. I felt awful. Someone who had never met me, who had never worked with me thought I was going to fire him.

John Harvey-Jones discusses his response to attempts to push decisions and responsibility upward:

> I remember the first meeting and it went something like "Thank God you've come, John, you're just the man we need, we've never had strong leadership before. You tell us what to do and we will do it." To which my response was "You're not going to catch me the way you caught all my predecessors . . . ." It was building a team that was necessary.

Whether the obstacles to change come in the form of rejecting direction from strong leadership, as was the case at Whirlpool, or an inability to perform at the level that the survival of Burroughs demanded, or from a long tradition of passivity and avoidance of responsibility as was the case at ICI, the transformational leader must deal with the resistance to change without resorting to the pitfalls of one-minute quick fixes. This is the first part of the revitalization challenge.

The resistance to change comes from the recognition that all change involves exchange. People have to break old habits and learn new ways of doing things. They must establish new norms and values, and in the process they frequently discover that their status and power in the organization are measured in different ways. These changes put in play the age-old conflict between the human desire for constancy so praised by the poets and the search for new experiences so applauded by philosophers. Resistance is the first reaction to change because people need time to assess the cost and benefits of the change to them.

The new direction often triggers many conflicting responses. The hope that the new plan will clarify a sense of direction is countered by the fear of the unknown.

The relief that accompanies a call to action brings with it a sense of anxiety that the right choice has been made.

The stimulation that change implies causes pressure as unforeseen consequences arise.

The happiness that people experience when they encounter new meaning and a new sense of value in their lives exists side by side with a sense of sadness at the loss of the values and sense of esteem that were earned by actions no longer valued.

We can analyze the reasons why resistance to change exists in organizations through the TPC framework.

Technical Reasons for Resistance to Change

Three major technical reasons for resistance to change are:

1. *Habit and Inertia.* Habit and inertia cause task-related resistance to change. For technical reasons, individuals who

have always done things one way have trouble changing behavior patterns.

2. *Fear of the Unknown or Loss of Organizational Predictability.* Not knowing or having difficulty predicting the future creates anxiety and hence resistance in many individuals. When computers are introduced for mid-level management and professional tasks, employees with established success records under a different system tend to resist this change.

3. *Sunk Cost.* Organizations, even when realizing that there are potential pay-offs from a change, are often unable to enact a change because of the sunk cost of the organization's resources in the old way of doing things.

Leaders can help the organization's members by reframing the way in which they think about their common problems. While Tom Murrin was president of Westinghouse's Public Systems Sector, he framed the quality and productivity issues for his senior executive team. In late 1980, after spending a year as head of a committee looking for ways to improve quality control and productivity at Westinghouse, he transmitted his new view of the world in a speech to his senior management group. He told them:

Frankly, gentlemen, my perspective of our competitive strength is tempered with caution and concern after gazing about the boardrooms, offices, laboratories and factories of our competition . . . . From Fairfield to Dallas, to Munich, to Tokyo and around much of the rest of the world, what I see is both exciting and alarming. In particular, findings in Japan scare the hell out of me . . . .

Murrin spent time at this meeting showing his managers videotapes of Japanese, South Korean, West German, and Italian factories and facilities to help frame the problem for them. He gave examples of how Japanese managers, with 100 percent U.S. workforces, were able to achieve dramatic productivity improvements. This included the Sony plant in San Diego and the Matsushita acquisition of a failing Motorola plant in Chicago. In both cases the product quality and productivity were comparable to plants in Japan and way ahead of U.S. competitors. Bill Coatsek, the president of Westinghouse's Construction Group at the time, stated:

When you visit Japanese factories and see everyone, but everyone, working like tigers to make that product more reliable at a lower cost, it's awesome. They even come back early from breaks. In factory after factory, everyone is trying to whip us. If we don't get that attitude we literally won't survive.

Once he had triggered the felt need for change at Westinghouse, Murrin then took the time to carefully provide a framework for achieving the changes. In Westinghouse's case, it involved applying proven Japanese ingredients for quality and productivity: the best facilities; 100 percent inspection of incoming materials; training for employees that stressed the why as well as the how; and closer cooperation among engineering, manufacturing, and marketing. An impressive array of technical, training, engineering, and internal and external consulting resources has been invested to meet Murrin's challenge at Westinghouse. As of 1985, the results remain mixed. There are some outstanding examples of success, while other parts of the organization continue to slide. Overall, Westinghouse remains vulnerable in the arena of global competition. But there is a sense of direction and hopefulness that can only result from the creation of a vision and the development of a strategy for achieving it.

Similar efforts are under way in many U.S. manufacturing organizations. General Electric's program to get managers to visit world manufacturing facilities did more than create a felt need for change. It helped managers develop a new technical frame for thinking about manufacturing. Providing people with technical maps to guide them in unknown territory is an important tool for transformational leaders.

Political Reasons for Resistance to Change

There are three major reasons for political resistance to change.

1. *Threats to Powerful Coalitions.* A common threat is found in the conflict between the old guard and the new guard. This came up at General Motors soon after the reorganization as described by Lloyd Reuss:

> There was a fear among those in the executive ranks that they would get run over with a steamroller by the new vehicle groups, but I think that things have changed so that they now recognize the role of the North American vehicle groups and realize that all the division and group organizations need to work together as a team.

2. *Zero Sum Decision-Making Resulting from Limitations on Resources.* In the days when the economic pie was steadily expanding and resources were much less limited, changes were easier to enact. Every part of the company stood to gain, as witnessed in past labor management agreements in the automobile industry. Now that the pie is shrinking, decisions need to be made as to who shares a smaller set of resources. The message from the CEO in most companies is to be more productive and innovative with less head count and less overhead. These zero sum decisions are politically more difficult to implement and stronger resistance to the change is the result.

3. *The Indictment of Leadership Problem.* Perhaps the most significant resistance to change comes from the fact that leaders have to indict their own past decisions and behaviors to bring about change. An example of this is the difficulty that Roger Smith faced early on in the course of change at General Motors. He had to indict his own past behavior as a member of senior management when he suggested that drastic changes were necessary at General Motors. Psychologically it is very difficult for people to change when they were party to creating the problems they are trying to change. In that aspect it's much

easier to come in from the outside, as Lee Iacocca did. He was
not indicting himself every time he said something was wrong
with the organization. Furthermore, he didn't have to risk step-
ping on the toes of his colleagues. In fact, he ended up firing 35
Chrysler vice presidents.

Leaders need to provide a bargaining mechanism and a process that will help key actors buy into the change process. Take
Westinghouse as illustrative of many U.S. companies. Merely
having a technical map to help managers work through the wilderness is not sufficient to mobilize enthusiastic commitment
for the journey. At Westinghouse, it is reasonable to assume that
political resistance was triggered because:

1. The proposed changes were threatening to people's fu-
    ture career opportunities. In fact, Murrin stated in his
    speech that an executive's future success would be mea-
    sured in terms of his or her ability to achieve improve-
    ments in productivity.
2. Some businesses in the Westinghouse portfolio were un-
    doubtedly in a better position to meet Murrin's produc-
    tivity challenge. Coalitions emerged, depending on the
    support that individuals felt for the new program and the
    probability that they would be able to meet the new
    goals.
3. The way in which the productivity improvements are to
    be funded—a small amount of corporate seed money and
    the balance from operating profits. There will undoubt-
    edly be increased internal competition for these scarce
    resources.
4. There was an indictment quality in the challenge. Wes-
    tinghouse management had been asleep at the wheel
    while foreign competition left them in the dust. It is a
    difficult psychological task to accept the responsibility
    for the failure and not to attempt to place it on events
    beyond the control of Westinghouse's management team.

The result of such resistance is inaction or even vociferous opposition to plans for change. Transformational leaders must come up with ways to work through this resistance. They must essentially provide the bargaining mechanisms that will bring key organizational members to buy into the need for change, teaching them a new way of calculating what is in their best interest. Thus Westinghouse executives must come to believe that the greatest payoff for them will occur if they help to implement this change process.

At the moment when Murrin delivered the message, most executives must have perceived more of the cost to them than the benefits; more of the pain than the gain. Executive compensation was tied to annual performance and yet Murrin's plan demanded sacrificing this year's bottom line to find the necessary money to finance the productivity improvement effort. It meant that executives were being asked to assign their bonuses to implement the change. This only exacerbated the indictment aspect of the need for change and undoubtedly was perceived by some managers as punishment for past failures.

Finally, to make the productivity program work, managers have to gain the cooperation of rank and file workers. This changed the existing power structure at Westinghouse. Unlike the company heroes of the past who were rewarded for being tough and nonparticipative and for making the numbers, the heroes of the future would be those most capable of convincing, jaw-boning, and cajoling the stakeholders to buy into the plan.

Cultural Reason for Resistance to Change

There are three key reasons for cultural resistance:

1. *Cultural Filters Resulting in Selective Perception.* An organization's culture may highlight certain values, making it difficult for members to conceive of other ways of doing things. An organization's culture defines that which people perceive as possible. Thus innovation may come from outsiders or deviants who are not as channeled in their perceptions. One crude way

of differentiating people is dividing them into those whose heads are "hardwired" and who cannot change versus those with "software" problems who can learn new behaviors and operate effectively in the new environment. In the AT&T system, those who are culturally hardwired, that is, who cannot adapt to the new change, are pejoratively referred to as "bellheads." No amount of training, coaching, or cajoling will change bellheads into entrepreneurial, marketing-oriented individuals. Most of our organizations undergoing transformations have their version of bellheads. At General Electric's Lighting Division, Ralph Ketchum's view is that:

I think there is a very slight change you can make in people. Sometimes you can get somebody in an organization that is pretty hardwired as you describe it, and say, "Look. Here are your strengths and weaknesses. We're going to bolster you up, we're going to plug in these kind of people beneath you . . . ."

Fred Hammer, who faced a very strong culture at Chase, holds a similar view. He was brought into Chase to build retail banking, but the culture of Chase didn't embrace retail banking. Hammer said that the typical Chase reaction to Bankers Trust selling its branches was a belief that Chase should do the same. He said:

> The culture had always been that we were the preeminent U.S. corporate bank. Basically, our international strategy followed our domestic strategy. We were a corporate lending bank, so why bother with all this expensive retail banking and branches, especially when you remember that all of the growth in the consumer business was through the acquisition of the Bank of Manhattan, which had lots of branches. But in the fall-out after that acquisition there was nobody left from the Bank of Manhattan at Chase. So in the retail dimension it was never going to do well. My challenge at Chase was, number one, to change the basic thinking of the people in the consumer area, and number two, to get this accepted by the rest of the bank so that they would give us the resources.

2. *Regression to the Good Old Days.* We often feel secure when returning to the past. However, transition requires people to give up the old ways of doing things. This became one of Roger Smith's early struggles. Cunningham talks about how Smith responded to the proposals for a massive reorganization, once the automobile market began coming back and things were getting better. It was a time when the cultural response put on tremendous pressures for a regression to the good old days. Cunningham said:

> About this time we were coming out of the recession and General Motors was again selling in volume and making money and was doing it in the age-old way. One of the things that I think was courageous on Roger's part was to say that we were going to continue to rock the boat despite the fact that we were back making a profit. He had the courage to say we may be doing all right but the changing dynamics in the marketplace necessitate a change in the way we do business.

Jeff Campbell comments on a similar tendency for regression to the good old days:

> We have a 30-year-old culture that we are trying to change. It doesn't change overnight, it gets insidious. It creeps back around the edges when you get things going. The better things get, the more people want to feel comfortable again. We had the idea that if we start to do the right kinds of things—changing the way we plan so that people would not be pressured to set goals that they know they cannot make—then we're going to see people respond by doing the right kinds of things instead of the wrong kinds of things. Second, there will be a tremendous surge of enthusiasm when they realize they no longer are tied to this treadmill.

3. *Lack of Climate for Change.* Organizations often vary in their conduciveness to change. Cultures that require a great deal of conformity often lack much receptivity to change. Most of our large corporate examples are no exception. Transforma-

tional leaders must recognize this and provide opportunities to create a climate for change. Part of it is doing the simple things, such as symbolic personal touches. Campbell describes a part of his approach:

> We knew what we wanted to do but you don't go out and tell everybody what you're going to do, you go out and listen for a while. . . . The way we structured the first batch of meetings was to go out in the market and meet with a hundred franchisees. We'd spend the first two hours listening. I'd ask them questions about where the business was, and we were pretty confident that as they talked about their problems, they would come to the same conclusion we had reached. We had the same problems and figured that the challenges they saw were going to be similar to the ones that we saw . . . .

After two years of success, Campbell had a problem similar to Roger Smith's of keeping people focused on the new agenda:

> They're making more money than they've ever made. They have forgotten the things that worried them two years ago. You tell them the long-term market's changing. We can look back at the last two years and we can all pat ourselves on the back and say it's great. But there are a lot of things we're still not doing right, and in the long term if you really want to be successful, if you want your kids to inherit your business, if we want the stockholders to still feel this is a valuable investment five or ten years from now, there are some things we're going to have to do and we're going to have to start now and here's what they are. . . . And that kind of fundamental change is going to take us three or four years. If it means that we have to reinvest some of those earnings, then we are going to do it. And everybody's going, yeah. Okay, but now we're really starting to come up against the resistance of the old corporate culture. In a lot of 30-year-old mindsets, the old way of doing things is so strong that they do not believe that you are serious and their behavior won't change.
>
> When you go back and say, "Why haven't you changed?" they will say, "Because it's not real. You really don't mean what you are saying. There'll be a profit crunch and all this extra labor will

be taken from us and it isn't worth changing because we will
have to change back." You begin to realize that articulation is not
enough. We're going to have to do some symbolic things and we
started doing that this past year. We said we're not going to grow
operating profits this year, stay flat, or even go down, we're going
to add managers to each restaurant because we're understaffed
and we're never going to get the quality we want unless we do
that and we are willing to take a hit on the bottom line. And they
all said, hah. They'll do it until the third quarter. Well, we did it
all year and we told Pillsbury up front we were going to do it. We
said we'll get you your 20 percent growth in earnings but that's
not how we're going to do it. We'll do it in other ways . . . .

Murrin's technical map implicitly contains a whole new set
of values and norms for the organization. Values of quality and
productivity jointly arrived at and held by workers and management are not frequently found in U.S. industry, where management requests are viewed as worker concessions. Many U.S.
executives continue to resist the notion that Japanese management practices lead to higher productivity. It is more comfortable to believe that the strength of the yen and the relationship
between Japanese industry and government allow them to
compete unfairly. More comfortable not because the Japanese
won't continue to dominate industries and markets but because
U.S. managers do not have to accept the responsibility for the
problem.

One of the first things a transformational leader must do is
determine which members of the management team can adjust
to the changing demands and which members cannot. It is
helpful to provide the opportunity to examine values, talk about
them, and discuss what needs to be changed. Managers, in
workshop settings, can analyze which aspects of the current
culture prevent them from changing the organization and devise methods of implementing new values to facilitate the
change.

Murrin helped the process along by serving as a role model.
He had all of his managers interviewed so that he could get

feedback on how his own style and behavior were incongruent with the new values the organization needed. This helped break down resistance. Jim Renier used an outside consultant to gather data from subordinates not only on his style but their own as well. He strongly believed that if you wanted to deal with resistance to change you had to start at the top. The process was then replicated through several layers of management.

AVOIDING THE SEARCH FOR AN EASY ANSWER

The transformational leader must constantly remind people why they are doing things. Jack Welch believes that U.S. managers' preoccupation with management tools, such as strategic planning, led to a loss of global competitiveness. It is not that planning is bad or that giving timely feedback to employees is destructive. It clearly is not. Neither of these techniques, however, is the answer to all organizational problems. The problem that arises is that people become enamored of techniques they master and skills they acquire so that they look for situations in which they can be applied. What results is the "little boy with the hammer phenomenon"—if you give a little boy a hammer he will soon find that everything broken could be fixed by hammering it. (This behavior pattern is not limited to the male of the species, since "little girls" also practice it.) Thus when we expose managers to the managerial grid, quality circles, zero based budgeting, dimensions of excellence, or strategic planning portfolio analysis we run the risk that they will seize and use it to try and solve all organizational ills. We are susceptible to snake oil claims because we live in a culture that seeks easy answers to fundamental problems. The following are some general guidelines for transformational leaders which can help them avoid being seduced by processes that are not focused on organizational problems.

1. *Have an Agenda.* Leaders have clear agendas—lists of things they need to accomplish to transform the organization. The agenda becomes an organizational anchor. The use of one management tool or another can be evaluated against a clear sense of what needs to be accomplished. For example, if an item with top priority on a change agenda is altering the style of management in the organization, as was the case for Tom Murrin and Jim Renier, then a program such as the managerial grid might be a useful tool to consider since it could help accomplish this goal.

2. *A No Easy Answers Norm.* The transformational leader must not permit anyone to attempt to implement panaceas. Frequently someone returns from a workshop or a training event having had an "ah-ha" experience. The person returns to the organization preaching the new gospel, but the evangelism can soon wear thin on those around the evangelist. The transformational leader must find a way to channel constructively their sincere enthusiasm while at the same time holding to the rule that there are no easy answers to the complex and dynamic problems facing the organization.

3. *Avoid the Overadvocacy Trap.* It is in the nature of most organizations that advocates for a change must oversell the concept in order to get it accepted. This creates a trap. First, it creates a sense of unreasonable expectations. Second, it sets in motion a set of political dynamics to perpetuate the new activity whether or not it succeeds. In the late 1970s many consultants, internal staff, and line executives oversold the idea of quality circles in order to get them accepted. Since those who assumed the advocate's role had made such a substantial investment in the acceptance of the idea, they were pushed to defend it even if it did not meet expectations.

The transformational leader must be alert for this overadvocacy trap and promote a more balanced view of what can be accomplished with a single program. The fact is that many things will work in little ways to improve an organization—but there are no panaceas.

Working through the trigger, felt need, resistance, and search for an easy answer challenges brings down the curtain on the transformational leader's first act. The second act will involve a careful diagnosis of the current state of the organization, along with the creation of a vision for the future.

ACT TWO

CREATING A
NEW VISION

4 DIAGNOSING THE PROBLEM

Long before the bottom line
indicates that the organization is in
trouble everything inside has gone
to hell in a handbasket.

JAMES RENIER

Americans are fascinated by images of great heroes. Thanks to endless books and movies, the expansion of the western frontier is coupled in our minds with the image of the legendary cowboys and lawmen and not with the families of settlers who painstakingly cleared the land and established communities. Our "superheroes"—Wonder Woman, Superman, Spiderman, and the rest—are not really like us. They arrive to rescue us from forces that would destroy us if it were not for their intervention. Thus it is not surprising that transformational leaders like Lee Iacocca have become national folk heroes.

These people fit right in with the romantic American notion of the heroic manager: they see a company about to collapse, come to the rescue with drastic action, quickly set the company right, and ride off into the sunset. The problem with the image is that it suggests a group of people who, like our superheroes, are benevolent "visitors." They differ from corporate raiders like Pickens, Icahn, and Jacobs, because they recognize the rights of constituencies—employees, customers, and communities—as well as stockholders. But they would not be part of the organization in the same way that its other members are. Like Superman, the outside hero bails the ineffectual mortals out of tough spots, but no disguise of business suit and horn rims will ever make him one of them. Mortals can admire him but never hope to emulate him.

This picture of the heroic manager is one painted largely by the press. Nothing, however, could be farther from the truth. We've found that an important element in effective corporate transformations is that the way they are carried out is the antithesis of the heroic style. Iacocca, to be sure, is heroic in many respects. Renier, Lawlor, and Blumenthal also inherited organizations in near crisis states; the actions to keep their companies afloat were indeed drastic. But they never pretended to be superhumans whose success was uniquely their own. On the contrary, they sought to empower others so that the necessary actions could be duplicated throughout the organization and, indeed, could survive their direct intervention and presence. Most did not seek the crisis but had it thrust on them.

For example, Blumenthal, Iacocca, and Lawlor did not realize the seriousness of the situations they were getting into
when they agreed to join their new organizations. Blumenthal
talks about Burroughs:

> I was congratulating myself because I had seriously considered
> not going back to private industry for all kinds of reasons, one of
> them being that I kept telling all of my friends that, hell, I had a
> good job when I ran Bendix, that was a good company, and the
> only kind of job I would be offered in industry would have been
> with a company that was sick—that had to be turned around. I
> really did not want to do that—or some kind of other problem
> with a small company. But I did not think there were too many
> large Fortune 100 companies around in search of a CEO where
> there wasn't a serious problem, and I had had my problems at the
> Treasury and I wasn't really interested in taking on another can
> of worms. So I kept saying, boy, I am the luckiest son of a gun in
> the world. Here I am handed this wonderful company—never
> had a problem—great industry, you know, growing by leaps and
> bounds. No problem of getting sales and I really had very little
> advance notice—none at all that there was any kind of problem. I
> was coming in to learn the computer business in a fine company
> and carry on a great tradition.

Iacocca talks about the situation he believed existed at Chrysler when he was talking with Riccardo about joining the company:

> I don't want to go into this blind, I said. I need to know how bad
> things are. I need to know where the company stands. How
> much cash do you have. What your operating plan is for next
> year. What your future products look like. And especially
> whether you guys really think you can make it.
>
> Our next two meetings were held at the Northfield Hilton in sub-
> urban Detroit. Riccardo painted a bleak picture, but one that
> I thought could be turned around in a year. I really don't think
> that John or anyone else at Chrysler was trying to pull the wool
> over my eyes. One of Chrysler's biggest problems, as I soon
> learned, was that even its top management didn't have a very
> good idea of what was going on. They knew Chrysler was bleed-

ing. What they didn't realize—and what I would soon find out—was that it was hemorrhaging.

Mary Ann Lawlor talks of her early days at Drake.

I worked for George Webster at Evelyn Wood Reading Dynamics. He was a lawyer and a Harvard Business School grad who put together the deal that saved Evelyn Wood. After he left there he decided to put together his own little conglomerate. He bought proprietary business schools in Boston and Washington as well as Drake Business School in New York. Drake at that time had five locations. The problem is he only looked at one location—the most modern facility. The locations he did not look at had desks with ink wells and iron legs bolted to the floor. There were electric typewriters but only at the 15 Park Row location. When he realized what he had bought, he hired me. So I came in as corporate managing director of the five schools.

Drake had had a respectable history from 1873 until after World War II, but by the late 1960s it was barely surviving on brush up courses. Webster thought the name was so terrific he would have an instant turnaround. The turnaround took longer than anticipated, and every time he put more money in or signed something he got more nervous. So it came to the point one day when we were at a meeting to renew a lease that I had negotiated with the landlord, when suddenly, Webster turned to me and said, "The board of directors met last night and named you president—you sign the lease." That's how I became president of Drake.

I had no idea how critical our financial situation was until Webster called me from Washington and said he couldn't meet our regular payroll the day before it was due. He said I don't know what you are going to do but I hope you'll figure out something. I used some money in a local operating account plus I took money out of the joint savings account that I had with my husband. Later, I insisted on control if I was going to stay. Then to raise money to improve our balance sheet so we could get national accreditation, I sold stock to the other three people on the management team.

These transformational leaders did not seek crisis situations—most expressed a desire to manage healthy companies and find their challenges in keeping them that way. But when the situation turned out to be more difficult than they had anticipated, they stuck with the commitments they made.

Managers need to think about Renier's short but profound comment that opens this chapter: the bottom line—"the numbers game" is only a scoreboard. It does not always accurately reflect the way the game is played. Healthy companies have the ability to capitalize on the good times and survive the bad times because their leaders spend their time essentially working as a team to face the competition outside of the firm. They do not expend significant energy fighting among themselves over issues of turf, status, and power. Nor do they spend time congratulating themselves on how good they are or assume that everyone who disagrees with them is wrong. Less well-managed companies, with luck and a relatively benign environment, will survive and keep the numbers respectable.

The first sign of trouble in today's more competitive business conditions is evidence that companies are reveling in past glories rather than looking for ways to adapt to today's hostile conditions. When a company examines all ideas that come from outside and automatically rejects those that do not coincide with internally generated conventional wisdom, the seeds of destruction have been planted because the conditions for self-renewal have begun to dissipate.

Many of our successful transformational leaders, like Franklin Delano Roosevelt when he developed the New Deal, did not have a clear vision of where they wanted to take their organizations. Instead, like FDR, they engage in "planful opportunism," the process of capitalizing on changing circumstances. They take advantage of "windows of opportunity," like Walter Wriston's plan of attack that enabled Citibank to overtake the Bank of America in the newly deregulated banking environment. Thus the same environment that enabled Citibank to become the nation's leading bank caused severe problems for Bank of America. Luck? Hardly. It's indicative of the phenomenon that is leading more and more researchers to look at the quality of top management teams in trying to explain the variance in organizational performance.

Another example of planful opportunism is IBM's late but aggressive entry into the personal computer market. Some observers maintain that IBM's management was motivated to a considerable extent by the need to keep Apple busy in what may well turn out to be the least desirable niche in the computer market rather than permit them to make inroads into IBM's more lucrative industrial markets.

Planful opportunism is the ability to turn unpredictable events into building blocks of change. Organizational transformation is not mere opportunism but creative, transformational strategy that more managers need to master if they are to operate successfully in today's competitive environment.

CONDITIONS FOR PLANFUL OPPORTUNISM

Conditions that facilitate planful opportunism involve diagnosing the source of problems. Transformational leaders look to four arenas to find the basic information they need to make a good diagnosis of their organization.

1. The leader engages in personal introspection to determine his or her strengths, weaknesses, and blind spots.
2. The leader facilitates analysis and introspection among a critical mass of individuals who make up the top management team to ensure that they work together for a common organizational goal and not against one another.
3. Organizational control systems must generate good data on the relative health of different aspects of the organization.
4. A careful scan of the environment must be made.

Good data are essential to the continued good health of the organization because the environment in which it operates is always changing. Thus today's solutions frequently are the root of tomorrow's problems. Transformational leaders must be sure that the organization has sensing mechanisms that provide early warnings of possible serious trouble. It did not take Blumenthal and Iacocca long to discover the extent of the problems they inherited. Blumenthal explained his initial discomfort with the state of Burroughs's health when he discovered that some of the conditions for planful opportunism did not exist in the organization.

> **Burroughs had the reputation of having been an extraordinary company. It hadn't had a down quarter in eleven years . . . . That viewpoint, however, was very quickly dissipated. I would say almost within the first week—I may exaggerate with the first week—but certainly within the first month. Because I began to sense that the quality of the people that were there, that I was meeting and talking to, seemed oddly at variance with the performance of the company. They were very unimpressive. Not only that but they didn't know the numbers. They didn't know where their profits were coming from—where they were making profits. They didn't have data; they didn't collect data; they didn't use computers!**

Transformational leadership requires several simultaneous levels of diagnosis. First, leaders must make sense of the organization's ability to survive in the competitive environment they confront. Second, they must be aware of their own abilities, motivation, and skills in relation to the organization's posture. Third, they must assess the individual capabilities, motivation, and skills of their key team members.

ORGANIZATIONAL FRAMEWORK

What makes a transformational leader's job so difficult is the dynamic and complex nature of large organizations and the unpredictable nature of the world in which they operate. Donald Schon states,

The first and perhaps most critical leadership task is framing the problem . . . . The process by which we define the decisions to be

made, the ends to be achieved, the means which may be chosen . . .
they must be constructed from materials of problematic situations
which are puzzling, troubling and uncertain . . . .

When Fred Hammer entered the Chase Manhattan Bank, he
spent a considerable amount of time getting the lay of the land.

> I basically feel the first year you have to keep your head down,
> you smile a lot and ask a lot of questions and then you decide
> what you want to do and how you're going to do it—timing,
> purpose, and rationalization. I was lucky with the management
> team at Chase because it was the first time that the bank was
> feeling a need for change . . . . By the end of the first year, it
> became apparent that we were losing money and to change that
> we would have to segment the markets and sacrifice share. This
> was a dramatic shift for retail banking within Chase: we were
> going to have to do less volume, be more selective about our
> customers, and we weren't going to grow. If we were going to
> grow, we were going to have to go nationwide.
>
> I came to that conclusion after looking at some hodgepodge
> data about our customers. We divided them into deciles and then
> tried to determine how much money we made in each decile. It
> turns out we made a lot of money in the first decile—the top 10
> percent. We made a little money on the second and basically
> broke even on the third and lost money on 70 percent of our
> customers. The first thing that became apparent was that we had
> to get our fixed costs down. But, the big thing was that we were
> going to price services in such a way that we would get rid of a lot
> of customers. We would not seek to do business with a broad
> spectrum of the potential customer base.
>
> As it turns out, it was not so important what we did but when
> we did it. Since virtually the entire industry raised their prices
> quickly after we did, we never got the bad publicity we ex-
> pected. We were beginning to develop the mentality of looking
> at profits, not just volume. This helped resolve a major question
> about the retail business at Chase, whether we were there to
> generate funds for use by the rest of the bank or to operate as a
> profit center. I said right away that we were a profit center.

Framing of the problem is not always conscious, yet there is
evidence in all of the interviews we conducted and in other

leadership studies we have analyzed that it was done. Each of our transformational leaders framed the set of organizational problems differently, yet all had a comprehensive and systematic approach. We use a framework built on the TPC system defined in Chapter 2. The TPC framework identifies the set of strategic tasks facing the transformational leader and therefore easily translates into a set of diagnostic questions. The three systems are briefly described next.

The Technical System

The management literature frequently offers advice to decision-makers on the technical challenges involved in running an organization. Leaders must choose their goals from among the feasible set of alternatives the organization could pursue and design the organization to carry out the chosen strategy.

1. *Mission and Strategy.* The most important technical task facing the leader is determining the appropriate product or service mix and market targets for the organization. Leaders are not equally involved in determining the content of strategy. Some, like Lee Iacocca at Chrysler, dominate the decision making in this area while others, like Jim Renier at Honeywell and Mike Blumenthal at Burroughs, are much more likely to be influenced by other senior executives when making decisions about their product service mix and market targets. The degree of technical expertise that the transformational leader brings to the discussion obviously affects the role that he or she will choose to play. Iacocca's early success at Ford with product breakthroughs like the Mustang established his credentials in this area, but his personality and experiences with Ford also played a role. When he started talks with Chrysler's former CEO, Riccardo, about the possibility of joining the company he said,

> Unless I had full authority to put my management style and policies into effect, going over to Chrysler would be a major exercise in frustration.

Mike Blumenthal's approach differed from Iacocca's. He describes the process that he went through at Burroughs:

> I just put together a team of seven or eight people. We sat down to figure out what we were going to do with this company. What are our goals? What's our position in the market? What are our strengths? What are our weaknesses? What can we capitalize?

At General Electric, where strategy issues span a large number of products and markets, Jack Welch and the other three members of the office of the CEO, Vice Chairman Larry Bossedy and Ed Hood along with Executive Vice President Paul Van Orden spend their time thinking about the relative viability of businesses in General Electric's portfolio and leave the determination of specific business strategies to the general managers running the more than 30 businesses in the GE/RCA portfolio.

Relevant data are collected from those in the organization whose opinion is most likely to be accurate.

The data are analyzed and plans are formulated optimizing the organization's long-term success.

The plans are communicated through the organization so that employees have a clear sense of what is expected of them.

2. *Organization Structure.* The leader's task is to design organizational structures which are technically sound in terms of the technology and response time demanded by the environment. What division of labor and what integration mechanisms will permit the organization to effectively achieve its mission? Blumenthal talks about these concerns in his early days at Burroughs:

> I started thinking about how to organize the company because I am not used to everything being related to everything else and I was looking for profit and loss (P&L) centers. I couldn't find any. It was all one giant P&L center. Everybody depended on every-

body else. I started experimenting with how to break the company apart and give some responsibility to individuals . . . .

This is where the fit between strategy and structure emerges. For example, in the late 1970s and early 1980s, many chemical companies found that uncertain supplies and rising prices of petroleum feedstocks placed them at a disadvantage in the commodity chemicals markets, where they were forced to compete with chemical companies owned by major oil producers like Exxon and Shell. They repositioned themselves so they would be less vulnerable to these external threats. For example, one large chemical company was organized as a matrix organization in which the different lines of business shared production and R&D facilities as well as marketing capabilities. This arrangement permitted substantial economies of scale which were critical in the price sensitive commodity chemicals business. The new strategy called for a move to marketing value-added products targeted to smaller market niches. The structure was changed from a centralized matrix structure to a more decentralized form that provided the lines of business with separate marketing capabilities as well as some separation of production and R&D. While there was more functional duplication in the new arrangement, it permitted managers to respond more quickly to market demands and was therefore consistent with the new strategy.

3. *Human Resource Management.* The final technical task the leader faces is to design a human resource system consistent with the organization's goals and structure. This involves a proper match between people and roles, specification of performance criteria for different organizational roles, a way to systematically measure the required performance, and control systems to ensure that staffing and development practices are capable of meeting the organization's long-term human resource needs as dictated by the business strategy.

Only in the most sophisticated companies do we see management's recognition of the strategic importance of effective human resource systems. All too often lip service is paid to the idea that "People are our most important asset," but company actions do not reflect the concern. Organizations that fail to evaluate the selection, appraisal, and reward systems when they wish to change the organization run the risk of producing organizational schizophrenia, as employees simultaneously try to achieve organizational goals and their own personal interests.

General Motors' managers spent a considerable amount of time and energy developing a set of criteria for evaluating people in the new organizational structure. Lloyd Reuss describes their process:

> We talked about the change process, what were the things that were really important if General Motors was going to succeed? And as Alex [Cunningham] said, all of a sudden, what were the givens: performance, profitability, return on investment. But that's sort of standard business school wisdom. Going forward, what were the new criteria? What kinds of things were really going to make a difference. We talked about competitive edge; we talked about quality of worklife; we talked about commitment to quality. And we used those criteria to choose our people. Because we had guys who'd be on everybody's first choice list from a technical standpoint who weren't there when some of the other criteria were considered . . . .

The Political System

Political activities are rarely talked about openly in an organization, but they frequently absorb significant amounts of senior management time. While the political activities that accompany decisions about resource allocation may not be discussed at management committee meetings, they are often the major topic of conversation at lunch, cocktails, and one-on-one meetings. These discussions frequently center on who is going to be promoted to an open position, what group is in power, who is going to influence strategic decisions, how budgets are going to be allocated across businesses or divisions, which functional areas have the inside track with the CEO, and who will benefit from the latest formula to distribute salary and bonus pools. The problem is that in most organizations it is culturally unacceptable to say that a given decision is political. Yet political processes are an inevitable part of the allocation of scarce resources. It is the task of the transformational leader to ensure that the processes produce results that further the organizational goals and that they are perceived as fair and equitable by the parties involved.

Clearly, the ability to decide what the mission and the strategy of the organization will be is a source of significant power. Technically focused textbooks and consulting groups advise organizations on how to do strategic planning, but they do not shed much light on how to allocate power in the actual strategic decision-making process. What levels of the organization should be involved in the process? Should technical decisions be made by those with technical expertise or by general managers? Should the chairperson make the decision alone? A set of decisions must be made to determine who will influence the formulation of the mission and strategy. In the absence of leadership on these issues, coalitions will tend to form to protect the personal interests of key groups in the organization. Decisions to enter new businesses or markets, to invest in start-up businesses rather than acquire an existing competitor, or to sell a "dog" business will affect some people's careers in a positive way while it will have an adverse effect on others. The allocation of budgets and people will depend on which choices are made in the strategic process, and it is a rare instance in which key players are indifferent about the outcome. Therefore, weighing the interests of one group within the company against those of another is an important part of the political decision-making process.

Transformational leaders must carefully think through how to allocate political power in the strategic decision-making process. The appropriate allocation will depend on an analysis of the interests of stakeholders, such as suppliers, board members, customers, employees, and management groups. The key variables are, who has the best information? and who needs to accept the decision if it is to be implemented? For example, when Lee Iacocca accepted the challenge to turn Chrysler around he wanted the ultimate responsibility for strategic decisions, but he clearly understood that he needed the cooperation of many constituencies. He spent a great deal of time lobbying groups in Washington to get the government to guarantee a loan. He placed Douglas Fraser, president of the United Auto Workers, on Chrysler's board and worked with management constituencies to get the cooperation he needed to lay off 20,000 white-collar and 40,000 blue-collar workers. He negotiated important concessions from dealers and suppliers to help Chrysler achieve its strategic objectives. Iacocca understood that if any of the key stakeholders felt the need to confront rather than cooperate with Chrysler during this period it would have been doubtful that the organization could have survived.

Transformational leaders like Jack Welch and Jack Sparks are trying to avoid crisis situations at General Electric and Whirlpool, but their success, like Iacocca's, could easily hinge on how well they manage the coalitions that emerge as they attempt to reposition their respective companies. Performance is always affected by the degree to which the leader effectively manages the organization's governance structures and obtains the cooperation of key coalitions within them.

Campbell understood the need to sell his program to franchisees who were unhappy with the way things had been run at Burger King:

> We said we're going to come out and we're going to talk to everyone once, and we're going to talk about where we are and where we think we ought to be. But first we were going to go out and listen to people. Now we knew what we wanted to do, but our franchise community was frustrated because, historically, they had not had much success getting anyone to address their problems. When I came on board I had enough of a reputation in

the system so that they felt excited but they still needed to beat me up. I had to go out there and give them a forum in which they could spill their guts.

Organization Structure. The technical issues in this area focus on how to differentiate and integrate the organization. The political issues involve the distribution of power in the organization. How much power should be exercised at corporate versus strategic business unit levels of the organization? How much discretion should subordinates have versus their supervisors? These decisions are reflected in the scope of decision-making authority regarding budgets and the selection and promotion of personnel. Thus when John Harvey-Jones identifies his task as "making leaders of ordinary men and women," he implicitly reveals a desire to decentralize power far down into the organization.

A second political design issue involves the distribution of power across organizational groupings. What is the relative power position of engineering vis-à-vis production, or production vis-à-vis marketing, or marketing vis-à-vis sales? These are political allocation decisions that distribute power across the organization and simultaneously affect individual careers.

The transformational leader must think of power along two dimensions—vertical and horizontal. Vertically, how centralized is the power in the organization? Horizontally, how equal are the divisions or functions in the organization? Iacocca moved to centralize power at Chrysler during the fiscal crisis, but in the fall of 1985 he announced a restructuring of the organization that would decentralize power. The purpose of this move, like the restructuring of General Motors, was to increase the flexibility of the organization and enhance its ability to embark on a strategy of diversification.

Human Resource Management. The other area in the political system is human resources. One of the most important tasks for a transformational leader to manage in this arena is the succession process. Decisions must be made as to who will get

ahead and how they will do so. In most organizations the nature
of the existing opportunities is such that there are more qualified candidates than there are positions for them. Promotions
are the most basic win—lose decisions the organization makes.
The level of political activity that surrounds them will correlate
with the relative scarcity for alternative moves. In some organizations the succession system is highly structured. For example, companies like Exxon and General Electric have a slate of
candidates for all key positions. The list has been generated by
a staff with considerable input from line management. When an
opening occurs, the choice must be made from among those on
that slate. This is in marked contrast to the majority of U.S.
corporations, where a much looser system is used. A vice president of personnel at a company with no formalized succession
system, when asked how decisions about important jobs were
explained to others in the organization, said, "We tell them God
did it." The answer is amusing, but the annual attrition rate of
25 percent of management and technical personnel that they
experience is probably less so.

The succession process and attendant politics tends to be
most visible at the top of the organization. If we look at the
recent successions in General Electric and Citibank we find
divergent approaches to these important events. At General
Electric, Reginald Jones worked hard to minimize the uncertainty that normally attends CEO succession. He managed a
process that produced not only a new chairman but also two
vice chairmen who could work together to guide the company.
The identity of these three individuals, chosen from a field of
seven or eight candidates, was known for 18 months before
Jones actually stepped down. At Citibank, by contrast, the identity of Walter Wriston's successor was still not known at the
time of a board meeting that was held 4 weeks before he retired. Indeed, the announcement was made only days before he
stepped down. One can be fairly certain that the level of uncertainty was greater at Citibank than it was at General Electric,
and that substantial time and energy were spent speculating on

who the successor would be and what each alternative would mean to the future of businesses, functions, and individual careers.

While the succession processes at Citibank and General Electric differed, their goal clearly was to produce the most qualified candidate as CEO. As we watch other organizations struggle with problems of CEO succession in the business sections of newspapers or in business weeklies, we realize that the psychological task of letting go is not always easy. For example, Harry Gray at United Technologies and William Paley at CBS groomed and dismissed a whole set of successors, ostensibly because they were not qualified for the job, but more likely because they were incapable of turning over to someone else the reins of companies they had built.

A similarly destructive process takes place when a CEO facing mandatory retirement is influential in picking an unqualified successor. The reason is that the outgoing CEO cannot accept the fact that the company could continue without his or her direction. Blumenthal describes the events that took place at Burroughs in the years before he was asked to assume the role of CEO.

> The company had been run for a long time by one individual. When that individual left, his successor was an obvious choice because he was the only possible choice, he was the president. He was the number two man, so he was sort of automatically promoted by the board to the top job. The board, being used to working only with that previous very strong CEO, had no real knowledge of anyone else—the CEO was going out reluctantly. His successor was at that point 62 and had two or three years to go until retirement. He stepped into the job and as he was moving toward retirement, the board became uneasy over the fact that they were really not very impressed with any of the other people they knew anything about, so they pressed strongly that maybe someone from the outside should come in. And that is how I came to be here.

The second political human resource task is the design and administration of reward systems. There are many variations in the way that people are rewarded. There is no evidence that the amount of money one makes is in any sense a measure of the organization's success or of the individual's relative contribution to the bottom line. Certainly, a perusal of *BusinessWeek's* annual list of the highest paid executives in the United States shows that the relationship between organizational performance and the amount paid to the chief executive is tenuous at best. The distribution of pay among levels in the company also varies considerably without any discernible pattern that would enable us to say the distribution was technically rational. Indeed, Blumenthal points out that when he took over at Burroughs he discovered that McDonald's pay as chairman had been comparable to other chief executive officers, but that the pay scales of those reporting to him were considerably lower than their counterparts in other companies. Clearly, this distribution is not meant to attract the type of people who are able to confront the leader on issues of importance.

Transformational leaders also must consider the impact that short-term bonus plans have on motivation and performance. When Tom Murrin told the general managers how important it was for Westinghouse to invest in improving productivity, he did not address the issue of how their bonus was being calculated. Certainly, general managers nearing retirement had little incentive to make the necessary capital investments in improving productivity that would not pay off for a significant time at the expense of this year's bottom line. Similar conflicts between organizational good and individual gain existed at General Motors during the decade of the 1970s, when the Japanese made significant inroads in the U.S. automobile market.

Finally, an important political issue in organizations involves the performance appraisal system. Who is appraised by whom and who sets the criteria are important issues because of the link that often exists between the appraisal issue and the distribution of pay and promotions. Indeed, an interesting conflict surfaces in this arena between the technical and the political systems.

Research on appraisal shows that a person's subordinates and peers are in a better position to evaluate that individual's performance and potential than his or her supervisor is. The original studies date back to World War II, when peers were better able to predict who would be a successful pilot than were the flight instructors. This finding, along with one that shows that subordinates also make more accurate judges than do supervisors, has since been replicated in a number of industrial settings. In spite of this knowledge, more than 99 percent of U.S. corporations are not able to tolerate politically a system in which peers and subordinates evaluate people in the organization.

Some leaders have decided to bite the bullet and deal with the political implications of appraisal systems. For example, Walter Wriston decided that it was important to evaluate how effective key managers were in managing people. Therefore, part of the appraisal of the manager is based on the results of an attitude survey administered to the executive's subordinates. Performance on these measures is used as part of the bonus calculation. The message from Walter Wriston is that making the numbers is a necessary but not sufficient criterion for a manager's performance. The use of this technique must be carefully monitored. The survey should be administered at irregular time periods to random samples of employees to ensure the validity of results.

At General Electric, data are also collected from peers and subordinates as part of the analysis of key executives' accomplishments. The data are collected and evaluated by a human resource staff ultimately responsible to the chairman and not to the general managers in the businesses. Such data collection must be handled in a way that protects subordinates from the possible abuse of power by supervisors in the event that the evaluation is not favorable. It must ultimately be supported by a philosophy that values equity and believes that superior performance by the individual provides the organization with a competitive edge.

THE CULTURAL SYSTEM

The first technical challenge that the transformational leaders face in the cultural arena is to separate out the relative impact that the values of philosophies of key decision-makers have on the choice of strategic alternatives. We are not suggesting that values should not play a role in the choice among strategic alternatives but rather that the value issues involved should be identified. This helps organizations avoid the scenario in which individuals distort technical analyses that support certain business decisions because they are philosophically opposed to them.

The leader's second concern in this area is to ensure that the organization's culture supports its mission and strategy. This is critical when a change in the strategy has occurred. AT&T, for example, must shift the values in the organization from those which support a regulated telephone monopoly to those which support a competitive high-technology business. The new culture must support innovation, competition, and profit. Westinghouse and General Motors are also involved in shifting the values in their organizations to those supporting a strategy based on productivity and quality.

Organization Structure. The leader must also align the culture with the organization's structure. An organization that moves from a functional to a matrix structure requires a different style of management. Since power is balanced on at least two dimensions in a matrix organization, the management style must allow for more open confrontation and negotiation of conflict as opposed to the more authoritarian style that accompanies a traditional chain of command in a functional organization.

A second cultural issue is the self-conscious development of subcultures to support different parts of the organization. Thus the leader must encourage a tolerance for the seemingly deviant behavior needed to foster high levels of innovation in a production oriented organization. To the extent that a variety of subcultures are required to effectively accomplish the organization's mission, the leader must design mechanisms to integrate them into a company-wide culture so that functional, geographic, or business subdivisions in the organization work to accomplish a common goal rather than expend resources to create personal fiefdoms. Companies like Exxon and IBM go to great extremes to create an organizational culture that transcends its subcultures.

The transformational leader must carefully weigh the advantages and disadvantages of integrating subcultures into an overarching corporate culture. Leaders in conglomerates like ITT and Gulf & Western have concluded implicitly that the price paid for maintaining such a culture is too high, whereas General Electric believes that such a culture is necessary so that senior management focuses on the need to do what is best for the entire company rather than for some portion of it at the expense of the whole organization. Millions of dollars are spent creating common ways of thinking and acting about issues. Much of this socialization is disseminated through extensive management development programs carried out at the management development facility in Crotonville, New York. In addition to formalized development experiences, organizations like GE, Exxon, IBM, and Hewlett-Packard rely on systematic rotation and movement of key executives to spread the gospel to plants and installations far removed from corporate headquarters.

Human Resource Management. The final area for managing culture is the human resource system. It is in this area that Japanese management has been more sophisticated and more attentive than American management. The Japanese have used the human resource system very skillfully to shape and reinforce cultures that provide the organization with a strong commitment to organizational goals. The process begins with the selection of people who are carefully evaluated as to how they fit in with and reinforce the dominant culture of the organization. In companies where this method is used, the interviewing process involves many people, and workers have a large role in the decision to select one of their peers.

Like their Japanese counterparts, American firms that are committed to maintaining their culture employ a careful screening process to candidates who are technically equal to assess the best fit in terms of values and philosophy.

As Fred Hammer found out, you can also systematically create dysfunctional subcultures in an organization. In his diagnosis at Chase he found that the retail banking subculture was going to be one of his biggest hurdles in transforming the organization:

> It took me about six months to figure out what was going on, what they were doing. I used to talk with a lot of people and then I would realize there was a timid quality about the human resources in this sector . . . I said, well these people are not going to lead us over the hill regarding change. But it was also evident that the rest of the bank had people that were outstanding, bright, well-educated, and aggressive. It was clear that this group was at a different level.

> The problem was exacerbated when all the lending authority was taken out of the branches the month before I arrived. After indoctrinating people that "real bankers" make loans, remember the culture of Chase was one that worshiped at the feet of lending authority, this decision figuratively emasculated branch personnel. Morale was devastated. It was not that the decision was wrong, but that the culture was one that stifled the growth of retail banking.

The second human resource tool for shaping the culture of the organization is the way in which people are developed and socialized. Organizations that use the human resource system to shape culture invest heavily in training and development. Much of this education is aimed at inculcating people with the dominant values of the organization. An explicit part of the IBM and GE training programs, for example, deals with company values.

Finally, the management of rewards is a potent tool to shape and reinforce the culture of the organization by promoting and compensating those who fit best with the dominant value of the organization. The human resource system can be a very powerful tool in making the cultural system congruent with the technical and political system.

THE ALIGNMENT TASK; ADJUSTING TO THE FUTURE

The transformational leader's task is to align the organization with its external environment. To do this, the organization's TPC systems must be adjusted to enable the organization to deal effectively with changing issues. The challenge for these leaders is to recognize that the drama is best represented as a dynamic jigsaw puzzle with pieces that need to be fitted together. The fit is never perfect and constant adjustments must be made. The extent of these adjustments depends on the relative stability of economic, political, and cultural factors in the organization's environment.

SELF-DIAGNOSIS

Transformational leaders know their strengths and weaknesses. Along with the organizational diagnosis, a process of self-assessment occurs. Like an actor approaching a new role, the leader must understand the scope of his or her technical skills and then decide what nuance of the role they will highlight. Jack Sparks's technical strength at Whirlpool was in marketing, not the engineering or production end of the business. Both Jim Renier and Mike Blumenthal moved into computer businesses needing revitalization without in-depth knowledge of computers. Blumenthal's technical expertise was in finance, whereas Renier brought an outstanding track record in imple-

menting a change effort in the controls systems division at
Honeywell. Lee Iacocca, however, had made his mark with his
product and marketing skills at Ford. In a television interview
with NBC News, Iacocca frankly assessed his strengths and
weaknesses when he discussed the options he considered in
the summer after he was fired by Henry Ford. He had offers to
run paper and steel companies, but he turned them down, because he thought it would take too long for him to learn a new
business. Iacocca's technical expertise, coupled with his need
to run the show, determined his decision to accept Chrysler's
offer.

Once technical capabilities are understood, the leader must
assess personal feelings about the exercise of power. If things
are to be accomplished in organizations, the leader must understand what motivates his or her own behavior and the behavior
of others in the organization.

Finally, the transformational leader must have insight into
his or her values—what is the source of the commitment that
must be made to the organization. When we asked Blumenthal
if he considered pulling out of the Burroughs situation when
shortly before he came on board he realized that the situation
was not what he had envisioned, he said,

> **No, at that point I was intellectually engaged. I felt I had com-
> mitted myself and I wasn't going to walk away. So I was in
> charge when the earnings for the first time went down.**

In his television interview, Iacocca also addressed the issue
of values when he said that he believed that everyone has to be
accountable to someone, and that his primary concern during
the crisis period at Chrysler was the 600,000 jobs that would be
lost if the company went bankrupt. His sense of values is also
apparent when he talks of the need to ensure that both the
sacrifice in difficult times and the rewards in good times are
equitably shared in the company.

No single individual is persuasive enough and energetic
enough to transform a large, complex organization single-

handedly. There must be a critical mass of managers in the organization who share the leader's sense of urgency about the need for change and who join in framing the problem. The same analytical issues, therefore, must be addressed with regard to this cadre of leaders.

The importance of a cohesive group of leaders is illustrated in Mike Blumenthal's reaction when he first learned of Burroughs's problems the summer before he was to take over as CEO:

> It seemed there were lots of problems. At this point I did not feel very qualified to deal with them because they involved technical issues and judgments—I really had no technical judgment—where was I going to get it from? I had reached the point where I did not trust anyone . . . I felt there were only two or three people capable and willing to give me honest answers if I asked them questions. . . . So by the time we got to the third quarter I realized there would have to be substantial change . . . . There would have to be a new team of people, since there were people here that clearly I could not work with.

It was also one of Lee Iacocca's first concerns at Chrysler:

> What I found at Chrysler were 35 vice presidents, each with his own turf. There was no real committee setup, no cement in the organizational chart, no system of meetings to get people talking to each other. I couldn't believe, for example, that the guy running the engineering department wasn't in constant touch with his counterpart in manufacturing. But that's how it was. Everybody worked independently. I took one look at that system and I almost threw up. That's when I knew I was in really deep trouble.

DIAGNOSIS: AVOIDING THE ONE-MINUTE QUICK-FIX SEDUCTION

The systematic, organizational, individual, and team diagnosis characteristics of our transformational leader provide the best antidote against the snake oil cures so readily used by U.S. managers.

Instant gratification is part of American culture. Managers are no exception. Over the years they have picked up and discarded hundreds of "management hula hoops" developed to solve fundamental organizational problems. Taylor's scientific management, time-motion studies, human relations gimmicks, management by objectives, zero based budgeting, quality circles, and Japanese management are a few examples of business's search for a quick fix.

The One-Minute Manager and all of its follow-up books are a symbol of this search. There is nothing wrong with the basic message, which is to set goals with your subordinates, give them positive feedback when they do something right and negative feedback when they do something wrong. There is also nothing new in these ideas. What, then, captured so many managers' fancy that they purchased more than a million copies? For many the seduction was that this was a simple "managing people" program that they could utilize—it offered a quick solution for difficult problems.

Unfortunately, difficult problems rarely lend themselves to simple solutions. The message is not harmful unless the manager sees it as a quick fix in a complex world.

Other quick-fix seductions (most of them did take more than a minute) that we have seen in the past decade include many of the strategic planning techniques, the recent focus on corporate culture, and the search for excellence. If properly interpreted and implemented, many of these prescriptions would have led to more effective organizations.

The more likely scenario, however, was similar to the reaction of many managers to *In Search of Excellence*. As the bad news spread about Japan's ability to achieve dominance in industries that the United States had controlled for decades, American managers looked for something that would make them feel good. After all, it was not reassuring to hear that the Japanese success story emanated from a societal culture that was very different from our own. *Theory Z* and *In Search of Excellence* arrived in the midst of this self-doubt with the reassuring news that U.S. companies, too, could be excellent.

Peters and Waterman wrote an important book. The focus was an attempt to identify the cultural characteristics of "excellent companies." Many managers latched onto the eight dimensions as a cookbook for success. Two quick-fix scenarios all too often emerged. The first occurred in companies where the CEO got a copy of the book, became upset because his company was not listed as excellent, and asked the management team to read the book and then go on a retreat to figure out how the organization could implement the eight dimensions of excellence. This approach is equivalent to finding an involved recipe for French pastry and copying the list of ingredients without noting the quantities, the method, or the baking directions, and assuming that the finished product will be a success.

A more sophisticated use of *In Search of Excellence* is as a catalyst for change. In some companies a great deal of excitement has been generated about the first stage of a change process. In this scenario, the CEO reads the book and comes to the conclusion that the organization should have a clearly articulated set of values. Many of the excellent companies identified by Peters and Waterman have their values explicitly stated and understood by employees. In this case the off-site meeting that follows the reading of the book is devoted to coming up with the 10 commandments of XYZ Corporation so that, like Hewlett-Packard, they can be widely disseminated to the employees.

Frequently, there is a very strong commitment on the part of the group involved in the development of the 10 commandments of XYZ Corporation. They return as it were from the mountain and ask those responsible for internal communication to tighten up the language and print a sufficient number of impressive brochures to distribute to all of the employees so they will know what the company's values are. And so ends the "excellence" program.

For companies tempted to write their own 10 commandments, it is useful to remember what happened when Moses came down from the mountain with the original tablets of stone. His people were involved in an orgy and were not terribly receptive to the new rules and values. Indeed, thousands of years later we are still struggling with the problem of implementation.

Implementation is a very difficult task. Going off-site for a few days to articulate the organization's core values is a good first step, as long as it is done with the realization that it takes literally years to implement new cultural values in the organization. It is not enough to distribute the message; it is probably more important to review the control systems in the organization to see if they reinforce the espoused cultural values. It is only when managers come to the realization that there are no quick fixes that they can start to transform their organizations with patience and hard work.

DIAGNOSIS: SETTING THE STAGE FOR CREATING A VISION

Perhaps the most essential component of a transformation is a vision of the future desired state. Transformations require a dream and require the organization to aspire to be something. Yet some way of assessing the current reality is also required in order to determine whether the vision fits with reality.

We have discussed the diagnostic portion of the transformation process as a linear process, but in reality it is a less ordered exploration. It is a period when hypotheses are generated and tested out with some data. Nevertheless, we argue that the basis for future action depends on this process of diagnosis. It's here that the capacity for planful opportunism is created. It readies the organization for its own renewal. Iacocca says that Robert McNamara, whom he worked for at Ford, was a master of diagnosis:

> McNamara knew more than the actual facts—he also knew the
> hypothetical ones. When you talked with him, you realized that
> he had already played out in his head the relevant details for
> every conceivable scenario.

Ed Thompson talks about new systems to frame the problem
at Schneider Trucking when he says:

> Our industry has been largely internally focused. We are going
> directly to the customer. We will do the work to define their real
> needs and set up partnerships and distribution. The temptation
> is to assume we know what's going to play out in our new envi-
> ronment and jump rapidly into the organizational and technolog-
> ical changes we already know about. This would be shortsighted.
> We have the opportunity to be data led rather than feeling
> driven. We want to know what our customers are thinking and
> what they need to do to be successful in their marketplace. This
> data collection and competitive analysis will take time at a point
> in our history when there is a pressure to move fast. As this piece
> of the picture clears up we will do a better job of formulating
> ways to organize around the cost and service desired outcomes.

Three principles emerge as we think about what happens
during diagnosis. Leaders can apply them in a variety of circumstances from very systematic, quasi-scientific analysis to
more artistic, intuitive problem solving.

Principle Number 1—Frame the Problem. The transformational leader must have a coherent view of the world so that a
diagnosis can take place. We have presented the TPC matrix as
one way to order the world. It enables leaders to focus on the
best technical alignment for the organization while addressing
the political and cultural alignment issues that may well determine the success or failure of the transformation process.

Principle Number 2—Collect Data. The transformational
leader is always collecting and analyzing data obtained through
vast informal networks as well as through systematic studies.

Perhaps the most systematic and formalized diagnosis occurred at General Motors. In September 1982, the General Motors executive committee created a special task force to study reorganization. Roger Smith selected John Debbink, former general manager of Delco Marine Division, to lead the task force, and called in McKinsey and Company as consultants. The mission of the study was to:

> Examine each element of the organization, particularly the structure and the systems that tie it together, so that they could identify where changes could improve their effectiveness. In short, they wanted to make certain that the organizational structure and systems provided them with the most effective delivery system.

A clear distinction was drawn between effectiveness and efficiency. Efficiency was defined as simply doing a task well; effectiveness was defined as doing the right task in the right way. The focus of the study was on effectiveness, knowing that efficiency was a natural by-product of an effective organization. A second aspect of the study was described by Roger Smith:

> A fundamental principle from the beginning was that the organization itself would generate the new organization concept. The ideas which are being implemented today in a very real sense came from the operating people in the corporation.

Over a 15-month period, more than 500 General Motors employees, representing all levels of the company, were interviewed and surveyed. These surveys revealed that while GM had certain strengths in its financial reserves, brand loyalty, dealer network, technical know-how, and people, it also had some key weaknesses. These weaknesses were identified as a poor decision-making process, product decisions that were not market driven, and lack of strategic planning.

One GM engineer characterized the problems from his perspective:

We had some really fine modern cars to offer. Things as good or better than the Japanese. But big executives from downtown would come in and point to the models and say "make this one and that one and that one." They were always the same cars, the muscle cars. It killed us when we stayed with them too long.

The study also discovered that GM's employees recognized that GM had to change and they were willing to help in that change.

What was needed was an organizational concept that would keep the strength while addressing the problems. A task force examined a wide variety of options before making its recommendations to the executive committee. As Roger Smith noted, "We did not start with a preconceived notion that we were going to do something."

Fred Hammer kept generating hypotheses about retail banking, but he would then test them empirically. He described one such incident:

> There was no question in my mind that we were very close to being the number one credit card bank in the country. We were the first bank to understand what the opportunities were. We could issue cards outside our banking territory. You know the old wives' tale that the only place you got credit cards was in your own bank, and the argument was that you can't issue these things out of your own area because as soon as someone gets into a financial bind, he won't pay you, he will only pay a local bank. Some of us did not believe that so we said let's test it. We put together a small, well designed test and we went to four states and it turned out that we had fewer collections problems than we had in New York. Then we checked delinquency and loss patterns because we wanted to make sure, since this would be a big step for us, and it turned out that the delinquency and loss rates were lower.

Principle Number 3—Dumb It Down. Complex realities must be reduced to a few central issues before others are asked to consider them. There is no inference here that the audience is incapable of understanding the full complexity of the diagnosis, but rather that people confronted with pressing operational problems will be more likely to respond to a parsimonious presentation of what changes the organization needs to make.

Ongoing diagnosis creates significant demands on an organization stretched to deal with operational problems, but it is a critical managerial process that frequently separates the best performers in an industry from those who are mediocre. Transformational leaders must find ways to motivate employees to stay alert to the early warning signs of danger and to the opportunities to gain on the competition and make the organization more secure.

5 CREATING A MOTIVATING VISION

The soul . . . never thinks without a picture.

ARISTOTLE

Transformational leaders must not only diagnose their organizations' strengths and weaknesses and match them against the environmental opportunities, but they must also find ways to inspire employees to meet these challenges. This vision of the future must be formulated in such a way that it will make the pain of changing worth the effort.

Dr. Martin Luther King created an enormously inspiring vision in his famous "I Have a Dream" address at the Washington Monument. In that speech he painted a picture of a United States that would be a better place. He talked about the little children, white and black, playing and holding hands in the rural towns in Alabama; blacks and whites working together in urban centers. That vision had a motivational pull. It created a positive image that people could strive for.

The challenge for transformational leaders is both to find and create a vision of an organization that is in some way better than the old one and to encourage others to share that dream. They must provide people with an image of what can be and motivate them to move ahead into the future they envision.

Jeff Campbell told us how he developed his vision for Burger King and shared it with his management group:

> While I was running the New York region, I was complaining to the then chairman about a number of things. He said, "Why don't you put your thoughts on paper?" Well, I wrote a memo that must have been 10 pages long. I said, "Here's all the things I think are wrong and here's how I would attack them." I never heard from him about any of it, but after I had been made president of Burger King, I said, "Hey, I've been thinking about this for a long time. I know what we need to do short-term," but as I thought about what we were and where we might go, a vision took shape. About one year into the turnaround, I was made chairman. We had a meeting of all the officers at Marco Island, Florida. I was sitting in my den thinking about where we had to go and listening to a recording of the theme from *Chariots of Fire* and I got an idea of making a speech about where we needed to go and punctuating it with music just to get the guys thinking about it. I know that sounds corny, but sometimes corny things work and I decided to go with my gut on this one.

So I talked about us becoming not only the best company in the portfolio, but the best convenience restaurant in America by 1992. I talked about what kind of a company we would be and the kinds of careers we would build for people. At the end I said, "I'm going to put on one more piece of music and I want you to think about everything we've talked about. Don't talk to your friend or look at anybody else. Just sit there a second and listen to the music and ask yourself if it's something you really think you can do and—if you really want to do it. Then, when the music is over, get up and I will be waiting at the back door to shake your hand."

I was pretty nervous, but when the music ended guys in their early sixties—not just the younger people—started coming back. You know it was a corny thing to do but what happened was magic. We had a 76 percent increase in earnings.

Campbell is an example of a transformational leader meeting an important challenge—mobilizing energy in the organization. While diagnosis prepares the leader and the organization for change, it is the vision that launches them into action.

Diagnosis is never enough, nor is ad hoc action a satisfactory basis for continuity. Certainly it does not give meaning to the organization nor form a coherent focus for the needs of the people in it, nor does it provide a structure to translate that meaning into continuity of organizational behavior. The point to note, therefore, is that each of our CEO's took charge of his organization and took it in a new direction . . . . Jones and Watson pushed into electronics, Wriston into consumer financing, McGregor into aluminum manufacturing, Hanley downstream into proprietary products, and Sulzberger into acquisitions.

When we look at these CEO's who took their organizations in new directions, we certainly find leaders who used diagnosis to assess their new business opportunities. But these leaders and the ones that we studied were able to effect transformations because they developed new frameworks for the future. This resulted in new standards, new values, and new ways of looking at the world and new kinds of actions. These leaders developed holistic visions of the future.

What may separate transformational from transactional leaders is that transformational leaders are more likely to be proactive than reactive in their thinking; more creative, novel and innovative in their ideas; more radical or reactionary than reforming or conservative in ideology; and less inhibited in their search for solutions. Transactional leaders may be equally bright but their focus is on how to best keep the system running for which they are responsible— reacting to problems generated by observed deviances; looking to modify conditions as needed and remaining ever mindful of the organizational constraints within which they must operate.

It is up to all of our transformational leaders to develop these holistic visions of the future for the organization and to stimulate a critical mass of leaders within the organization to do the same.

Jack Sparks did not arrive at the helm of Whirlpool when that company was in the valley of the shadow of death. But he did have a vision that involved transforming the way Whirlpool did business and in the process making it stronger in the face of competition.

I set out to change the image of the corporation from a conservative operation with some marketing skills to a marketing operation with some manufacturing and engineering skills . . . . I will know when I get there because you will see more excitement, you will see people really trying to accomplish things. You will see a better operation in total and of course you will see the things that go along with that, like growth. In fact my goal is . . . a very sophisticated organization with a broader vision.

One of the first things I did as CEO was take all the officers down to Washington for two-and-half days to meet senators, congressmen, bureaucrats—even take a tour of the White House, the Executive Building—because these guys were so out of touch with what was going on in the world, I was the only executive

officer in this corporation that was doing this kind of thing . . . I
wanted these guys to know you're in a big, grown-up world.
There's more to it than Michigan, Indiana, Illinois, and Arkansas.
I hope to have a more sophisticated team.

Jack Welch is a transformational leader who keeps articulating and reiterating his vision. In speaking with his managers
four years after becoming CEO he told them:

That drive to be number one or two, to be more competitive in an
ever increasing competitive world, has got to be at the forefront.
And I don't mean static competition. We asked every person who
comes into a meeting in our place to be sure to have a session on
competitiveness in the first 15 minutes of the meeting. Immediately the bureaucracy got fired up, memos went out, let's get
those damn static strategic planning pages out again . . . who are
the five competitors? What is their share? How many employees
do they have? . . . They didn't look at the dynamics of what
these competitors will look like in 1990, what moves would you
make if you were running those companies. How many plants
should they close? What investments should they make? What
they should do? . . . that's what competition is all about. Competition is about 1990, not some strategic planner's view of today.
So we desperately want to take a look at our competition in a live,
vibrant, passionate way. At what they are going to be doing to
beat the hell out of you over the next five years . . . . In the end
that drive to be number one and two is still the biggest focus we
must keep in this company, and yes it is going to get tougher and
tougher and tougher and tougher. As we move down this road we
are playing in an ever increasing competitive world . . . .

You can't feel "I am at GE and therefore I am safe." GE is not
safety, your own competitive business is safety, winning in your
markets is safety. GE has no wall around it that can protect anything . . . . Candor is calling it as you see it . . . dealing with it,
getting it up on the table . . . talking about it here with people
who can do something about it, not people who can commiserate
with you about it . . . .

We are concerned both with what the characteristics of motivating visions are as well as the process transformational lead-

ers use to transmit that vision to others in the organization. Creating a vision is much more than traditional, rational business planning. It involves both right and left brains—both intuition and creativity. It is holistic in its view of the organization, dealing with business strategies, values, inner political relationships. Thus, in order to achieve an organization driven by vision, transformational leaders need to call into play a new set of leadership skills.

HOLISTIC VISIONS

The vision is the ideal to strive for. It releases the energy needed to motivate the organization to action. It provides an overarching framework to guide day-to-day decisions and priorities and provides the parameters for planful opportunism.

A successful vision has a tension that's the result of its having been created both from intuition (right-brain thinking) and logical analysis (left-brain thinking). This is not an easy task. Managers often resist right-brain activities.

Alex Cunningham describes the birth of the vision at General Motors. It was a very intuitive and organized process that laid the groundwork for the greatest transformation of GM since Alfred Sloan's leadership.

> Basically it was very simple. The first key word that everybody said was "effectiveness"—we wanted to create a more effective organization. The next one we hammered on was "responsiveness" and that's responsiveness to the market, to the customer. So we wanted to be more effective, we wanted to be more responsive. And those two words really sum it all up. Responsiveness was our ability to react both with product and timing to the demands of the marketplace, effectiveness was to do things in a better manner. Then that brought in all the things that go with effectiveness—being able to do more with the same number of people, and so on . . . .

Transformational leaders talk about visions as an evolving phenomenon. For example, Ed Thompson, of Schneider Transport, talked about the development of a vision for his company:

> We started the process with a rather structured approach. We picked a time period out three to four years to get us out of the influence of the pressures of the current state. We worked to make statements of what we would look like at that point—revenue levels, number of employees, equipment types, maintenance and support systems, technology and operating methods, desired customer base, and so on.
>
> As we involved more people in the process the focus shifted and became more mature. For example, working through a lot of the human dimensions generated direction. We explored new ways to align and empower people. You know in service industries like ours over half our people touch the customer in some way each day. We really have some ideas on new ways to do the human side of trucking. The vision also grew as we pushed ourselves in areas like building in an ongoing change orientation and viewing ourselves as innovators in asset management. We kind of picture that this visioning will be an organic or ongoing part of our work. We are getting more and more of our people involved.

Mike Blumenthal talks about his vision for Burroughs—six years after he became CEO:

> It's amazing to me as I look back on it now, because when I look back I realize that I went by the seat of my pants. Today it is very clear and tomorrow I will leave for a press conference in New York where we are announcing major new products. I would say the vision has evolved. In preparation for the speech I will give tomorrow I looked back at the speech I gave to this group back in the spring of 1981 and to the speeches that Paul Stern and I have given since that time and I realize that you can see a trend. There is no one flash—no one moment when the vision is established. The vision has evolved helped along by executive retreats—we went to Vermont for three days, we went to upper Michigan for three days and we went to the Homestead for three days.

The recurrent theme as these transformational leaders talked about the development of a vision for the organization is that unlike the vision of a founder/entrepreneur, visions in large complex organizations tend rarely to be one person's dream but rather the expressed commitment of a group.

Jim Renier explains it in the following terms:

> Developing a vision in a big organization I believe is a completely different process than developing a vision in a small entrepreneurial business, because there are many possible visions as opposed to a vision. In a large organization you must get the whole organization to buy in. You can't just say, we're heading for this place or that with an immediate buy in. We're apt to end instead with a bunch of people reacting with something like "listen to that smart bastard." What you've got to do is constantly engage in iterating what you say and what they say is possible. And over a couple of years the different visions come together. If you try to jam them together on day one in an organization like this, it will not work.

In these cases the vision was a complex collage of what their organization should strive to become. It included a basic component of business strategy (namely markets, product, and services) but it also included a strong sense of how the organization should be structured and the part that the human resources would play.

A vision is motivating for two reasons. First, it provides the challenge for which the organization and its members strive, it is the reach for excellence and the source of self-esteem for the members.

The second purpose is to help provide a conceptual road map or a set of blueprints for what the organization will be in the future. Utilizing the metaphor of erecting a building: the vision starts with the architect's renderings—the idealized project that inspires people to move ahead—and then specifies the particulars that will be needed to get there.

At the core of the vision is the organization's mission statement. Since the organizations we are discussing have an economic, rather than a normative purpose, we frequently find that the mission is not clearly articulated. This may be the reason it is so difficult for people to develop a sense of purpose about their membership in these organizations apart from their own career goals and economic security. It is frequently the absence of a sense of purpose that causes organizations to fail in their efforts to bring about needed change and to gain needed commitment from employees. The Japanese understand the importance of developing a sense of common purpose, and much of the commitment they gain from their employees results from organizational socialization processes that clearly outline how the parties involved share responsibility for the survival of the company. Japanese employees are told that their job security depends on the economic viability of the firm and that both management and workers must always do their best to ensure a safe future for all. When we interviewed Jim Renier, he spoke at length about the need to involve employees in a discussion of values if organization revitalization is to occur:

> **Productivity had gone to hell. And we had an angry workforce. The best thing I could do was go talk to those folks and let them take a measure of my sense of values, because what they were rebelling against was a sense of values. They were not rebelling against anyone in particular. Their attitude certainly said, hey, we aren't bitching about pay or benefits. They love the company, you know, the image of it. What they were basically saying is, "Something has happened to truth, trust and respect. We don't like that."**

> **The problem is that quality goes to hell when that happens, because when you work in an environment where truth, trust, and respect are absent, you have no respect for yourself anymore. You don't feel like quality, and I contend that people who don't feel like quality can't produce quality, either. Quality comes from people who feel like quality. I think it all comes back to that, it really does.**

> **My greatest concern for the United States stems from the increasing narcissism and the idea that everyone should look out for themselves at the expense of others. I believe that until this**

> country returns to the values of truth, trust, and respect for one
> another as opposed to the current paddle-your-own-canoe values
> we will be unable to solve our basic economic problems. You
> know, I think this country can go into decline just as other great
> nations have declined. To me this is not a religious issue. It is
> just plain empirical fact. You go through history and that is what
> history teaches you.

Many American firms that have been labeled paternalistic
have basically had the same concern for their employees as was
voiced by Renier. IBM, whose core value is "Respect for People," developed the concept of lifetime employment during the
Depression, and employees understood that the promise was
part of an exchange between the worker and the company that
could be kept only if the firm continued to prosper. Somewhere
in the intervening decades this understanding has eroded in
many organizations. A colleague of ours, Vlado Pucik, who was
born in Czechoslovakia and has spent a great deal of time in
Japan as a researcher, pointed out that in America it is more
legitimate to display enthusiasm rooting for one's favorite
sports team than it is to be enthusiastic about one's job. Our
people show an eagerness to be part of the organization when
they are hired. We can only wonder what we do to breed the
enthusiasm out of them in the workplace. Thus a major challenge for transformational leaders is to develop missions for
their organizations that enable all stakeholders to commit themselves to the survival of the venture.

ELEMENTS OF THE VISION

Vision has two fundamental elements. One is to provide a conceptual framework or paradigm for understanding the organization's purpose—the vision includes a roadmap. The second important element is the emotional appeal: the part of the vision
that has a motivational pull with which people can identify.

Both the cognitive, intellectual understanding and the emotional pull give the vision meaning. Fundamental or quantum

change requires shifting the basic assumptions, values, and paradigm that the organization uses for problem-solving. This is true whether creating a new paradigm for world competitiveness a la Jack Welch at General Electric, or a new vision of the trucking business in a deregulated environment at Schneider Transport, or Jeff Campbell's new image of Burger King. In all cases it is a basic shift, a breaking with the past that is replaced by a new vision.

The notion of a holistic vision is at odds with most practices in organizations that utilize a static planning model rather than the projection of images in visions of the future. If one were to go randomly into the Fortune 500 companies and ask for any documents that capture the future of the organization, one would most likely be handed the strategic plan.

Most strategic plans are kept in thick three-ring notebooks. The majority of them are filled with short, concise mission statements followed by strategic objectives, followed by hundreds of pages of data on market share, return on investment, return on assets, manufacturing, productivity, engineering figures, and so on. It's not surprising that an outsider doesn't get a vision of the future by reading through this material.

If, however, you randomly interview senior management and ask them to describe the future organization, there is often great variance between their own intuitive, verbal vision of the future and what's captured in the planning documents. Again, it is like carefully examining the blueprints of a complex building structure and trying to get a visual image of what the finished project will look like. An artist's rendering of the building lacks a great deal of the technical detail that is an actual part of a structure because attention is given to creating a model with the purpose of communicating the concept and the architect's vision.

Why Visions Are Motivating

People regulate much of what they do by following fairly standard routines. There are more complex areas, problems that occur less frequently and that involve some degree of uncertainty, such as meeting new people, entering new organizations, dealing with a subordinate who is having a problem, or running into problems with the business. In these situations, we develop what some social psychologists refer to as scripts.

A script is a set way of dealing with different problems. Some of us have specific ways in which we enter new groups and get to know people. Others have specific scripts for dealing with peers or when faced with a new project. These behavior patterns become embedded in our minds and form a part of our self-image, a part of our behavioral repertoire. Over time, they define our self-worth and self-esteem. To alter these scripts we must go through the psychodynamics of change described by Bridges—that is, go through the transitions which include working through the endings or disengaging from an old script. As with other transitions, there's confusion. Frequently, it is impossible to begin this process unless we can first write a new script based on a new vision of the future. Without the vision, we tend to get stuck in the middle of the process of change. The old behavior pattern, or the old script doesn't work, but no new one has been found.

If we think of making difficult life transitions of any kind, we must imagine or develop a vision of what it's like to live on after the death of a loved one or what it will be like to put a life together after a divorce or after having been fired. To be revitalized we need to get in touch with something that will pull us into the future. These same basic dynamics operate in the work setting, when we dramatically redefine global competition and put a whole new set of demands on management in terms of how they'll manage people, resources, and their competitors.

Organizations are made up of thousands of people, each with his or her own set of psychodynamics. Thus, at the organizational level, it is important to go beyond the technical view of the future most often captured in strategic plans—the product market mix of the organization, how it's going to be organized, and so on. If people are going to visualize themselves in the future organization, they need a vision of what the political system will be like, who will be influencing decisions, who will have power, how much power they will have, how people will get ahead, and how the rewards will be allocated. They will envision themselves playing out their own personal agendas in the future political environment.

Underlining all this will be the values. What are the norms going to be like in the future? What values will be needed to drive the business strategy, what will be the style of management, how will people treat each other, what kind of people will be selected, what values will be used as a screen for admitting people to the organization and permitting them to climb the corporate ladder? Thus the vision needs to incorporate the TPC systems of the organization.

Not all of our transformational leaders define their visions in such holistic terms. Nevertheless, as we've seen them articulate and refine their visions, it is clear that they provide glimpses of all three of these systems. Jim Renier at Honeywell started with the value system and clearly articulated role models. He mobilized the workforce around a new set of values about the way people were going to be treated. At the same time a great deal of energy went into redefining the technical strategy for Honeywell Information Systems, articulating that there would be integration with the rest of Honeywell and control systems. That certain mainframe computers would depend on product developments of NEC, not only Honeywell driven product developments, and that people with different skills and values were going to get ahead. Control systems people were coming over from that side of Honeywell to take key positions in the computer business, people with entrepreneurial flair were moving ahead, and bonuses were going to be allocated differently.

When we look at Welch at General Electric, we see him stressing the need to be competitive. GE people had to achieve a dominant position in the industry if they wanted to stay at GE. Beyond that, he began to articulate a set of cultural values that were going to be important in implementing that strategy. And as his vision unfolded over the early years of his chairmanship, it was clear that a different set of stars had begun to emerge at General Electric. Some of the people gaining power came from the inside, some from the outside. Some traditional managers were being moved aside. Different criteria were developed for distributing rewards. After three or four years, Welch's vision of the company he wanted General Electric to be in 1990 began to come into focus for more and more people.

Finally, in his fifth year, Welch led the largest non-oil acquisition in U.S. history when he initiated the purchase of RCA. This move lent credence to the theory of quantum change that he had been espousing at General Electric since he became chairman.

Frederick Hammer at Chase laid out five strategic goals as the technical part of his vision, then went on to make some key announcements and political moves that signaled who would play the principal roles in the organization. He also shook up the value system with his entrepreneurial flair and his lack of concern for organizational level; he sought information and counsel from people he felt had the knowledge and expertise to evolve creative solutions to Chase's problems and opportunities. Once he developed a clear sense of where he wanted retail banking to go at Chase, he was able to depict a vision of the future and to paint pictures that would motivate his subordinates and stimulate each one to develop his or her own vision.

Mary Ann Lawlor backed into her transformational leadership role at Drake in much the same way that Blumenthal did at Burroughs. She did not realize the extent of the crisis until after committing herself. She was motivated to persevere and to get others to join her in turning Drake around by creating an image of an organization that would do good while providing its managers with career opportunities they might not otherwise have. She developed a clear vision of what Drake would look like after it was accredited, the range of services, the values that it would pursue, and how the organization would be structured in terms of ownership and management power. Jeff Campbell believed that Burger King could be the preeminent convenience food company in the world. Like Lawlor, he developed a vision of a very entrepreneurial culture in which power and rewards were shared by many.

At General Motors, Alex Cunningham, Lloyd Reuss, and Bob Stempel created an overarching vision for General Motors' North American group, but they had spent a great deal of time the first couple of years convincing others in the organization of the need for change. Their view is that they need a critical mass of visionaries at the top of that 360,000 person organization, Buick-Oldsmobile-Cadillac and Chevrolet-Pontiac-Canada.

John Harvey-Jones, a visionary who had a great deal of fun shaking people up and trying to shift paradigms and scripts at ICI, reported in his interview that the management meetings he ran were marked by frequent laughter. He sees the primary thrust of his vision as the cultural shift needed at ICI, even though his first years were spent in technically pruning, reshaping, and repositioning the organization.

Lee Iacocca's great success in turning Chrysler around was due to his ability to create a motivating vision of the new Chrysler Corporation while simultaneously tearing 60,000 people out of the workforce. He was able to get those who remained excited and signed up by helping them understand the new business strategy, the new niches they were going after, the importance of productivity and quality. He was able to negotiate deals with the UAW, the bankers, the government, his own management, his board, the dealers, and the suppliers, and make them all see in that vision how they would get something out of the turnaround. As he communicated this vision he also began laying the foundation for a new culture at Chrysler. The irony of Iacocca's success in turning Chrysler around is that it created tremendous pressure in 1985 and 1986 for him to develop a new long-term strategy for the company that was not based on crisis.

Across town at General Motors Corporation, Roger Smith started out as a real sleeper. Many people saw him as a traditional financial man coming into the chairmanship. They anticipated an emphasis on control, not innovation, but he fooled them. He acquired EDS, Hughes Electronics and the Servicing Business of the Northwest Corporation, and The Colonial Group C.G. of Core States Financial Corporation. He launched the most significant reorganization of General Motors since the days of Alfred Sloan and oversaw the launching of the Saturn organization. Smith has created a vision of a high-tech, somewhat diversified automobile company. At the same time he sent signals about the new political structure, the new vision for who's going to get ahead at General Motors. He started a major cultural change to get the bureaucracy out of the company and to stimulate more entrepreneurial behavior and participation.

John Akers at IBM is the transformational leader for the next decade. Soon after he became CEO, he announced his goal to transform IBM into a $185 billion company driven by software and systems rather than hardware. This transformation will require major reorientation and reprogramming. Individuals will be asked to write new scripts. The dilemma will be that the company is so successful and so profitable that the urgency for change will be difficult to create.

Urgency was not a problem for Ed Thompson at Schneider Transport. Deregulation forced Schneider to create a new paradigm for what business they were in so they could dramatically reprogram the way that that business was carried out. Through a participatory process, this vision was developed and shared throughout the organization.

What's common in all these cases is that the leaders kept working at a holistic vision. None of them had a vision of an ideal organization appear to them in a dream, but all of them knew the importance of being able to visualize the organization in the future. All of them shared that vision with the organization and continued to articulate, develop, and elaborate on it.

Michael Blumenthal described the process of developing a vision at Burroughs.

I tend to gather six or eight people around me and we talk about everything, we're very open. I'm very open and I listen to them, and I travel around and talk to a lot of people, and then eventually I try to enunciate what it is that we have learned and I suggest that this is what we are going to do. And then people react to it and at the end I say, okay.

We develop a set of priorities which involve first of all strengthening the product line, closing the holes, and managing the company in at least rudimentarily intelligent fashion, with some numbers, some forecasts, introducing variance analysis, getting some kind of financial measurement, assigning responsibility for decision-making farther down the organization. Beginning to talk to people about what it means to take responsibility, what it means to match authority with responsibility, and how to find the right balance in taking individual responsibility and yet being a member of a team . . . . They agree that that's really what we ought to do.

THE PROCESS OF VISIONING

The architectural metaphor provides an easy way to think about the transformational leader's job. The great architect is much more than a technician. There is a strong element of creativity involved. Yet the creativity goes far beyond the production of something aesthetically pleasing. Buildings are created to serve some social purpose. Architects evaluate one another's work not only in terms of its creativity but also to the extent that form serves function.

Similarly, the transformational leader who creates a new organization can and should be evaluated not only in terms of the ability to bring a dollar to the bottom line but also in terms of the social purposes for which all organizations exist. Transformational leaders who build organizations to serve all the stakeholders achieve excellence.

These creative endeavors require thought processes that are in many cases the antithesis of most management training and practice. Even though there is still some controversy over the scientific adequacy of describing left-brain and right-brain thinking, we will use this categorization as a shorthand for two kinds of thought processes—the left brain being the linear, analytic, systematic, conscious thought processes and the right brain representing the creative, intuitive, instinctive thought processes. It is in the right brain that fantasy and dreaming take place. Vision implies the ability to picture some future state and to be able to describe the state to others so that they begin to share the dream.

Managers are not encouraged to fantasize and visualize. As a matter of fact, the environment they operate in discourages these activities. They are encouraged to use analytical financial, marketing, and production skills—those supported only by left-brain activities. Even the strategic planning process in most organizations is a linear, left-brain activity that does not lead to a vision of a future state but rather results in an extrapolation of current market share, return on investment, or production figures several years into the future. It is as if there was no difference between an organization of x size and an organization of $x + y$ size or $x - y$ size.

Clearly the picture painted by Michael Blumenthal of what transpired at Burroughs as it grew in the 1970s shows the problem with this linear type of extrapolation. It is as if the architect had no overall sense of the building he or she was trying to create and felt that adding a room or several rooms without rethinking the whole would not pervert the artistic intention. It is interesting to note that none of our transformational leaders credited the formal strategic planning process as the source of their vision. For Jack Sparks, who introduced the concept of strategic planning to Whirlpool, the vision came after years of mulling over the kind of organization that Whirlpool could be, and after his constant interaction with people in other organizations and academics. The vision was his; and the strategic planning process became the vehicle for implementing that vision, not its source.

The challenge for the transformational leader is to be able to tap the right-brain vision and then be able to systematically develop blueprints until the TPC matrix is fully articulated in terms of the desired state. In this way, change can be implemented.

GUIDELINES FOR RIGHT-BRAIN VISIONING

All of us have engaged in some type of right-brain activity in our lives, but there are no simple ways to teach it. Children clearly demonstrate the ability as they turn blocks into skyscrapers, forts, houses, and other edifices. Teenagers spend countless hours imagining suave exchanges of conversation with members of the opposite sex, or picturing that perfect athletic performance and being carried off the field on teammates' shoulders. Orators and authors frequently paint vivid pictures that continue to move us as adults. One of the basic problems that we encounter in organizations is that it is culturally illegitimate to fantasize and dream about the future. If the idea cannot be presented in great rational detail it is dismissed as a halfbaked scheme. Yet we have seen that transformational leaders begin journeys on roads that are not always clearly marked. Creativity cannot flourish in a highly critical and defensive environment. Levinson and Rosenthal described the process by which the leaders they interviewed created the climate for visioning by permitting employees to take risks:

The leader provides permission to risk, thereby encouraging autonomy by offering support and collective decision-making efforts, and the encouragement and resources to support that permission. If organizations are to satisfy human purpose, then the leader must not only have a cause but must also create a structure that both supports the development of the bond to the corporation and becomes an instrument for its continuity. Even promises of lifetime employment have no meaning if a business does not remain in business . . . . They put their money where their mouths were. The risks they took were not

foolhardy: the men were not gamblers. The risks were based on care-
ful thought, but ultimately choices had to be made that were beyond
demonstrable logic. The leaders fell back on intuition—"my viscera"
as Watts put it. All of them could have been wrong.

And, of course, some of them inevitably were wrong some of
the time.

How to Foster Right-Brain Visions

We start with the premise that all people can create visions,
although some people may have the skill developed to a greater
extent than others. The transformational leader's challenge is to
unleash as much potential for visioning as possible for people
in the organization. A couple of techniques we have used successfully in organizational settings are described, including the
following case described by Professor Russell Ackoff of the
Wharton School, who led the Clark Equipment Company
through a visioning process that demonstrates the power of normative, right-brain planning. Ackoff explains:

On Wednesday, January 28th, 1985 the Clark Equipment Corpora-
tion and AB Volvo of Sweden announced their intentions to form a
joint venture in which they would merge their Clark Michigan and
Volvo BM divisions. This will create one of the largest construction
and mining equipment corporations in the world. The story behind
this announcement merits a book. A brief commentary can hardly do
it justice. But it is worth a try.

In 1983, Clark Michigan, which had not performed well during the
recession, initiated a major effort to plan itself out of its mess. It
began by formulating that mess: the future that it would face if it
continued its then current practices and policies, and if its environ-
ment did not change in any unexpected ways. The future that was
revealed by this analysis spelled doom for the division. In the time
available to it, it could neither generate nor acquire the resources
required to redirect its future.

Rather than give up in despair, Clark Michigan's management then prepared an unconstrained design of an ideal competitor to the two giants that dominate the industry, Caterpillar and Komatsu.

Next, again without constraints, Clark Michigan's management considered which companies in its industry, together with itself, would most closely approximate the ideal company it had designed. Three organizations were identified. These, together with Clark Michigan, resided in four different countries on three different continents.

Armed with this concept and design, Clark first approached Daimler-Benz, which owned the Euclid Truck Company, and in almost record time arranged to acquire that company. Clark had already begun discussing a joint venture with Volvo BM, the construction equipment division of Volvo AB. Volvo displayed interest in the concept but naturally had a number of concerns. Clark then proposed that a team be formed to address these concerns by preparing a detailed design of the proposed joint venture, and evaluate its financial prospects.

Volvo agreed. The ten-man team that was formed consisted of the general managers of Clark Michigan and Volvo BM, their production, marketing, financial and engineering managers. This team began by producing a more detailed design of an ideal joint venture than Clark Michigan had prepared. Then it prepared as close a feasible approximation to this design as it could. The requisite financial analyses were carried out. They revealed significant financial advantages to both parent companies.

The joint design team presented its findings to the executives and boards of the two parent companies in the fall of 1984. They approved the design and made the commitment to it at the end of 1984.

In addition to producing an exciting design that elicited confidence in it, the designers welded themselves into a homogeneous management team that had overcome all the major cultural differences that initially separated the two parties. By working closely together for six months, they even reached agreement on who should occupy each executive position in the new company.

Through this cooperative design process the team anticipated and dealt with almost every problem that can arise in a joint venture. This enabled the two parent corporations to make their commitments with a degree of confidence that seldom characterizes initiation of a joint venture.

What happened at Clark Michigan would be absolutely impossible with normal planning. But starting with a vision of where you ideally would like to be, it works. There is one reaction to the vision once it is formulated and it is the heart of this whole thing. It happens in every organization. When the vision actually is brought into being, they say: "My God, we can have most of what we really want." And that is a recognition of a fact that is not normally believed, namely, the principal obstruction of where you are and where you would like to be is you. When we plan it is always focused on external obstructions that are keeping you from achieving: competition, government, manager and so on. We are our own principal obstructions to what we want. By visioning the ideal, you find you can get most of it. It becomes like the holy grail of the Crusades and motivates people to overcome themselves.

Creating a Vision of the Future

People can be encouraged to project themselves into some future time period by asking them to write an article to appear in their favorite business publication describing the organization five years from now and the role they played in the transformation of the organization. They are asked not to talk about the changes and their accomplishments in a rational linear format but rather to use a journalistic style in describing how the projected organization differs from its present state. Since journalists engage our interest by using words to paint graphic pictures, the exercise forces executives to abandon the terse outline with bullets backed by data that they favor when they make presentations to their peers and superiors. While some people resist trying this activity, it is useful to ask that they do what all writers ask us to do when we begin to read a story— willingly suspend our disbelief. Criticism is to be reserved for the finished product, not for the process. Once involved most people find the activity enjoyable, for it makes legitimate an activity that we find pleasurable—daydreaming.

Identifying the Themes

Once the article is completed, the individual is asked to iden- tify both the personal and organizational themes in the article. It is useful to be able to discuss the article with someone who can be used as a sounding board.

Creating a Common Vision

In large organizations this activity can serve as a springboard for reaching a consensus about the organization's future. Strate- gic plans frequently focus people's attention on quantitative projections, and that can lead to arguments about their accu- racy. Lost in the shuffle is a discussion of whether the basic thrust underlying the numbers is the correct direction for the organization to take. This exercise tends to focus attention on the overall direction of the company—what would it look like if the plans were to succeed? The leader can gain valuable infor- mation from such an exchange about the degree of consensus that exists among key decision makers in the company. The result can be a vision that most of the team shares, or it may result in a less democratic decision, which the CEO under- stands he or she must sell to the team.

Creating a Mission Statement from a Vision

A vision contains an implicit mission statement, for embedded in every vision is a sense of what kind of a company we want to be at some point in the future. When Jack Sparks spoke of a more sophisticated, aware management team at Whirlpool, he could begin to identify the values such a company would espouse. Blumenthal was explicit about the things that the "new Burroughs" would and would not do. The themes that comprise a mission statement were embedded in their visions.

Developing a Leadership Agenda

Once the vision has been created and the mission statement has been articulated, a transformational leader must develop an agenda. This agenda will contain a set of priorities that are necessary if the dream is to come true. If the vision and mission statement have been developed as part of a team exercise, each member of the team can work up a personal agenda setting priorities for himself or herself.

The major benefit derived from this exercise is that it provides a culturally acceptable way for many people to tap into their right-brain thinking. While the cultures that support people engaged in artistic endeavors permit a greater deviation from rational norms than we find in cultures geared to business organizations, the use of a business media fantasy is one to which most executives can relate. As a matter of fact there is a videotape of Jack Welch filmed at the Harvard Business School soon after he became chairman of General Electric, in which he ends by telling the audience what he would like *Fortune* or *BusinessWeek* to write about him in 1990.

Another technique is that used with the senior management team at Detroit Diesel Allison, where the top management team was attempting to develop a vision of the organization in the future. In preparation for a two-day workshop, each of the ten senior executives was asked to picture his or her ideal organization three years into the future. They approached the activity in a left-brain way. Each drew an organization chart, specifying some of the characteristics of the roles, and how things would be carried out. Essentially, they developed a set of blueprints. When they arrived at the workshop, they were asked to engage in an exercise that opened them up to right-brain vision-ing activities. They were put in pairs, with half of them as-signed to the role of reporter for *The Wall Street Journal*, writ-ing a story about Detroit Diesel Allison three years into the future. The other half of the group was to fantasize what they would say to that reporter. The results of this exercise were similar to those obtained when executives are asked to write scenarios. After the "interviews" were presented to the group, organizational and leadership themes were extracted and a bridge was made to a fairly disciplined left-brain planning ac-tivity.

THE LEFT BRAIN: TPC BLUEPRINTS

If the right brain is responsible for the vision, which we have compared to the architect's building model, the left brain is analogous to the architect's blueprint. The blueprint must con-tain a detailed set of specifications so that the building we erect is structurally sound. The TPC matrix provides a frame for the blueprints. As the leadership articulates a vision, it can begin to develop the specifications that must be met by that future orga-nization. The leaders can be asked to develop a qualitative statement of what will exist and to list whatever quantitative measures are appropriately associated with the qualitative statement. For example, in the mission and strategy area, the product market matrix can be created for the organization along with return on asset figures, market share, and so on. In the mission/strategy/political area, a map of the key power figures, whose cooperation is needed to successfully run the business, can be created. In this arena the organizational processes for dealing with coalitional differences about the appropriate strat-egy for the organization should be addressed. The future values of the organization in the mission/strategy/cultural area should be articulated as the final part of a discussion about the mission/strategy processes in the organization.

The goal of this activity is to have a set of working drawings that will lead to a set of transition plans. The architect must now devise a construction plan that will enable him or her to create the right-brain vision *and* the blueprints.

WITHOUT VISION, NO REVITALIZATION

One message should be clear in this chapter: leaders are responsible for the creation of a vision, and the vision provides the basic energy source for moving the organization toward the future. The vision is conceptually complex because it mirrors the organization. Staying with our architectural metaphor, we can talk about the difference between designing a building to fit a specific site and renovating an existing structure. Both are creative endeavors, but the design of a new structure is clearly the easier task because it is frequently more difficult to imagine what can be when confronted with what is. We are limited and constrained by the current structure, and it is often harder to visualize how it can differ in both function and form.

The difficulty comes from the inability of the architect to assess the total structural soundness of the building before work begins. Just as Jim Renier talked about the fact that deep-seated organizational problems often exist before the numbers go down, so the architect of a renovation project is frequently forced to guess about the condition of the wiring, plumbing, and support structure until the walls are torn out. The renovation is also complicated by the fact that the existing tenants may have to live in the building while it is being renovated. The inconvenience frequently results in second thoughts about the wisdom of the decision to rebuild the structure.

Our transformational leaders are closer to the architect dealing with the problems of renovation than they are to the architect dealing with the problem of creating a new structure. It is the entrepreneurs who designed and built new organizations in places like Silicon Valley and Route 128 and who have been responsible for most of the growth in jobs in the United States in the last decade. The honeymoon in these growth industries, however, may be over. In February 1985, John Young, president of Hewlett-Packard, presented a report to the White House documenting America's growing competitive vulnerability to foreign competition. And many highly respected companies, such as Texas Instruments, Apple Computers, and Intel, find themselves contracting rather than growing. The Young report focused on problems in a number of areas that included the adversarial nature of the relationship between workers and management; the declining percentage of GNP devoted to the research and development needed to create jobs in the civilian sector of the economy; the seeming inability of U.S. companies to master modern manufacturing techniques, a problem undoubtedly exacerbated by the high cost of capital here relative to other countries; the fact that antitrust legislation in this country places pressure on those companies in a position to compete with the integrated Japanese and Korean companies; and the need to address the deficiencies in America's trade policies vis-à-vis the current world competitive situation.

These companies thus join much of smokestack America in facing the need to find new ways of coping with an environment that is increasingly hostile. Competition means constant adaptation, and the truth is that all companies will have to be lean if they are to survive in the competitive arena. Every job that we ship overseas so that an organization can survive places additional strain on the fabric of our society. We cannot afford to abandon any of our industries. We must find the will and the resources to transform the losers into winners again. This is the challenge faced by transformational leaders.

MOBILIZING COMMITMENT: GETTING PEOPLE SIGNED ON TO THE MISSION

6

Formulating a vision for the future of the organization is a creative and important task. Communicating that vision through large complex organizations can provide transformational leaders with a herculean challenge.

In 1983 Fisher Body, one of General Motors' largest divisions, employed over 75,000 people at 28 locations worldwide. At that time, Fisher Body designed and fabricated automobile bodies. Once a car's outward appearance was determined by GM's design staff, Fisher's design engineers and craftspeople redid the design, detailing and testing every part, feature, and material to be used in the car body. Next engineers, craftspeople, and die designers determined the most efficient way to fabricate the parts, and production engineers worked out the assembly details. Once these tasks were completed, metal fabricating plants stamped out the body parts. Trim plants produced the interior fabrics and hardware plants produced the necessary small components. Finally the assembly plants assembled, rustproofed, insulated, and painted the car bodies. The people were technically proficient and the process worked, but in 1984 Fisher Body was dismantled. Why? On January 10, 1984, Roger Smith, chairman of General Motors, and James McDonald, president, announced the corporate reorganization of General Motors. The North American car group was split into two integrated car groups that were to function as self-contained business units. Each group would be totally responsible for entire products and processes, from basic design engineering and development to manufacturing, assembly, and marketing. A third group in the initial phase of the reorganization would be the body and assembly group comprised of Fisher Body Division, General Motors Assembly Division, and Guide Division. As the reorganization progressed, Fisher Body, General Motors Assembly Division, and Guide Division would be absorbed into the two car groups.

Charles Katko began the process three days after the reorganization was announced by convening a conference of 104 key executives from the body and assembly group to discuss the reaction to the news and invite their questions and input. During this conference, he expressed his commitment to the proposed changes and stressed that the reorganization was adopted solely to make the company more competitive and not as a vehicle for further layoffs. He invited all those present to participate in the process of helping the company achieve this desired goal by becoming a united team. He stated at the meeting:

> **I need your help . . . not only in communicating but also in building trust and credibility especially now . . . in the midst of this change . . . if we show our employees we care about them they will begin to trust us and ultimately they will begin to believe what we tell them about competitive position and quality.**

To demonstrate the need for employee participation in the reorganization, the conferees were asked to break up into 12 small groups, with each group including a mix of Fisher Body, Assembly Division, and Guide Division people. Each of the group then chose one of the 12 issues which Katko had identified regarding the reorganization. These 12 issues were:

1. How can we establish a meaningful feedback system for our people during the transition?

2. How should we be involved as a senior executive group for body assembly in the entire transition process?

3. What do you see as problems and pitfalls with our new organization [including the transition]?

4. What kind of communication strategy should we establish during this period of transition?

5. What advice do we have for the group vice presidents?

6. What guiding principles, ethical standards, do we want to establish for the new organization?

7. How can we transfer our divisional pride to pride in the new organization?

8. How can we build an effective working relationship among GMAD, Fisher, and Guide people?

9. What is our role, the people in this room, in making number 8 happen?

10. What problems might be experienced by the implementation teams and how might they be minimized or avoided?

11. When and how should we bring the UAW into the process?

12. Given the complexities of the transition, how do we keep the business running smoothly?

The groups met separately to brainstorm strategies for the issues they selected. Each made a presentation to the whole group later in the afternoon.

On February 6, 1984 Katko held two general meetings for 800 employees of the Fisher Body Division and 1000 employees from General Motors Assembly Division to inform the hourly workers personally about the change and to field their questions. Finally, he established work study groups which were to formulate plans for implementing the needed changes. All the teams were brought together for meetings in April and May to compare notes and see what everyone had been up to.

Katko believed that a key element in the growth of team spirit is mutual trust: employees trusting management to conduct business in a humane manner that considers their needs and concerns, and management trusting employees to work together with them to help the company succeed. He outlined three steps to build this trust.

1. Demonstrating one's commitment to the change process

2. Having effective two-way communication

3. Seeking employee participation and involvement in the process

To instill commitment on the part of employees, he empha-
sized that they needed to understand that they were involved in
a logical organizational change. Therefore, all managers must
understand what the changes are, communicate this information to their employees, listen carefully to them, and be as responsive as possible to their informational needs. Fisher Body
managers followed these principles during 1984, sending information to the body and assembly group implementation team.
Work group chairpeople were encouraged to seek out those
best able to aid them in addressing their particular issues, no
matter what their positions in the company. Workgroups interviewed employees at all levels of division, information that
influenced critical decision-making came up through the division.

A second area of managerial concern for Katko was the need
for speed in communication. He didn't want anyone affected by
the change to hear important information from external sources.
He said:

> I am afraid that too many GM people found out about the
> changes from the media first and I do worry a lot about this. We
> probably did a much improved job of communicating the
> changes down through the organization this time but we still
> have to improve a great deal as we go forward. Hit and miss
> communication can only diminish our efforts to build employee
> trust.

To avoid this pitfall, Katko enlisted the aid of his director of
public relations, Dick Wilmont, in instituting an efficient and
timely communication system. The system was designed to
generate information, further understanding, and communicate
official changes immediately before the media could do so. Its
basic components included a new organization newsletter; employee feedback through drop boxes, Katco staff meetings, and
question-and-answer sessions at employee assemblies; rapid
and thorough communication through middle management;

CRT bulletins and public address announcements; electronic mail; and videotapes of important meetings and presentations.

In these early stages of reorganization, workers worried about basic, personal concerns: What am I going to be doing? Whom am I going to be doing it for? Where am I going to be doing it? Katko addressed questions through various communication media. When asked the question, "Since Fisher Body is breaking up, will the individual have a say about which group he or she goes to—the Buick-Olds-Cadillac or Chevrolet-Pontiac-Canada group?" Katko's response was:

> I don't like to refer to Fisher Body as breaking up. I prefer to refer to Fisher Body as becoming a part of the big or small car groups. As to the choice of which car groups individuals will be joining, each of you have particular assignments and some of these assignments are more involved with the large or small group. It's logical then that you would go with the group that you're most involved with. We need to look at the experience and talent each individual has and fit them into the group that best suits them. Most moves will consider both the work the individuals are involved in and the needs of the large and small car groups. (At this time early in the year, the Buick-Olds-Cadillac group was often referred to as the large car group and the Chevrolet-Pontiac as the small car group. Since that time that designation has been dropped.)

When asked how the people of the Fisher Body Group felt, Katko commented:

> Fisher Body has played an important role in product design and development in the past. We see Fisher people having an important role in the new structure. The same need for input still holds.

Katko kept the communication lines open so that people could talk openly about symbols and changes. A seemingly trivial symbol, but one that was treated with respect, was this question from many of the workers: Are we going to be changing the signs on the facility and what will they say? The response from Katko to this question initially was, "Not soon. We don't know yet. The matter is still under consideration."

By the fall of 1984, Fisher Body had been dismantled and people had been reassigned across the two car groups—a rather amazing feat as the people involved were charged up and excited and committed to the new organization, at least in the short run. This was surprising when one considers that Fisher Body was reported to have the strongest old boy network in General Motors and was noted for protecting its own even at the expense of other units. A large group of dissatisfied old timers could have made the reorganization extremely difficult as they rode out their final years until retirement in the new situation. Another factor that could have inhibited team building was Fisher's unique area of expertise, but Fisher design teams were transferred intact into the new car groups. Finally the Fisher name, with its long and proud history in General Motors, was likely to remain in the organization in one form or another. As McDonald stated:

I would say that the name Fisher Body will always have an identity in General Motors. How it is to be preserved is something we still have to determine.

Charles Katko was credited with having done an outstanding leadership job in transferring the identity and commitment of the workers to the new organization. He had worked himself out of a job; he moved on to become the group executive for the bus and truck group at General Motors.

This is just one illustration of the transformational leaders' challenges in the 1980s and the 1990s. Not everyone will be dismantling organizations. Nevertheless, many will be transforming groups into something different, and we can learn a great deal from cases such as Katko's, in which a basic understanding of the psychodynamics of change and group process enabled him to pull off a transition successfully that many thought would be a real blood bath and could have hampered General Motors for years to come. As in the Fisher case, mobilization of commitment means giving hundreds of people in the organization the incentive to create visions of the future that they find motivating. This is what John Kennedy did when he challenged the thousands of NASA engineers to get a man on the moon before the Russians did, and what Martin Luther King's "I Have a Dream" speech did for lawmakers and citizens.

Mobilizing commitment involves a dual challenge. One half of the challenge is to unhook people from the past, the other is to get them hooked on the future and revitalized. We will provide examples of some of the transitional vehicles that leaders seem to use successfully.

LEADERS AS STEWARDS: HELPING PEOPLE THROUGH TRANSITIONS

Jim Renier assumed the role of transformational leader at Honeywell Information Systems in September 1982. He came over from the control side of Honeywell to become vice chairman of the corporation and president of Information Systems. Once Renier recognized the psychodynamics involved in the change process he was better able to carry out his transformational role. By framing the problem this way he began to understand the difficulties people had in reorienting their thinking and realized that change could not be pushed through the organization. The true test of leadership came in serving as a steward of the change process, which enabled people to unhook, refocus, and develop a commitment to the new vision. He succeeded in getting a number of key people to assume the responsibility for transforming various parts of the organization.

At General Motors, Alex Cunningham, executive vice president of General Motors North America, was charged with the restructuring of the car divisions. He began the process by involving the managers who would head up the new car divisions, Bob Stempel and Lloyd Reuss, in a workshop based on the transformational leadership framework. This provided an understanding of the psychodynamics that thousands of GM managers and employees would have to work through if they were to navigate the transition from the past successfully.

When Jack Welch first became chairman of General Electric, he laid out an agenda for change and worked hard to win converts to the vision. By 1984 the psychodynamics of change were surfacing in many parts of GE, and there were many ambivalent feelings about what Welch was trying to accomplish. Some of these feelings were captured in the *Fortune* article that named him the toughest boss in America in 1984. In the long run, Welch's success may depend not only on his ability to ram change through the organization but on his ability to provide the necessary support for people to work through the organizational transition.

Whether the transformational leader explicitly recognizes and frames the change process in the organization is not important. It *is* important, however, that the leader intuitively understand the need to provide space and support for people as they work through the transition.

Jack Sparks is very conscious of the fact that he is the symbolic leader who must keep himself at the center of the change process. He says:

> I keep a high profile. I write something every month. I've got people reading books, I've got seminars going on and I'm always opening these things up. They all know how I feel, the whole atmosphere I'm trying to create is that we are going to upgrade, we are going to be the best, we're going to earn it . . . .

John Harvey-Jones at ICI describes himself as being in the middle of the transition. He states:

> I have two more years. My process for the five years was the first year, reset up the board and build a team, set in a new budgeting

system. Set in a system for doing strategic reviews. Years two and
three were for going through every business in the group and
every territory in the group and setting a clear strategy, by which
I mean a one line strategy, that is, grow in Japan or operate for
cash or disengage for this, etc. A one line strategy. The next two
years are meant, as far as I'm concerned, for trying to change the
culture farther down the outfit. I've been trying to change the
culture during the past two years, but I didn't figure there was
too much value in trying to work with it until it was clear where
we were going.

One of the kinds of cultural change is trying to open up the
recognition that people are all vulnerable and make mistakes,
and we can learn from them. Harvey-Jones described one situation:

We had one disaster this year where I went back to the CEO of a
business and said, "It wasn't your fault," because we asked him
to do something and while he wasn't doing it in quite the way we
had envisioned he was headed in the right direction. We had
made a mistake in what we had asked for. . . . It's pretty unusual for the chairman to say "I screwed up," and even more
unusual for his colleagues to tell him that he had. But they did it
nicely. We take three or four times out in the year to review what
we are doing and how we are doing it . . . . I think it is important to develop the ability to be self-critical.

Cunningham talks about some important things the people at
General Motors learned during this process:

I think that the lesson was that organizations and structures and
plans on paper are one thing, the implementation of the pragmatic world is something else and the degree of flexibility you
need to have in your mental outlook towards that is important.
Some things happen more quickly than you would have hoped
and many things of course, don't. Consequently the thing is a
humanistic development program, because there is always the
tendency to be disappointed at the speed and rate of change. And
you've got to understand that the rate of change goes at its own

pace and it is driven by the people in the organization, and it is better to have a little slower rate of change that is developed by people and bought into by people in the organization . . . .

PROVIDING THE MEANS FOR TRANSITION

The dynamics of working through endings, transitions, and new beginnings are so compelling that those with sufficient power and resources will often spontaneously create the structures and vehicles they need to effect the transition. CEOs faced with a major change often seek help with endings and new beginnings. They set up task forces, hire consultants, and analyze the current situation to find out what went wrong. They will throw up trial balloons and spend six to nine months supporting themselves in the transition state. They will not make commitments to the future nor will they unhook from the past, but they will go through a series of exploratory activities. Reginald Jones's activities at General Electric, in the two-year period that preceded the election of Jack Welch as his successor, are a good example of dealing with a transition. Jones spent a great deal of time identifying the possible candidates for chairman. He felt that there were seven or eight people at GE qualified to succeed him, but he also wanted to be sure that he had a team in the office of the chairman which could work together.

Jones used a vehicle he called the airplane interview to effect the transition. He began to focus organizational attention on the issue of who would succeed him as chairman of General Electric by arranging a series of meetings with each of the seven or eight candidates who had been identified as possible successors. He did not announce in advance the purpose of the meetings, so when he opened each one, every candidate was surprised. He created a scenario and asked each the same question. The scenario was that Jones and the candidate are riding in the GE plane, it crashes and the two are killed. The question was "Who should be chairman of General Electric?"

Jones claims that some of the candidates tried to climb out of the wreckage, but he would not let them. In the next several hours they talked about the candidate's perception of the challenges that GE faced and who among the GE executives would be most capable of helping the company to meet those challenges.

Jones claimed that the information he obtained was invaluable. Not only did he get their perception of the company's future but he learned a great deal about the chemistry among the top group at General Electric, "Who could work with whom and who absolutely despised whom." He did not take notes or use a tape recorder, which he believed would have inhibited the exchange, but rather went back to his office and wrote up or dictated the conversation as soon as it was over. Several months later he repeated the interviews, but this time he announced in advance what the meeting would be about and the candidates arrived prepared with notes to back up their analysis of the situation.

Jones waited for some time and then set up another set of meetings with the same group. This time he had slightly altered the scenario but the question remained the same. The new scenario was that Jones and the candidate were riding in the GE plane when it went down and Jones died but the candidate survived; the question now was, "Who should be chairman of the General Electric Company?" This scenario produced more valuable information. Jones discovered that some immediately responded, "I'm your man," whereas others "did not want any part of it." He then repeated this scenario in a set of meetings in which the candidates knew in advance the subject of the meeting.

At the same time that Jones was collecting information from the group of potential successors, he also was discussing his impressions with several senior executives who would be retiring with him and with Ted LeVino, who headed up the executive management staff at General Electric. Finally, months before he would retire, he named three of the group to the office of the chairman. No one knew at this point who would be chairman and who would be asked to serve as vice chairmen. This not only gave Jones and his advisors an opportunity to see these men in their new roles but it gave the board of directors an opportunity to learn something about them and the way they operated.

When the decision had been made, Jones met with each of the candidates separately for what he describes as difficult meetings with two of them, since he had to say, "We would like you to be vice chairman not chairman of General Electric."

This process was clearly time consuming, but Jones believed that one of the most important tasks he had as a leader was to prepare the organization for the transition that would occur when he retired. He recognized that the conditions that General Electric would face in the coming decades would be vastly different from those that had existed during his tenure at the company, and the selection of a chairman would serve two purposes. It would select the person best able to deal with the changing environment and it would help focus organizational attention on the issues that General Electric needed to address if it were to continue to be a world-class competitor.

The process also provided the leading contenders for the chairmanship with some time for personal transition. The gradual nature of the process and the collection of data from a broad group prevented a mass exodus from the senior management ranks at General Electric. It also provided Welch, the new chairman, with substantial support from both the top management group and the board since they had had an opportunity to know what he would do if elected to the post.

Jones intuitively recognized the importance of symbolism and ritual and the psychological ramifications of this transition for both the organization and the key executives who had played an important role in General Electric's past success. He understood that he was dealing with strong emotions and feelings, as well as technical evaluations of skills and competencies, and finally he grasped the importance of forging a team capable of mobilizing commitment to a new order.

One interesting thing about our transformational leaders is that they try risky things. They also are attuned to the importance of symbolism and to using their intuition. Once Jeff Campbell had become clear in his own mind about the vision for Burger King, he was preparing to share this with his people. He described some of his earlier activities to develop commitment. He gave big bonuses. He gave all employees credit cards at Burdine's. One of the most interesting things he did was to reward the ad agency. He described this in the following way:

> Our ad agency was at a meeting where we were recognizing the outstanding effort of many of our employees. We called them up on the stage, and gave them a surprise gift—a watch, because, we said, "You guys really contributed to this success in a big way." Then we said, "We have something else for you," and we handed our account executive a check for a quarter of a million dollars. He was astonished—and he called the chairman of the agency, who could not believe we would do something like that. No one gives ad agencies bonuses but I think it really was a way of getting an extra effort on top of an already superlative performance.

HOW PROTAGONISTS HAVE DEALT WITH THE CHALLENGE OF MOBILIZING COMMITMENT

There are some identifiable strategies used by our transformational leaders to mobilize commitment in their organizations. They fall loosely into four groupings. These are not totally distinct, and many of our leaders use multiple strategies, but we will illustrate these four in the following section. They are:

1. Planning as a commitment-generating vehicle
2. Education as a commitment-generating vehicle

3. Changing team composition
4. Altering the management process by which problems are framed in the organization

Planning in Order to Generate Commitment

Fred Hammer. Once Hammer had stabilized the retail banking arm of Chase Manhattan Bank, taking out costs and laying the foundation for profitability in the short run, he was ready to mobilize widespread commitment to a new vision—that of a strong consumer banking sector. He chose as his vehicle a nine-month planning process, in which the top 25 managers, along with literally hundreds of their subordinates and staff, worked on the design of future businesses and structures for those businesses. People were assigned to task forces to run a variety of businesses as temporary organizations. In addition to their regular ongoing assignment, they would be part of a planning group made up of members that cut across many of the existing departments and businesses.

These planning groups met regularly, had regular reviews both by Hammer and his team inside consumer banking as well as key corporate staff people from Chase. They were expected to do 50 percent more work during this period. Their regular jobs had to be done, had to be done well, and, in many cases, they had to squeeze out half-time commitments to the planning and development work. People worked long and hard but morale was extremely high.

During this process, people were able to understand for themselves the need to change past behavior, and they were able to get excited about their vision of future businesses for consumer banking. By the end of the planning process, there was a great deal of excitement and ownership for the future. The technical plan that resulted from the process was probably not very different from one that could have been written by Hammer and a couple of key people nine months earlier. The difference was the mobilization and sense of ownership on the part of the many people who had been involved.

Ed Thompson. Thompson was leading Schneider Transport when deregulation called for rapid change. This trigger did not draw an immediate response from all the key players. As the alarm bells continued to sound, however, a sense of the degree of change required sank in. This facilitated the goal setting or vision development.

At this point Thompson viewed his leadership task as having to get and keep the attention of a whole array of stakeholders, each of whom had become accustomed to focusing only on a piece of the whole business. Thompson had to keep everybody involved and working through their piece of the transition phase:

> You know one of the hardest things for our organization was to see how things were fitting together during the change period. We have several groups doing important work on sales, operations, computer systems, equipment engineering, driver involvement, new location start-ups. Often the work was done at different locations. It all had to fit and flow together. Out of necessity we developed a number of things which facilitated this important view of how single pieces of work fit into the larger whole— we used temporary task forces, had large report meetings, rotated people onto different teams, promoted some drivers to management to facilitate work across the interface, brought sales people in from the field to share marketplace reality with driver groups. We held business training and communication sessions for our employees almost every week for two years. The line and support people who led the sessions just had to see the whole to perform well. We included union leaders. Customers made presentations. This transition phase from where we were to where we needed to be had to be done well. On the one hand we had major cost reductions to make in our existing operations and on the other we had to start up new operations across the country in fresh ways. Service to our customers had to remain consistent during the change period. In the end we concluded that it was as important for all involved to have as clear a vision of the fit of the

major moving parts in the transition phase as it was for them to be holistically in touch with the future vision.

Thompson's activities here were much like Fred Hammer's, keeping the pots stirred, listening to people, encouraging them, helping them think through and arrive at conclusions that maybe he himself had already reached but which they had to own themselves.

Mary Ann Lawlor. The strategy pursued by Lawlor was very similar to that followed by Hammer and Thompson, namely the mobilization of her key managers to plan through and implement their own change strategy. She told us how she kept the key people motivated in those early days at Drake.

> We used to drink wine on Friday night to congratulate ourselves for getting through the week. Sometimes someone would bring in some fancy food and we would pretend we were successful. The bonds in the group were very important. We felt that we were doing something special and we were having a great time doing it and who knew when we were going to cash the pay checks we held for weeks at a time. It was almost like being in combat. I think I got an appreciation for what men feel about one another when they have been in battle.
>
> I had this feeling that I was leading them but I was also dependent on them. There was no way that I could do what had to be done simply by issuing orders. Of course, I did issue orders, I used to write memos day and night, I was always writing memos but if I didn't stop and have a drink with them once a week they never would have done it. So it was like combat—awful while you're going through it, but the relationships you form are terrific—we all developed a sense that we knew where we were going—we knew what had to be done.

Management Process and Framing the Problem

Other transformational leaders seemed to have obtained the most leverage in gaining commitment to the vision by helping reframe the way people thought about the business and by altering the management process. They changed the way in which meetings took place, agendas were set, and other procedures were done.

At General Electric Lighting, Ralph Ketchum was the individual who was able to reframe the way GE thought about the lighting business. Rather than think about lighting as a commodity business, he began to introduce marketing and price leadership strategy into his manager's thinking. Ketchum did this through a process of careful education, which involved building into the management area the use of marketing data and new information systems, and establishing a new style of management in meetings and agenda preparation.

Jeff Campbell at Burger King also broke the frame of the past and began to have his managers identify both emotionally and intellectually with the idea of Burger King as the leader, not the follower in the industry. This meant actively encouraging people to open up and focus in new areas.

John Harvey-Jones in London altered the identity of ICI from a commodity chemical producer to a company much more focused on value-added products, a global company with tremendous investments in the United States, with a fast growing pharmaceutical arm. He altered the management process by reducing the number of deputy chairmen and pushing accountability down into the organization.

Changing the Composition of the Team

The commitment of the key players at the top is absolutely essential to making the transformation take place. Jack Sparks at Whirlpool altered the team composition in the top three or four ranks of Whirlpool by offering a set of golden windows. Several hundred Whirlpool managers took advantage of the early retirement and golden handshake opportunities. The managers who remained were those committed to helping Whirlpool through the transformation.

In another part of Michigan, at Burroughs, Mike Blumenthal faced a more painful process. He used financial incentives like golden windows and golden handshakes to retire many managers. But at the top there was no way to avoid some firings. Of the top 21 people at Burroughs, all but a few were eventually brought in from the outside by Blumenthal. Obviously those brought in were likely to be highly committed to both Blumenthal and the new mission for Burroughs. At Chrysler, Iacocca fired 35 vice presidents and brought in 14 of the managers he had worked with at the Ford Motor Company. This type of wrenching change at the top does not come without its price. It gains rapid commitment to the change process, but it tends to create a we/they syndrome between the "insiders" and the "outsiders."

Some of the ambivalence at Chrysler and at Burroughs is the message about how you get ahead. In both of those organizations individuals question whether a personal link to the top person is a necessary, if not a sufficient condition for advancement. And there is also a concern that the experience of having managed in the "old" Burroughs or the "old" Chrysler might not be considered as a ticket to the top.

Another extremely interesting transition vehicle involved the use of insiders rather than outsiders to change the composition of a top management team. It happened at General Motors in 1984.

The year before the actual reorganization at General Motors took place Alex Cunningham was given the responsibility to plan how the reorganization process would work. He reports that once the plan was approved in principle by Roger Smith and Jim McDonald, part of the conversation that followed went something like this:

> "Well, I'm glad you guys like the concept, but if you're going to let us do it you've got to let us pick the team, because if you don't do that, don't ask me to have any part of it." This was because if we had done it the way we usually did, you would have had a whole bunch of people pick favorite sons by reputation and per-

sonal knowledge. You don't get a uniform team that everyone supports by doing it that way. We basically went through a process where we took every top job and wrote the criteria of that job, and then took lists of our top executives who fitted them to some degree, and then evaluated them by the criteria on a weighted scale basis. Bob Stempel, Lloyd Reuss, Charles Katko and I ran the team that did this.

Before describing the process it should be pointed out that Bob Stempel and Lloyd Reuss joined the team in a very interesting fashion. First, their initial reactions to being selected were indicative of the radical way that General Motors was going about the reorganization. As Stempel commented:

One of my reactions was that it was the first time in General Motors that somebody said, "You're going to get a new job but I don't know what it is, but you're going to help write the book." That had never happened to me before, because I knew exactly what all the jobs were that I was going into, and what was required, and how to do them. As a matter of fact, Lloyd and I for a long time didn't even know where we were on the organization chart.

They were told that they were on the team and that each one was going to run one of the major car groups. However, Cunningham told them that they might be running either group, and that over the first few months they were going to be working together in selecting the top teams that would work for each organization. Each of them was to pick two teams, one if he was going to run the Buick-Olds-Cadillac group and another if he was to run the Chevrolet-Pontiac-Canada team; and they were to help each other in selecting those teams. The purpose of this, according to Cunningham, was to build in some checks and balances so that they would not necessarily select the people with whom they would feel most comfortable. This process forced each of them to think carefully about what he would do if he had the business and also forced them to look at their own strengths and weaknesses as managers.

The group went through a careful process of identifying what each of the organizations would need to be most effective and what qualities each of the key positions would demand. Then they began to match people against the established criteria. They did a number of very interesting exercises during this process, one of which is described by Cunningham.

> Then we did something else without looking at the results of scores. We went back and took the same people, because in an organization like this good people surface. In fact, we all generally pick good people. We had nine out of ten that we agreed on, and we took all these people and without any judgment of score said, hey how do these guys stack up against one another? Each of us ranked them in order. Then we put those rankings up on the board, noting who had done each list, and began talking about them. It became obvious there was a lot of agreement among the people doing the evaluations. Then when we put those together with the subjective scores, there was almost a perfect correlation. You almost said, "Hey what did we waste our time doing the exercise for?" except that we had new criteria that had never been there before: what was the guy's attitude toward quality, for instance, had never been one of the evaluation criteria. What are his quality of work life and people attitudes? These had never been in the ratings before, either. But the same people who surfaced on a subjective basis were there on an objective basis.

In developing these criteria, Lloyd Reuss commented:

> We arrived at these criteria by asking ourselves what we needed in the new organization, what kind of managers we were looking for. We talked about the change process, what were the things that were really important if General Motors was going to succeed. And what were the givens: performance, profitability, return on investment. But that's sort of standard business school stuff. Going forward, what we talked about were the new criteria, what kind of things were really going to make a difference. We talked about competitive edge, we talked about quality of work life, we talked about commitment to quality. It's one thing to say, yeah I'm a quality guy. It's another thing to say, "He really is a quality guy." And we used those criteria to begin to sort them

out. Because we had guys who had been on everybody's first choice list from a technical standpoint, but who weren't there when some of the other criteria were considered. We've had candidates about whom somebody would say, "Well, in my experience he really doesn't meet this new criterion." "You're right, he's a great guy in the old frame, but not in the new."

Alex Cunningham stated:

In fact, when we were all through this process and we met with Jim McDonald, the president, to review our selections, several times he asked us, "Well, what about Joe? You know he's always been one of our best" and we'd say, "Well, yeah, he was on our list but he didn't shake out and here are the reasons he didn't shake out. . . ." Again, we had this analysis on the weighted point average and you could see that the guy was low in scores against some of the new criteria we'd set.

In discussing the participative process of creating these top teams it became clear as Stempel said:

The great advantage in doing this exercise was when you were faced with a possibility, you really got serious because the understanding laid down was once you commit to the team you can't change it, you're in bed with it. And you have to look at it very seriously. And what that did was begin to make you assess in each operation if I'm there what team do I need to do the job. It was kind of a check and balance to make sure we felt we had the right guy for the job.

Stempel's colleague, Lloyd Reuss, said:

I don't care who you are. If your boss is going to give you the team and say, "All right, this is your team, you go out and do this job," you're not going to have nearly the commitment you would if he says, "All right, there's a pool, now you put your team together and it's yours." It was no holds barred. We looked for talent anywhere in the organization, overseas, in other parts of GM.

The feeling on the part of the top group is that the process worked so well in picking the people who report directly to them that they were eager to use the process in helping subordinates pick *their* subordinates. Alex Cunningham describes the process and tells why it's so important in the following terms:

> The process becomes selfish because you know that you have to perform and you want to perform. You want this thing that we've started to be very successful. I certainly want it to be successful in the worst way and so do the rest of the guys involved. It's selfish to want to get the best possible people regardless of where they come from or anything else about them, because that's what is going to make the thing a success. That's a powerful motive, you know, that you can't deny. When you have a total organization that's not dynamic and you're just picking people one at a time to fill a slot, you can afford to take a second class pick, even though in reality you shouldn't. The rest of the organization will carry that individual, so any less than top performance will not make such a great impact. But here you really had this task at hand, you just had to pick the very best people you could.

And as Bob Stempel stated:

> It was clear that one of our objectives implicit from the very first meeting, was that we were going to change, and that meant reducing the number of layers of management, improving our span of control and our effectiveness. So you couldn't afford an extra nice guy, or one more guy on the team, you really were looking out to be lean, to be effective. So you really started to go for the talent.

A year later this process is still cascading down inside those organizations. There is evidence that the teams being created are high-commitment teams, that in the process of selecting people they have engaged individuals in a number of visioning exercises to help fit them to the future. One of the ways of helping the screening process was to have candidates for different slots write *BusinessWeek* or *Fortune* articles of the future, using their personal visions.

Educational Vehicles for Managing the Transition

At CIBA-GEIGY, Don MacKinnon spearheaded the introduction of a management development program for the top executives. Over a one-year period they ran hundreds of executives through a strategic thinking workshop. What made the program unique was the fact that the chairman and the president were present at every single one of the two-week sessions for most of the time. Each of these educational sessions became an important vehicle both for team building and for gaining commitment to a new way of operating at CIBA-GEIGY. The incredible amount of time and energy spent by both the chairman and the president at CIBA-GEIGY is seen as one of the best investments they ever made, since it resulted in a great deal of commitment and mutual understanding of where the organization is going in the future.

Another CEO who values education as a change tool is Jack Welch at General Electric. He spends time at every one of the senior executive programs run by General Electric in its Crotonville education center, sharing his vision of the company's future, talking about the culture change, and working with people several layers down in the organization whom he normally would not have the opportunity to influence directly.

Another example of a leader who developed an educational experience to help with the process of organizational transformation was Jim Renier and what came to be known as the Gainey Farms experience.

In fall 1983, approximately one year after he became president of Honeywell Information Systems, Jim Renier announced his vision for the business to the press, the financial community, and the top 150 executives at Honeywell Information Systems. The business vision included reliance on a Japanese company for some of the elements of the mainframe computer business, NEC, and an intention to integrate with the rest of Honeywell. These moves were dramatic shifts from the past.

While the press gave wide coverage to Renier's strategy for staying in the computer business, there was not a great deal of enthusiasm or commitment for these changes on the part of his top management team. As a matter of fact, the climate could accurately be described as one of cynicism, skepticism, depression, and questioning. There was low morale and little esprit de corps. If Renier could not mobilize the commitment of this group there was little hope that his new strategy would succeed.

Renier recognized the need to help his top management team through this transition. The vehicle he created was a leadership workshop designed to confront this group supportively with their concerns about the future and to mobilize them to become transformational leaders in the parts of the organization they led. While there was a great deal of ambivalence on the part of Renier's staff and senior executives about the advisability of such a high-risk workshop, Renier decided to go ahead and take that risk.

THE EXECUTIVE LEADERSHIP WORKSHOP: CREATING LEADERSHIP MOMENTUM

As a result of his involvement with team workshops, Renier recognized the need to provide some of the same experiences for a critical mass of senior managers who would have to take on new leadership roles to revitalize the business. A one-week leadership workshop was developed and launched in November 1983 for the top 25 executives. The objectives of the workshop were:

1. To provide the individuals with feedback on their leadership style along the following dimensions: goal clarity,

goal commitments, standards, responsibility, recognition, and teamwork.

2.   To foster teamwork among the key executives aimed at transforming Honeywell Information Systems.

3.   To further the cultural change process within Honeywell Information Systems by helping people to work through the endings and transitions.

4.   To mobilize a critical mass of executive talent to take on the leadership responsibilities needed to successfully change the business.

The assumption was that the workshop would create a temporary system to serve as a prototype of the new culture Renier wanted to implement at Honeywell Information Systems. This new culture would support individuals engaged in open and honest confrontation, would recognize individuals as having needs for self-esteem and responsibility, and would commit Honeywell Information Systems to winning in the marketplace through teamwork.

The transformational leadership framework provided the organizing concept for the workshop. There were activities designed to support both the organizational dynamics of change as well as the personal or individual dynamics of change. It was assumed that members of the top management group had conflicting feelings about committing themselves to Renier's agenda for change. Clearly, if they stayed, they would have to go through some painful endings, including disidentification and disenchantment with the past.

Some of the highlights of the workshop follow.

Since much of the culture of an organization is preserved and passed down in the form of stories, myths, and legends that represent key values, the workshop began with each participant telling two stories. One story was to represent a value that the individual thought was worth preserving at Honeywell Information Systems, the other a value that the individual thought should be extinguished. After they had heard each story, the group would explicitly state the moral. In the process of sharing these anecdotes the group began to see more clearly the things individuals were committed to perpetuating and what they wanted to change.

Each individual used the transformational leadership framework to conduct a TPC analysis of his or her part of Honeywell Information Systems, identifying the major leadership challenges.

Individuals were presented with data from their subordinates about their leadership style. Their self-ratings were compared to those of their subordinates and to national norms. These data provided a powerful stimulus for self-analysis and individual plans for change.

Individuals shared their leadership agendas in team meetings as a way to begin the work of team building and to reinforce a norm of openness and collaboration.

Teams worked on designing the "new" organization. Each group took one key management process (e.g., strategic planning, financial reviews, talent reviews) and analyzed its current practice as well as how it would have to be changed to support the new Honeywell Information Systems culture. These analyses were presented in the form of two skits, which were acted out in front of senior management. The first skit showed how the management process currently works, focusing particularly on its negative aspects, and the second skit looked at how it would work in the future. Developing these skits required a higher level of trust within the group than a more conventional presentation and was meant to reinforce the values needed in the new culture. A great deal of fun and creativity was generated in the process, and senior management responded with a clear statement that the skits contained action implications for them.

A number of different learning modalities were employed. Part of the team building exercises involved the groups in a mini-"outward bound" experience. They were confronted with a set of physical challenges much like a military obstacle course. To accomplish these tasks successfully required team planning and cooperation. The climax of the afternoon involved scaling a 12-foot wall. After each exercise there was a group discussion of learning and reactions both at an individual level and at a team dynamics level.

Individuals were involved in exercises that required both the development of a vision and the action plans needed to realize that vision.

People who need to work together were encouraged to negotiate deals with one another. The negotiations often took only a few minutes, although some lasted much longer. In some cases, individuals who had been fighting for years agreed to change their behaviors so that they could support each other and the organization. In other cases, individuals who had never been interdependent joined forces to try and effect change in the future.

Outcomes of the Leadership Workshop

Personal Impact.   Perhaps the most important part of the workshops was the impact on the personal lives of those who participated. Numerous individuals have shared accounts of how they have changed the way they deal with other people, including members of their family.

Deals Negotiated with Other Managers.   Many of the deals negotiated with other managers to accomplish leadership agendas have been carried out. The result is a new spirit of teamwork and cooperation.

Motivating Subordinates to Change.   The majority of the workshop participants went back to their jobs, met with their subordinates, and designed activities that would move the spirit and learnings from the Gainey Farm experience down through the organization.

New Stories, Myths, and Rituals.   The Gainey Farm experience has created its own set of stories, myths, and rituals that have become symbols of the new culture and the new way of operating. People often refer to "doing things the Gainey Farm way."

Pressure for Change Up the System.   The workshops have created a continual pressure to respond to action plans proposed by the participants. Gainey Farm provides momentum for the top management group to continue to press for change.

A Shared Bond.   Those who participated in the Gainey Farm workshop have developed a collegial bond as a result of the common experience.

Leadership Agendas.   Everyone leaving Gainey Farm had a written, articulated vision of what he or she is going to try to accomplish. They thought about how they are going to get commitment to the visions they created and what steps they are going to take to implement their agendas.

Pressure to Change the Human Resource Systems.   As a result of the Gainey Farm experience, there has been increasing awareness and commitment on the part of key executives to make the human resource system a vehicle for committing the organization to the new vision and, most importantly, for institutionalizing the new culture.

Mike Blumenthal also relied a great deal on training as a process for generating commitment. He dealt with endings and new beginnings.

> We had "funeral" stories. We also had stories about people who had done it right. We instituted leadership training, we talked about individual versus group responsibility. We also spent an enormous amount of time and money in training. I encouraged people to talk openly, brought in consultants who tried to analyze why people wouldn't talk openly at meetings. We had meet-

ings and talked about how to have meetings and how to talk
openly at them.

GUIDELINES FOR THE TRANSFORMATIONAL LEADER

Managing Your Own Transition

The president of the Bell operating company we talked about
earlier is in no condition to provide leadership to the rest of the
organization until he has personally struggled through much of
the transition. He may find it helpful to involve his top management team in the process of working through the psychodynamics of change rather than working through the transition
alone, but he must not deny the process to himself. To do this
the leader must admit that the emotions that accompany endings exist and be willing to invest the energy needed to resolve
the issues involved. The process usually requires a support
system, trusted individuals with whom one can float trial balloons and who will play devil's advocate as the leader works
through the process. Many leaders attempt to tough it out alone
and as a result they are never able to accomplish the needed
transition.

The leaders who come into the organization from the outside
will not carry the emotional baggage of the insider about the
need to change. But neither will they share the feelings of
others about the past. They must provide the necessary support
systems so that others can make the transition to the new vision.
Dynamic individuals tend to be impatient and turnaround situations contain their own sense of urgency, but it is impossible
to bring about stable lasting change unless people are allowed
to work through the psychodynamics of change. You can modify
behavior in the short run, as was the case at ICI and Chrysler
when they were in danger of failing, but this modification was
simply a conditioned response to the threat of extinction. If we

take a closer look at events that unfolded at Chrysler in 1983 and 1984, when the company showed a profit for the first time after 10 consecutive quarters of red ink, some of what appeared to be commitment turned out to be merely compliance. Iacocca's present challenge, like John Harvey-Jones's at ICI, is to forge the necessary commitment from organizational members in the absence of immediate threats.

Supporting the Top Group's Transition

To leverage change through a large organization, the transformational leader needs a dedicated group of people at the top. It is a mistake not to ensure that they have the necessary support to work through the process of change. For example, Alex Cunningham was on the task force at General Motors that spent over a year discussing the pluses and minuses of alternative organizational designs for the company. The task force served as a vehicle for him as he worked through the endings and transition. It was important for him to recognize that the others below him who were going to have to implement the new vision had not had the same opportunity. One of his roles as leader was to provide the top management team with the time to work through their feelings. This is not easy in a business environment not used to dealing with emotions—one where the troops marched when the orders were given. His ability to provide the necessary support, counseling, and help enabled his top cadre to work through the transition.

Mobilizing Commitment from the Entire Organization

The final guideline for the transformational leader is to have a plan for gaining the commitment of a critical mass of people in the organization. Here the symbolic aspects of the leader's role become critical. The communication of stories and myths representing the new culture is important, as is the acknowledgment that people need to have some space to work through these changes. At Honeywell, this has resulted in a program for change aimed at hundreds of middle managers below the top 150. From 1984 to 1985, these people developed and articulated their own leadership agendas and worked to finish the endings phase in order to embark on new beginnings.

In managing the commitment process, Mary Ann Lawlor made use of some of the tools we talk about later in this book on the institutionalization of change through the human resource system—particularly through the reward system. But these were being used not as the final institutionalization of the change but as tools to facilitate the commitment process. As she describes it:

> I would give them raises when I could. I gave them promotions whenever I could. Everybody got titles. We also used incentives. We needed to build the gross. Whenever I could I put people on gross incentives—very simple gross incentives. For people who were the administrators of locations, we would look at what they brought in during the same month last year, and we would give them 10 percent of any increases they achieved this year. Very simple, everyone can figure that out, they don't need those machines, right? And we worked on 10 percent of the increase for a couple of years until we sort of hit a plateau and I couldn't grind it out of these people anymore . . . . We had to find new ways to challenge people. When Diane moved into the top operating spot she brought a new energy, especially to the motivational effort.

The challenges laid out in this chapter are among the most elusive, subtle, and complex in the transformational process. They are also among the most undermanaged in most organizational change processes. In *Managing Organizational Transitions,* Albert proposes four processes to help organizations through transitions. We think they sum up the leader's task well:

1. *Summarize the Past.* A summary is an abbreviated history of the past. If it is to create a sense of closure, it must summarize

the meaning as well as the objective facts of the past. The hopes and dreams of the participants as well as their accomplishments . . . . To create a sense of closure, a summary of the past need not be true, but if not, it must be a believable fiction.

2. *Justify a Change.* Provide sufficient reason for doing something new . . . . Justification must state why this change is necessary or desirable and why it is necessary and desirable now.

3. *Create Continuity between the Past and the Future.* Since revolutionary change will always be resisted, motivate change by the promise that at least some valued elements from the past will be preserved and will continue in the new arrangement. . . . Some provision must be made to mourn the loss of a valued past. To manage change, one must accept this task or ensure that there are no survivors.

4. *Eulogize the Past.* One cannot leave a valued course of action without acknowledging, giving expression, and celebrating the worth of what is left.

Mike Blumenthal's view is that a commitment to the vision and the mobilization of positive energy really don't come until there is some success. He feels that:

> It became positive when the numbers became positive. Nothing succeeds like success. Lee Iacocca got successful when he started selling more cars. Mike Blumenthal only became a hero at Burroughs when it became clear that the products were better and the customers wanted them and we were reporting increases again. Then suddenly it worked. Before people were skeptical. So the flow became positive as the results became positive. The most difficult period was when people would tell horror stories that were already three, six, even nine months old. You're already beyond that but you're still saying how awful it is. Only when you are through that pipeline and you are coming out of it and you're really in the daylight that suddenly people say, you know, by God it's working. It's the same thing when we bought Memorex, and people said it was a foolish undertaking and it would really drag us down. Only when we started making money

people said it was a good purchase. So now everybody's saying, Blumenthal's strategy is right . . . .

Transformational leaders, having accomplished the task of getting individuals excited about the possibilities that exist in the quest for a new vision must turn their attention to the act of creative destruction, which involves dismantling the old organization and building one that can accomplish the dream.

ACT THREE

INSTITUTIONALIZING CHANGE

7 CREATIVE DESTRUCTION: REWEAVING THE SOCIAL FABRIC

. . . it's almost like a political revolution, and I thought in those terms once . . .

JACK SPARKS

Once transformational leaders create a vision and use it to mobilize individuals in the organization, they must turn their attention to designing new organizational structures and processes so that the vision can be achieved. Changing an organization requires more than changing individual attitudes and behaviors. The roles, the networks, and the formal structure of the organization must be reshaped. The transformational leader becomes a social architect, using the tools of social relations and structures to design a new organization.

One of the greatest pieces of social architecture was designed by the founding fathers of the United States. James MacGregor Burns describes it as follows:

Critical and creative . . . those words sum up the feat of the Founders. Because they could stand back from the existing political system and examine it critically, because they were not content to patch up the existing Articles of Confederation, because they could rise above the usual level of pragmatic brokerage; transcending their immediate interests even while powerfully motivated by their educational, social and economic backgrounds, they brought off a striking act of creative leadership as they reshaped the constitutional and political leadership of which they were a central part . . . .

They designed a system built on a very clear and explicit set of assumptions about people, ". . . they were neither illusioned nor disillusioned about people . . . they assumed that all these qualities, good and bad, manifested themselves in varying degrees, at varying times, under varying circumstances." As a result of this view of human nature—that people were capable of both good and bad and that the circumstances could be created which would bring out more of one than the other—they were clear about the need for trade-offs and checks and balances. This was demonstrated by the creative leadership of Madison, who would not allow the system to be built on "parchment barriers" that could be easily broken through. "He [Madison] found his barriers in one of the most enduring motivations among humans—ambition—and he channeled the powerful effects of ambition through a marvelous system of sieves and conduits so that power in government would be fragmented, balanced, and defanged . . . ."

Thus, as Burns argued, the real goal of transformational leadership is in what it does for its human members.

The essence of transformational leadership is the capacity to adapt means to ends—to shape and reshape institutions and structures to achieve broad human purposes and moral aspirations. The dynamics of such leadership is recognizing expressed and unexpressed wants among potential followers, bringing them into fuller consciousness of their needs, and converting consciousness of needs into hopes and expectations . . . the secret of transforming leadership is the capacity of leaders to have their goals clearly and firmly in mind, to fashion new institutions relevant to those goals, to stand back from immediate events and day-to-day routines and understand the potential and consequences of change.

It may seem a bit presumptuous and overpowering to hold up the act of the founding fathers as the role model for industrial transformational leaders, whether it be at the CEO level, at senior management ranks, or down through the middle levels of our organization. However, the reality is that they do provide the right role model for the type of process that needs to be followed, namely critical and creative leadership built on the dictum that guided these early Americans: "Think like men of action and act like men of thought."

Transformational leaders face a challenging social architectural problem, not one of de novo institution building, but one of major renovation. For in the process of envisioning the new out of the old, one must appreciate the constraints and opportunities offered up by the past and fit the demands of the future with them.

The challenge for transformational leaders is to move from the vision to a viable set of blueprints so that a long-term, enduring set of behaviors can be made part of the organization. Furthermore, to continue the architectural metaphor and limit it to the vocabulary of renovation, we are talking about taking an existing building and transforming it in some major way. In the architectural field this might be exemplified by the renovation of some of the old mills in southern New Hampshire that have been turned into office buildings housing high-technology firms and exciting shopping areas. The shape of the old entity limits and constrains but does not determine the future identity.

Examples of corporate renovation are found in the Motorola transformation, the conversion of the Singer Sewing Machine Company into a high-tech aerospace and defense company, and the recent appearance of IBM in the personal computer market. When IBM decided to enter the market it required fundamental change in its research and development and production and marketing arms. Unique organizational configurations were designed to make this possible. There was a need to accommodate new political relationships that would empower a different set of actors, and to support a culture that differed from the dominant culture in the firm at the time. The transformation was more successful than most had assumed possible.

A contrasting example was the attempt by Exxon to diversify through Exxon Enterprises into high-technology businesses through acquisition. The social architecture needed to create this transformation never appeared. Instead, innovative entrepreneurs floundered in the same environment that oil and gas executives thrived in. Political turmoil within the subsidiaries turned technological leadership into technological followership and ultimately into the demise of most of Exxon Enterprises' high-tech businesses. In the absence of changes in the social architecture of the organization, the experiment had failed.

CREATIVE DESTRUCTION

All of us are enmeshed in vast webs of social relationships. These social networks both define who we are (father, mother, boss, colleague) as well as who others are in relation to us (son, daughter, subordinate). The transformational leader must creatively destroy and then reweave the system of social networks to create meaningful change.

It is not surprising to find that many of our transformational leaders are outsiders to the company or new to the job when the transformational process begins. Certainly a leader who has been in place for some time has the more difficult task in assuming responsibility for revitalizing an organization. Such a leader is enmeshed in an existing network of friendships, political alliances, and work exchanges, and at the same time must envision a network that will more effectively support the organization's future direction. The vision must include a sense of who will work with whom, who cannot get along, who can adapt to the changing reality and who cannot. Formulating the vision is difficult, but reweaving the social fabric of the organization, breaking old ties between people, and establishing new ones is clearly the more challenging task.

A critical time for understanding the role of social networks in any organization comes when there is a transition of leadership at the top. For example, when Akers succeeded Opel as chairman of IBM, the media talked about the shift in focus that the change represented for the company. Opel was perceived as someone who rose through the ranks at IBM on the basis of a strong technical background. His focus was primarily internal. As such it was particularly suited to a period in which IBM devoted its energies to the development of the personal computer and the necessary organizational infrastructure to support this quantum change in its marketing strategy. Akers, on the other hand, is seen as someone with superb marketing skills. His principal focus has been external, and as such particularly suited to a period in which the company's principal challenge will be to maintain its dominant position at home and deal with the growing protectionism it faces abroad.

The press also spent a great deal of time speculating about the succession issues at Citibank. There was a feeling that one would be able to predict Citibank's strategy once one knew whether Wriston's successor would be John Reed or Thomas Theobold. If it were Theobold, then the traditional bankers still held the power at the bank. But if Reed were to become chairman, it would be an indication that Citibank saw its future in further diversification in the area of financial services. From the perspective of the TPC framework, excellent companies contemplating a succession at the top must ask not only whether an individual's technical competencies fit the company's strategic challenge of the next decade, but whether the networks in which the individual is enmeshed will play a significant role in his or her ability to execute a given strategy. We have argued that the leader must be able to mobilize a critical mass of the organization to effect a transformation. A leader need not be loved to gain this commitment, but he or she must be respected. While most strong individuals make some enemies in the course of a career, the number of these should be limited or it will be difficult to accomplish a leadership agenda.

IBM had an established track record in making smooth management transitions and a culture built on consensus and lifetime employment. Citibank, on the other hand, does a great deal of hiring from the outside and is not perceived to have a highly structured succession process in place. However, it has defied the media's dire predictions that once a candidate was chosen, chaos would result. There has been no significant defection of key personnel at Citibank in the months following the announcement that Reed would succeed Wriston as chairman, despite the fact that Reed was only 45 years old at the time, and may well hold the position for 20 years. Wriston has not as yet talked about the events surrounding the selection of Reed, but clearly a great deal of attention must have been paid to the key stakeholders and to the existing social networks inside the organization to effect so smooth a transition.

Certainly the way in which Jones handled the succession of Jack Welch to the chairmanship of GE is an excellent example of network management. It was apparent that Jones was massaging, manipulating, and trying to control social networks through this process. While Jones had placed GE in the enviable position of having seven or eight qualified candidates for the position of chairman, it was clear that not all the contenders for the top slot would stay and effectively work for the winner. Yet Jones perceived that he needed not just one but at least three of the contenders to serve in the office of the chairman. Furthermore, for the team to work well they not only had to get along with one another, but they had to be accepted by the board and the management group that represented those directly reporting to the office of the chairman. Thus it was clear to Jones that building a coalition to support the future GE team was a major political task.

The "airplane interview" gave Jones the insight he needed into the chemistry among the top contenders and it also let him know who did not necessarily want to be CEO. After the cut was made, three of the seven were appointed vice chairmen and continued to work together as peers for a period of 14 months. This gave the board and management groups ample opportunity to observe the styles and priorities of the team before the transition was made. Jones's ability to use sociometrics to map the consequences of different configurations on parts of the company resulted in a remarkably smooth transition to a radically different style of management. Jack Welch was cut of a different cloth from his patrician predecessor, but Jones was able to give good reasons why this 46-year-old, outspoken entrepreneur, who held a Ph.D. in chemical engineering, should become chairman of GE. And he convinced a critical mass of people that the person they needed if the company was to prosper in the years ahead was not someone like himself but someone who could lead the company through a period of rapid technological change, an individual whose style would enable him to reshape the organization to meet the increasing pressure of global competition.

While IBM, Citibank, and General Electric are examples of successful coalition building, there are many examples of plans that have soured because of inadequate attention to these issues.

In one case, an organization was facing a turnaround situation. It fired a president and promoted his successor from within the company. The problems started when a senior vice president, who had been the new president's peer, disagreed with the direction he was setting for the company. He engaged in foot dragging and in some cases actively sabotaged the new strategy. Every time the president attempted to bring him into line, he would turn to his contacts on the board and they would influence the chairman, who would get the president to back off. It took more than 18 months for the president to build the support he needed to force the resignation of the senior vice president.

Another interesting transition problem occurred when a diversified company decided to develop its executives by exposing them to a variety of business experiences. Two new vice presidents were assigned to an existing division with a double agenda in mind. One was for the two new vice presidents, one in marketing and one in manufacturing, to join the management team in a stable business and provide it with new perspectives that would help revitalize their organization. The existing management team, however, knew very well that the two vice presidents were there on pass-through assignments. Their two- or three-year stint with this business would be a developmental experience and they would move on; the rest of the team would stay. The CEO's vision was to inject new blood into businesses and simultaneously develop a cadre of management who could be moved around the corporation. The plan failed because there was insufficient attention paid to building the necessary coalitions. The vice presidents ended up fighting tooth and nail with the existing management team until one left the company and one was transferred to another business.

Thus the challenge in transition management involves more than the individual dynamics described in previous chapters. The same sort of dynamics occurs in relation to other people. We have roles to play that are defined by others, and they have expectations of us. People exist in networks made up of boss, peers, subordinates, family, and friends. All of these people expect certain behavior from us, and these expectations at times may be in conflict. Individual networks are connected—the people we interact with are embedded in their own networks; it is like a large fishnet with TPC ties. Thus communication and exchange among individuals are made up of different flows—information, influence, and some emotional ties like friendship or shared values.

Networks are central to getting things done. It is through networks that we define much of our self-image or self-esteem. The absence of significant networks is seen as a sign of social maladaptation. People run adrift without social anchors. Emil Durkheim described the lack of meaningful network ties as *anomie,* or a sense of meaninglessness. Organizations in transition engage in a risky business of creating anomie purposely for many of its members. Networks are broken in the hope of forming new ones. A transformational leader must manage to foster a new set of social networks with new flows and ties.

Transformational leaders need to provide guidance for this macrolevel transition challenge. It is one that builds on the psychodynamics that have previously been described. The importance of networks is pointed out by a number of our protaganists. Jack Sparks at Whirlpool said:

> It goes back to people . . . it's almost like a political revolution, and I thought in those terms once . . . I told them, we're not leaving this lodge until we agree to the objectives. This is what will drive this organization. I then went on the circuit to sell 2000 of our management people, though I only really need 40 committed people. It's like the Communist party. I don't need all 2000 committed. Give me 40 people and I can run this company . . . .

Sparks's sentiment was echoed by Lee Iacocca:

> The kind of people I look for to fill top management spots are the eager beavers. These are the guys who try to do more than they're expected to. They're always reaching. And reaching out

to the people they work with, trying to help them do their jobs better. That's the way they're built.

So I try to look for people with that drive. You don't need many. With 25 of these guys, I could run the government of the United States.

At Chrysler I have about a dozen. What makes these managers strong is that they know how to delegate and how to motivate. They know how to look for the pressure points and how to set priorities.

Ed Thompson talked about the need to manage networks to accomplish the strategy of repositioning the cost base of the unionized portion of his company:

It was obvious that industry labor negotiations had, over the years, gotten driver wages and fringes out of line with the new realities in the industry. We made the decision to work with our drivers and the union to develop new behaviors that would result in a cost-effective operation rather than walk away from them; most had played a role in building Schneider. The approach we used was to cluster the work required into four "channels." We trained our young management group to think about managing these important channels or clusters separately and simultaneously. We had to manage a behavior change in our driver organization, aggressive negotiations with the Teamsters, the development and focusing of our own internal organization, and make changes in our cost-service package for our customers. We selected the right people to head up the major changes required in each "channel," then charged them with the additional accountability of assuring network synergy across four channels. For example, the progress in negotiating wage and benefits concessions and gaining separation from the Teamsters' National Master contract was very dependent on intelligent and careful progress in the driver "channel." The union locals had to see the drivers in an OK place before they would budge. The drivers had to be put in touch with the realities of the new industry economics through exposure to work being done in the customer "channel." The internal organization had to sustain a positive health and spirit as they managed some real tough issues faster

than ever before. Without their capacity to integrate and see that
they were improving and growing as we approached the vision, a
less than positive spillover from this "channel" would halt progress with drivers and customers. It was tough for our young
organization to buy all this integration and network synergy
when they saw prices dropping and felt the awesome accountability of providing the leadership to prepare the driver organization to see that a 15 percent pay cut, and more productive involvement in managing variable expenses like fuel usage, and
maintenance was the correct and desired behavioral future state.
Although the notion of delegated simultaneous channel management was, to say the least, a bit abstract, we didn't have time to
work each "channel" in series. The good people at all levels
surfaced, grew, and delivered. In the end it worked. We did
achieve the holistic goal of repositioned costs, a separate and
more productive contract, realistically involved drivers, and a
stronger overall organization. During the middle of the change
period our vice president of human resources commented that it
seemed like a giant junior achievement center. I'll tell you that I
think more creative solutions were developed in a group's own
"channel" because of the need for their work to fit, support, and
accelerate work being done in other areas. Someone coined the
term "tough involvement." I guess it fits.

It is clear that Sparks, Iacocca, and Thompson understand the
power of networks and the fact that the right individuals have
tremendous leverage on the remainder of the system.

THE TECHNICAL-POLITICAL-CULTURAL NETWORKS: OLD AND NEW

As Henry Mintzberg and John Kotter have shown, general managers get their work done through hundreds of network relationships. Most of these are informal. Effective general managers use chance encounters in the hallways after meetings and
during meetings to keep constantly reinforcing their agendas.
They engage in planful opportunism around the network. The
transformational leader not only uses the networks but must

also envision a new and different set of network relationships to get a job done. Mike Blumenthal talked about changing the nature of network interactions at Burroughs:

> I wanted to change the kind of response where someone avoids taking responsibility by pointing the finger at someone else. Sometimes they would see me react sharply—like when they would say, "Well, I sent that piece of paper to Jones." And I would say, "Did you call Jones?" and they would reply, "Well, I called him but he didn't call back." I would point out that they were the project manager and they had the authority to knock heads together—"Did you knock heads? You've got the authority and the responsibility to do it. The fact that you put a piece of paper in his box does not absolve you of that responsibility."
>
> The problem, you see, was that in the old Burroughs, when "father" asked what did you do, you could say I sent it to the other "son." It's not my fault, I left it in his box. I want them to know that's not OK. They have got to grab that guy by the scruff of the neck and say, "Wait a minute, our obligation is to get that product out on time, and to have it work, and to have the right quality, and the problem is stuck in your box but I am responsible, so let's get it out."

Thus a critical part of transformational leadership is an understanding of the complex nature of social networks and how they operate.

Politicians use networks, they're the primary tool of their trade. Perhaps two of the most notable manipulators of people and networks were Fiorello LaGuardia, mayor of New York City in the 1930s, and Robert Moses, who for almost half a century was the single most powerful man in New York. According to Robert Cairo, Moses

> developed his public authorities into a political machine that was virtually a fourth branch of government, one that could bring to their knees governors and mayors from LaGuardia to Lindsay by mobilizing banks, contractors, labor unions, insurance firms, even the press and the church into an irresistible economic force.

Both LaGuardia and Moses were obsessed with power and a desire to transform New York. Unfortunately, they saw people as pawns. It's instructive to view them as bad role models for our transformational leaders in the way they both subtly and at times brutally used and misused social networks. It is interesting how the two interacted.

The mayor's intimates noticed that while he liked to push people around, he only respected those he couldn't push. I think he put on a great deal of his brutalities to test people out. C. C. Burlingham observed, if they could stand up against him it was all right. But if they couldn't they were in bad luck and Moses could stand up against him better than anyone else.

It is interesting to note how Robert Moses made sure who had power in his network. One illustration was brought out by Cairo.

Moses destroyed the source of Curren's power, his friendship with the mayor. He did so, Curren charges, with a tactic that would have been familiar to Ansley Wilcocks and Judge Clearwater, who felt Moses had used and discredited them with Al Smith. He lied, Curren says, he lied about me to LaGuardia. There was, Curren says, a whole series of lies that gradually poisoned his friendship with the mayor. Once, for example, Moses told LaGuardia that Curren had disobeyed LaGuardia's specific order to certify a disputed civil service list of authority employees although Curren had in fact done so. And LaGuardia without bothering to check the facts, flew into a towering rage and wrote Curren a letter that stung him deeply.

Transformational leaders must understand the workings of networks. They are an important part of the social architecture. Leaders also must be subtle manipulators of the networks. But to qualify as transformational leaders, they must not treat people as pawns, simply because excellent people refuse to be treated that way. Thus bludgeoning people and the use of lies are not appropriate tactics for our transformational leaders.

NETWORKS IN THE TRANSFORMATIONAL PROCESS

Organizations are conceived as clusters of people joined by a variety of links. These clusters transmit:

1. *Goods and services.* Raw materials, marketing research support, financial and accounting services, and people themselves among groups within the company.

2. *Information.* Regarding the organization and its environment.

3. *Influence.* Both formal orders and informal attempts to persuade.

4. *Affect.* Exchanges of friendship among individuals.

Formal structures or prescribed networks consist of people who are clustered as a result of organizational design; they are in departments, work groups, and committees. Informal structures or emergent networks, such as coalitions and cliques, arise without organizational sanction. Prescribed networks are typically represented on organizational charts. Clear distinctions are made here between prescribed and emergent networks to emphasize the point that within organizations there exist a multitude of interpersonal work arrangements, which arise out of many possible types of relationships. Only a portion of the organizational structure is prescribed. Thus unplanned structures and behavior patterns generally emerge in all organizations.

Among some managers, and in much of the management and organizational literature, these emergent structures and behavior patterns have been misleadingly labeled "the informal organization" and are often assumed to be something undesirable. They are in fact neutral and take on desirable or undesirable characteristics depending on how they are managed. For example, in some research and development departments prescribed organization charts are not maintained because all the work is done through the emergent networks—groups of people who will interact in a number of ways, depending on the demands of the task.

The examination of information networks—who exchanges information with whom—provides concepts and tools for analyzing the technical aspects of organizations. In order to understand how research gets accomplished in R&D organizations, one needs to map the information exchange networks. Then it is possible to discern organizational problems that arise when scientists who exchange information with outside scientists and who develop new ideas that could contribute to the R&D effort are not well linked with one another. These scientists do not make the contribution they could make to organizational innovation—they do not share information with their colleagues because they do not interact with them.

The examination of influence networks—seeing who influences whom about what—provides the concepts and tools for political analysis. For example, at Ford Motor Company, Henry Ford probably pulled together a coalition of board members to support his decision to fire Lee Iacocca. To fully understand the event, one would need to map out the networks around Henry Ford and identify the exchanges that took place between Ford and those he persuaded to back him.

Finally, the culture of an organization is best analyzed by uncovering the friendship relationships. It is largely through these relationships that the values and norms of the culture are disseminated and reinforced. Much has been written about the influence that first ladies like Eleanor Roosevelt, Rosalynn Carter, and Nancy Reagan have exercised on their husbands' presidencies. Similarly, Mary Cunningham's influence on the decisions that William Agee made at Bendix has been the subject of much speculation. But in most organizations it is not the spouse but friends and colleagues who hold positions of confidence and who exercise influence outside the prescribed networks. For example, both of us were meeting with the president of a large research company one day when he talked about his "kitchen cabinet," which consisted of four people. Three of the names were immediately known to us, but the fourth was a mystery. We had to find a detailed organization chart, which showed the missing member of the cabinet to be someone without significant organizational rank but who obviously enjoyed considerable organizational influence.

Reginald Jones spoke of the people in the organization whom he felt he could trust, mostly staff members who would be retiring at about the same time he would. These were people with whom he consulted about the issue of succession at General Electric. When Lee Iacocca came to Chrysler he brought with him 14 high-ranking Ford managers. Their willingness to leave Ford for a troubled company was a good indication that Iacocca was more than simply a boss to them. They believed in him and placed their loyalty to him above their loyalty to Ford. In turn, Iacocca placed them in positions of key responsibility at Chrysler because he trusted them and he did not know who at Chrysler he could trust to carry out his plans. He used them to leverage the changes he wanted to make in the culture.

It is crucial that transformational leaders have an understanding of the multiple networks that exist in organizations, the overlay of one fishnet with another for the transfer of information, influence, and affect from individual to individual. Sometimes the individuals share all three, while at other times they share one network but not another.

By having a reasonably good idea of what networks exist and who influences them, the transformational leader can gain a great deal of leverage. This means that management by walking around is not a random activity. Grabbing the right person in the hall, or sharing some information or encouragement, are actions that will probably have an impact on different cliques and coalitions in the organization. The challenge for transformational leaders is not only to use the networks but simultaneously to transform them.

CREATIVE DESTRUCTION AND REWEAVING OF SOCIAL NETWORKS

The implications of social networks on transition management are profound. Social fabrics make up the network of TPC systems. The technical system is largely held together by work-related informational exchanges among members of the organization. The political system is made up of influence exchanges, while the cultural system is held together by exchanges involving shared values among organizational members. In order to change an organization, networks must be dealt with in each of these three systems.

The adjustments that take place involve breaking and re-forming the information, influence, and affective links in organizations. The major determinants of changes in informational links are shifts in the task demands of the technical system. The major determinant of change in influence networks is the shift in the balance of power among organization coalitions. Finally, changes in the culture of the organization are most likely to alter affective links.

The transition period involves maintaining certain relationships, creating new relationships, and breaking off some old relationships. To add to the complexity, the pattern of maintaining, breaking, or creating networks varies for information, influence, and affective networks.

Transformation of the technical systems in the organization will be accomplished primarily through the information networks. This transformation will be accomplished by deciding which linkages in the information networks need to be maintained and which need to be broken, as well as what new ones need to be formed. These changes, however, will affect the influence networks as well.

The same is true when the transformational leader changes the power distribution in the organization. This change occurs primarily through the influence networks. However, once the influence networks are changed, it will have a secondary impact on information and affective networks.

Many of the leaders we spoke with intuitively understood the nature and complexity of the networks they managed. John Harvey-Jones spoke of ICI:

> I basically believe that I am not clever enough to run a company of this size and complexity. For example, I am not a scientist, so what on earth am I to do with the research policy of this company, which is key to our success, apart from saying that I want one? I have to use a teamwork approach. One of the problems this company used to have was that the previous chairman did not spend the time I spend managing the team, and, as a consequence the people down the line got conflicting messages. So, one of the things I have done is to place the highest possible priority on getting my team to agree as to what our policy would be. And I was prepared to subordinate my views in order to get commitment among us. And, indeed, in my first six months there were two things I passionately wanted to do which I did not do because I could not carry my colleagues with me. I didn't test it by taking it to the board, I could have driven it through the board because my nonexecutives would have backed my judgment, but I would have lost my colleagues and the things I wanted to change would not have worked.

Another master of the art of managing networks is Lee Iacocca, who was able to map the complex networks that included government, unions, management, suppliers, and dealers who would have to change the way they did business with Chrysler if he was to get the loan guarantees needed to turn the company around.

TRANSITION VEHICLES FOR MANAGING NETWORKS

The most critical part of a trapeze act occurs when one trapeze artist lets go of a partner and flies through the air to the hands of another trapeze artist. The ending, the transition zone, and the new beginning are all well defined. Failure to execute this maneuver properly can have grave results. It is interesting that in a trapeze act the ending—the "take-off"—has a tremendous influence on future events. It limits and constrains the arc and the distance that the trapeze artist can fly through the air but does not totally determine it. If the ending is a little bit off, the trapeze artist can change the body rotation, arch the back a little bit, and make some minor adjustments during transition so there can be a successful new beginning. It is clear that all three phases are critical to the success of the act.

The transformational leader is like a trapeze artist. There is a point at which the break with the past must be made. The past certainly limits and constrains the future, but it does not totally determine the new beginning. Constant adjustments need to be made during the transition so that the links that were broken can be replaced with new ones. The danger is that the transformational leader can throw an organization into ambiguity, uncertainty, and chaos if he or she doesn't make the adjustments needed to reweave the social fabric and create a new beginning. It is precisely during this transition period that the greatest network demands are made on the transformational leader. People are not clear where to get critical information. The norms and values are not totally clear. Friendships often get broken. Jim Renier spoke about this process at Honeywell:

> At some point you've got to loosen the reins, delegate. You've got to get the whole organization to practice this, to get you there. At the moment we have painted a picture that is not as clear in its detail as I would like . . . .
>
> It's almost like being on a battlefield in a fog. It's too much to ask the commander to describe the terrain as if the fog wasn't there. I don't have all the answers, but we've got to be willing to listen and say, well, someone else has seen through part of the fog so we'd better listen carefully to that person.

Given the nature of the transitional task, the most central problem is political uncertainty. When political uncertainty is high it becomes the major focal point for people's energy, because it is most directly and fundamentally linked to the survival of individuals in the organization. The ultimate political act in an organization is the decision about who will stay and who will go. Thus one of the most salient points to keep in mind is that when political uncertainty is high, transformational leaders will find it virtually impossible to work on technical or cultural issues, even though they may need attention. Something must be done to reduce the political uncertainty first.

HOW OUR PROTAGONISTS REWEAVE THEIR NETWORKS

When our protagonists approach the task of reweaving the social networks, one of the major variables is whether the leader is an insider or an outsider. Obviously, when a new leader comes into an organization he or she brings a vast network that will probably be different from those of existing employees. Thus Fred Hammer's appearance at Chase Manhattan Bank brought with it an interesting mix of external links in not only the areas of financial services but also in the computer industry and the manufacturing sector. Blumenthal, who had served as Secretary of the Treasury, came into Burroughs with an extensive external network. He brought a trusted colleague, Jerry Jacobson, who had worked with him at Bendix, to serve as his right-hand man. Jacobson became vice chairman of Burroughs. Ed Thompson, on the other hand, came to Schneider Transport from the outside but did not bring former colleagues with him. He appears more or less to have left his network at the door, the direct opposite of Lee Iacocca's transfer of his top management team from Ford. Finally, Mary Ann Lawlor found a network within Drake when she came—and she brought in some new members as well.

The leaders who came from within their organizations dramatically reshuffled the networks but did not bring anywhere near the number of outsiders into the network that outside leaders did. We found clear differences in the way that outsiders approached the task of reweaving the social networks when compared to the insiders.

Outside Protagonists

Fred Hammer spent the first several months mapping out the networks at Chase Manhattan Bank. He did a great deal of management by walking around, visiting branches, talking to people. He also roamed the halls of Chase headquarters, getting to know key individuals, figuring out who needed to talk with whom to get things done. He then focused on the inside of his organization to develop credibility in the wider Chase political system. He looked for high leverage actions that could gain him credibility and political access outside his own section of the bank. His real agenda was to build a strong, aggressive, nationally focused consumer banking group at Chase. To do this he had to clean house and have his organization in good working order. He dug in and did this, closing branches, making things more efficient. It was interesting to watch the way he used networks, especially in the second half of his tenure at Chase, when strategic plans for the national expansion were being formulated. He played the role of a very skillful politician. Inside his own organization, he created the cross-cutting task forces we described. From a network perspective, this formed a whole new set of linkages among people that cut across traditional functions and encouraged collaboration on the new vision Hammer had forged for the organization. This turned out to be an excellent way to help unfreeze and unhook people from old alliances, and produce new coalitions and networks in the organization. But because this was a planning activity, it provided a neutral zone or transition space of about nine months where people could maintain the old links and begin to build some new ones. These task forces met every week and in some cases daily, had review sessions with Fred on a frequent basis, and interacted with members of the rest of the bank while they went about their regular job.

Hammer understood that getting acceptance of his plans depended heavily on laying the proper political groundwork. He actually had management by walking around time built into his calendar to deal with the senior management at Chase. He spent several hours before and after key executive meetings opportunistically roaming the halls at One Chase Plaza. This was especially critical because Hammer's office at the time was located in a building 50 blocks north of corporate headquarters. His day at headquarters provided one of the few opportunities for him to bump into people. He would drop in and visit with those who were available and talk to them about the future, about how they viewed the strategy for consumer banking. In addition to working the informal networks, he staged a number of strategic review sessions in which he brought senior functional people from the corporate offices to provide feedback and input into the strategic planning process. In this way, he kept them informed and coopted a number of them into being his allies when the plans were formally presented.

Michael Blumenthal and Lee Iacocca both pursued similar network strategies. The initial breaks or unfreezing in the old networks were jarring and rather brutal. Both individuals showed a great deal of compassion for the individuals who could no longer perform their jobs, yet both of them felt it necessary to remove almost all of the senior management team. They both developed strong outsider teams at the top. Blumenthal appears to have been much more sensitive than Iacocca to the integration of those teams into the wider Burroughs culture. He was very careful to let them know that they were not to create a we/they attitude and put down the old Burroughs people. This is in stark contrast with the brash, aggressive style of the Ford team, which created a great deal of animosity during the turnaround situation due to their style and the way they treated the Chrysler executives. But in both of these organizations a whole new power structure was grafted on and is still in the process of being disseminated through the organizations.

Ed Thompson and Mary Ann Lawlor provide a third example. They made extensive use of existing networks and people in their organizations and tended to blend in a few outsiders, but they spent most of their attention on identifying the key people in the existing organization and figuring out how best to utilize their talents.

The Insider Protagonist

Alex Cunningham, Lloyd Reuss, and Bob Stempel spent the first 18 months of their tenure creating a participatory process for reweaving the networks within the two car groups at General Motors. Even though the explicit focus of their selection process was on finding the right individuals for the roles they were to play, it had the secondary consequence of breaking up old-boy networks at General Motors and providing an opportunity for people to participate in the creation of new networks. The process described in the previous chapters, in which the executives engaged in a participatory team identification process, has been followed and has cascaded down into the organization. It provided a transition vehicle for members of management in the car groups at General Motors to create new networks to which they are highly committed. People who pick their own teams have a vested interest in the appropriate development, encouragement, and molding of resources.

Whirlpool is as inbred as General Motors. It has the added challenge of being a much smaller company in a much more isolated setting. Thus Jack Sparks's reweaving of the social networks has been focused on reshuffling the existing players rather than bringing in outsiders. The first position in the top ranks of Whirlpool to be opened to an outside search was for a chief financial officer. The rest of the senior management came from within. Sparks spends a great deal of time, however, changing those networks. The golden window that resulted in the early retirement of several hundred managers opened up a number of key senior management slots for young people. Consequently, there was a great deal of rapid upward movement; the top of Whirlpool now, three years after Jack Sparks began his tenure as chairman, looks totally different than it did when he started.

If we look at the General Electric Lighting Group we notice that Ralph Ketchum, who heads the group, did most of his selection from among the General Electric pool of executives, although he did hire a marketing executive from Procter & Gamble. Nevertheless, the coalition that manages the Lighting Group has shifted dramatically under Ketchum's leadership. Their old-boy lighting power structure still exists, but the conflicts are not overt, and the new network is being created by evolution, not revolution.

At Honeywell, Jim Renier, as president of Information Systems and vice chairman of the organization, totally reconstituted senior management. The network was jarringly changed to start with when Renier came in from the control side of Honeywell, following the departure of the former president. Renier rapidly changed a number of key positions, systematically bringing in executives from his former division, the control side. By the time he turned the day-to-day operation of Information Systems over to Bill Wray, another control system executive, the top management team of Honeywell's Information Systems was made up totally of people from Control Systems, with the exception of the financial manager. These changes fit with the strategy of integrating the two Honeywell systems by switching people with long-term careers from one side of the house to the other. The scene had been set for the integration to take place.

John Harvey-Jones at ICI and Jack Welch at General Electric both operate in companies that have had a strong tradition of developing their own managers. Going outside in either of these companies would be a dramatic testimonial to managerial failure. Therefore, the reshuffling and reweaving of networks is done with the existing players. However, once we get below the top couple of layers at General Electric, we find that Welch did bring in a number of outside executives. John Harvey-Jones made do with his existing crew, but early retirements and significant reshufflings changed the complexion of the ICI top echelon.

Finally we have Jeff Campbell, who in reorganizing Burger King brought in executives in the senior ranks, moved people from one role to another, and simultaneously learned to work the existing old-boy network that ran the regions and made the organization work on a day to day basis.

SOME PRESCRIPTIONS

The world is, of course, complex. Relationships among people are not technical, political, or cultural. Usually there is some mixture of all three. To plan for a transition, however, we will argue that it is useful to pull these three apart analytically, so that we can be very clear about the technical information flows between people that are needed and what changes are required. We would also want to be clear about the political influence flows and the effective cultural flows that go on in the organization. Transformational leaders use a variety of tools to analyze these flows.

The technical plan should be based on a work-flow analysis that identifies who needs what information from whom at what point in the process to get the job done. Work units should be clustered to get groups together who need to interact most frequently and then provide integrative network vehicles such as liaisons, matrix, or other ways of coordinating the work between groups.

In the political arena, it is important to identify the following elements:

1. Target individuals and groups whose commitment is needed for the change to happen
2. The definition of the critical mass needed to insure the effective implementation of the change
3. A plan for getting the commitment from a critical mass of employees
4. Some kind of a monitoring system to track changes in the political system

The first step is to do an analysis of key influential people to determine their current attitudes toward the desired change. Then determine where they need to be in order to carry out the transition successfully. It should be noted that in order to change an individual politically, it is important to assess the networks in which that individual operates, since it may be easier to effect change by working through other people.

Cultural transitions demand that we deal with some of the most elusive elements of the transition process, for embodied in the culture are people's beliefs, values, and norms. These generally cannot be changed directly; they certainly cannot be changed by fiat but must be worked on over long periods of time in redundant ways. However, the leader who wants to change the culture in the organization should start with a network analysis that includes:

1. Identifying the cultural values and beliefs that require changing
2. Identifying the gatekeepers of the organization's current culture, that is, who are the most important guardians of the norms and values, and whose support will be most critical for the new culture to succeed
3. Defining the critical mass of cultural gatekeepers needed to change the culture
4. Developing a plan for getting the gatekeepers to feel a

need for cultural change and start to work toward such a change.

5. Developing a monitoring system to support the change process

In this analysis, it is important to identify those elements of the culture that need to be maintained, those that should be eliminated, and those that should be introduced. Then a specific plan is needed to build links to the gatekeepers to change their values and beliefs.

Loosely Coupling the Networks that Manage Transition

The TPC networks are often worked simultaneously by the transformational leader. A single event could contain a technical message, a political message, and a cultural message. The important point for the transformational leader is that he or she has some understanding of how these agendas are working. Furthermore, networks, perhaps more than any other aspect of the organization, are worked through planful opportunism. With a vision and an agenda, a chance encounter can be used to reinforce an important value or to give a political message.

But this planful opportunism can be enhanced. For example, the famous Hewlett-Packard "MBWA" (management by walking around) is an illustration of the constant working of social networks, as is allocating a certain amount of time out on the floor interacting with the workers. At Hewlett-Packard this was done and continues to be done primarily for cultural reasons. Nevertheless, the technical and political networks are continually massaged at the same time.

Several years ago we conducted a study of an R&D organization. A staff department expressed a desire to serve the line organization more effectively. We collected data from the line organization about how effective they perceived the support unit to be and found that there was room for improvement. We also found that line organizations that received their information from face to face meetings with staff units, rather than by telephone or by memorandum, felt the staff units were more effective. We suggested that the unit attempt to increase the amount of time it spent in face to face contact with line managers. Programs such as "Walk a memo" and "Take a client to lunch" were instituted. Eighteen months later, when data were again collected from the line managers, the perceived effectiveness of the unit had increased significantly. In addition, the unit was asked to sit in on meetings where key decisions were made involving their areas of expertise, rather than simply being asked to implement the decisions once they had been made by the line.

Maintaining networks clearly provides an opportunity to increase organizational effectiveness. The transformational leader must skillfully use a variety of ways to enhance the networking capability of the organization by understanding that

1. Physical architecture and physical space are important network tools. The architecture controls the flow of traffic and increases the probability of meeting among people. Where people are placed and traffic flows, as well as the location of offices and conference rooms, are important vehicles for network management.

2. Transferring people from one network to another is not just an individual act, because those people bring with them their linkages to others. A multinational corporation used movement of key executives around the world as an organization design tool to build and maintain global networks. Similarly, as in Honeywell's attempt to integrate the control and information system sides of the house, the greater the number of transfers between the two units, the more informal or emergent networks will be created to break down the cultural, political, and tech-

nical barriers that currently exist between the two groups.

3. Temporary systems such as task forces or collateral organizations can be created that bring together groups to work on a new task. In the process, new alliances and new networks are formed.

4. Finally, the transformational leader can introduce new management practices designed to help the organization develop new network ties. One such tool is the role analysis technique which specifically focuses on role sets. Individuals define their job and what they need from others in their role set and conduct negotiation sessions in which the members of the role set agree to exchanges to facilitate the work. This makes the linkages in their network explicit.

It is up to the transformational leader first to understand social networks, then to do a diagnosis of the current and desired state, and finally to call on the multiple set of tools needed to execute the difficult trapeze act of letting go and reaching the new beginning by breaking old ties and constructively building new ones.

THE LEADER AS SOCIAL ARCHITECT I: MAKING BUREAUCRACY BEHAVE

8

If you imagine a Fortune Hall of Fame, an entrepreneur's mecca, a picture of Henry Ford hangs on the wall. What did Henry Ford do? He invented the assembly line—a technique to get a group of people to work together better. That requires something else besides an entrepreneur coming into the system. Look at the Japanese who are making those kinds of innovations today, like letting blue collar workers do inventory control so that they don't need the white collar bureaucratic overseer . . . . So entrepreneurs are not enough to make the innovations work, we need the right social environment . . . .

LESTER THUROW

215

Transformational leaders institutionalize the vision by reweaving the strategic rope: the technical, political, and cultural strands must be combined to make the bureaucracy behave. It is foolish to talk in terms of doing away with the bureaucracy in large complex organizations; the challenge, instead, is to make it drive the organizational goals. This struggle to revamp complex bureaucracies is at the core of Act III of our transformational drama. Jack Welch talked about the organizational design challenge at General Electric.

> So called skunkworks, in my opinion, can be Band-Aid solutions to a fundamental problem. Nothing less than a reorientation of the culture away from incrementalism is needed in big institutions. Quantum thinking must become a way of life, not a one year, one or two product program, but a decade long, total company process.
>
> In the end the bold step must and in fact will work. In the end the same system, the same bureaucracy, when challenged, will bring together the technical resources in creative thinking and will rally around to make sure it does work . . . .

GE's culture is undergoing quantum change. To ensure its global competitiveness, the new culture must be institutionalized. The challenge to Jack Welch is to create the social architecture that will do that.

John Akers faces a similar challenge at IBM. This extraordinarily successful company is restructuring its bureaucracy to meet the challenges that Akers envisages. The new social architecture is already unfolding. David Sanger chronicled these changes in a recent *New York Times* article:

The most dramatic and far-reaching example of IBM's new commitment to risk has been its creation of the independent business unit. These IBUs are specifically designed to operate completely outside Armonk's orbit. Unencumbered by the slow and sometimes stifling corporate bureaucracy, the goal is to give the small units the freedom to experiment, to bet their capital and talent on new and untried solutions, in short to be entrepreneurs.

Peter Drucker lionized Alfred Sloan in his 1946 book, *The Concept of the Corporation*. But by 1966 Drucker believed that Sloan's concept of the corporation had become "fuzzy beyond recognition." Again, taking the dysfunction out of a once successful bureaucracy is the challenge facing Roger Smith at General Motors.

The water shed, in the view of many observers, came in 1958 when Frederick Donner, a financial man with no operating experience, was named chief executive. Under his iron fisted rule, the operating divisions became mere instruments of corporate headquarters.

No one was more convinced that the bureaucracy was a problem at General Motors than Roger Smith, who argued for a return to Alfred Sloan's principles. The major reorganization that resulted is most visible in the creation of the two new car groups. With total decision-making authority pushed closer to the customers and to operations, General Motors has become more responsive to both consumers and competitive pressures.

Finally, at Honeywell we find Chairman Edson Spencer and Vice Chairman James Renier driving a restructuring that will require new groupings, structures, political governance, and cultural systems.

The organization design challenges facing transformational leaders are enormous. The technical issues range from identification of new areas of strategic leverage that often entails turning commodities into value-added products and creating new markets, to globalization via joint venturing; recasting the corporate headquarters role and structure to cut down on excessive overhead and ineffective control systems; and revamping financial allocation systems which don't manage the long- and short-term trade-offs well.

The political issues start with the redefinition of the CEO's role and the reallocation of decision-making authority to empower the organization. Thus we see Iacocca, Smith, and Welch shifting more and more decision-making authority to the organizations below them. Other political issues include addressing the issue of the dual citizenship role for multiple business organizations where the balance between what is good for each business and what is good for the organization needs to be struck. Transformational leaders develop conflict resolution mechanisms that encourage healthy debate to resolve differences.

Finally, the cultural design challenges include balancing cultural diversity with values shared throughout the organization. At GE, where the diversity of the business portfolio results in tremendous cultural diversity, the leadership challenge is to create a set of shared values to serve as the normative glue. Another cultural dilemma is the changing nature of the psychological contract between the organization and the employee. The implicit contract of "lifetime employment" for loyal service is being buffeted in a marketplace where job security depends on the organization's ability to survive.

For transformations to be successful, leaders need to examine the alternatives in organizational design, political governance, and value systems to support the restructuring. We will explore why structure is important, how to frame the social architectural problem, and the use of the TPC framework as a tool for institutionalizing the new vision.

WHY WE NEED STRUCTURE

Rene McPherson, who led Dana Corporation, is a folk hero to many managers attempting to change modern corporations. The legend starts with the fact that he threw out 22.5 inches of corporate policy manuals and replaced them with a one-page philosophy statement. McPherson won the reputation as "the man who got rid of bureaucracy at Dana Corporation." A more accurate assessment was that he streamlined and changed the bureaucracy guided by the old architechtural dictum "form follows function." He made it function in service of the work that needed to be done. The problem is that many of the bureaucratic forms in today's organizations do *not* follow function. Instead they follow historical precedents and protect political turf, often at the expense of the technical goals of the organization. Most of us can cite at least one example where the organizational structure was gerrymandered to create a "job" for a long service employee who had lost out in a bid for another position. Structure is important. It channels and orchestrates behavior in the organization. Thus we need to understand why bureaucracy frequently becomes its own worst enemy. Often management hasn't taken the time to adjust the structure to fit the new organizational mission. Bureaucracies that go untransformed inevitably suffer from what the sociologist Robert Merton called "means ends inversions." That is, what initially started out as a means to an end becomes an end in itself. Filling out a particular form starts out serving a useful end. Over time, the original need no longer exists, but the form keeps getting filled out because it has always been done that way.

Some of the inflexibility is caused by those who have power and don't want to give it up, even when the technical demands on the organization shift. One way to sum up the problem of bureaucracy (or any system for that matter) is to point out that today's solutions have embedded in them the next round of problems, and that what makes for good fit and alignment at a particular time will probably be out of sync under another set of conditions. Yet the forces for resistance are such that it is extremely difficult to dismantle the structure and reassemble it in a more effective way.

Creating an effective structure is clearly a necessity. In the short run strong leaders can override the bureaucratic structure. Lee Iacocca's management team made things happen at Chry-

sler in spite of dysfunctional bureaucratic systems because of
the severity of the crisis and the strength of their personalities.
But in the long run it is the bureaucracy that endures. It does so
because the way in which Chrysler hires, develops, and ap-
praises people, the financial systems, and other control systems
affect thousands of people every day and direct their behavior.
When faced with a conflict between what they are told to do by
top management (be innovative, focus on the long term, etc.)
and a system which day in and day out rewards them for just the
opposite (conformity, short run results) they will do the smart
thing. They will say the right words about innovation and long-
term objectives but continue to behave the way they always
have to get the rewards they value. Furthermore, this double-
talk leads them to a deep-seated cynicism about top management and themselves, resulting in a "do as I say, not as I do"
culture. Transformational leaders must reduce such cultural
schizophrenia by designing rational structures.

We will look at social architecture along three dimensions:
technical, political, and cultural. We will focus on how the
transformational leader can tie them together so that the organization has structural integrity.

HOW TO FRAME THE SOCIAL
ARCHITECTURAL PROBLEM

When transformational leaders decide to redesign their organizations they often discover that there are several phases to the
process. They need a map to guide them through. Fred Hammer started by facing the issue of how profitable the bank's
branches were. Along the way he found he had to reduce the
number of branches, develop a centralized facility that could
handle the paperwork, automate the teller process, develop an
aggressive marketing program, and begin a study to group
branches into regional zones to gain benefits from the consumer
community. Hammer commented:

> First, we were organized functionally and that is absolutely anti-thetical to my way of doing things: I don't like that. I knew we were going to have to make some basic changes. We were going to reorganize the businesses in such a way that we could have businessmen running them with responsibility for decisions. Now that was a problem, since there were some pretty senior guys that I was not willing to give businesses to . . .

When Mike Blumenthal assumed control at Burroughs he too was dismayed by the lack of profit centers and the attendant difficulty in holding people responsible for their actions. Harvey-Jones also moved to develop control systems that pushed accountability down into the organization.

The critical variables in a successful organizational design are control and guidance in the face of uncertainty. Organizations must be designed either to reduce uncertainty or to absorb it. If we go back to a classic definition of an organization as the rational coordination of people, information, and technology around some common purpose to produce an output, then we can see that concepts like predictability and control are important. When the organization is faced with uncertainty, transformational leaders need to respond with constructive problem-solving. Successful problem-solving will either reduce the uncertainty or create conditions that will equip the organization to deal with a high level of uncertainty. For example, if General Motors is uncertain about the quality of cars coming off the production line, it can tighten the specs and build in more control systems or it can create systems for constant problem-solving about quality by using mechanisms like autonomous work teams that have responsibility for quality control. These teams take actions, such as stopping the assembly line when mistakes are made and correcting them; in other words, these teams have a much more built-in self-control.

We assume that there is uncertainty in all three of our basic organizational systems—technical uncertainty, political uncertainty, and cultural uncertainty. Technical uncertainty is related to areas of the organization's efficiency and effectiveness, political uncertainty is related to the allocation of power and resources, and cultural uncertainty is related to the values and belief systems of the organization.

TECHNICAL UNCERTAINTY

There are many reasons why technical uncertainty exists. In the United States, transformational leaders identify the globalization of the economy as a major source of uncertainty. Even prior to the RCA acquisition GE was a reasonable microcosm of the U.S. economy with businesses in what it calls three circles: high-tech, service, and core. Uncertainty is increasing in all three circles: the high-tech factory automation, plastics, and medical systems businesses are competing with both West European and Japanese firms; the core businesses, such as lighting, turbines, and locomotives, are in the same situation. The service businesses vary: GE Credit along with the newly acquired NBC are domestic businesses, whereas GE Information Systems is international. Faced with growing technical uncertainty there are two basic paths our leaders can take.

Reducing uncertainty can be accomplished by getting out of a business and redeploying the assets. At GE the divestitures of Utah Mining and GE housewares both represent uncertainty reducing strategies, and this will continue to be a viable tool for dealing with uncertainty as more of GE's businesses fail to meet Welch's strategic objective to be number one or two in their respective industries.

Another way to reduce uncertainty is to try and design it out of the organization. This approach is labeled a mechanistic design strategy. Mechanistic approaches to dealing with uncertainty are attempts to reduce uncertainty by building in predictability. Thus the extreme use of bureaucratic procedures like standard operating procedures, strict planning, and control systems, are vehicles for reducing uncertainty in the organization. One could use slack resources to create coordinating or gatekeeper positions that would absorb uncertainty from the operating units. These solutions run counter to the current trend toward leaner, more agile organizations, with decision-making close to the site of the expertise.

Indeed, the problem with the mechanistic approach is that it succeeds best under conditions of moderate technical uncertainty. Once there is too much uncertainty the system gets overloaded and breaks down. The more the system applies the old bureaucratic routines which do not fit the new environmental conditions the more the situation deteriorates. This happened at General Motors in the late 1970s when the company attempted to work harder at the traditional solutions to productivity improvement, product innovation, and marketing problems. The result was devastating—red ink appeared on the books for the first time in decades. The alternative strategy to reducing uncertainty is to enhance the organization's capacity for self-adjustment by learning and adapting as it goes along. This architectural strategy is referred to as an organic approach.

Organic systems absorb a high degree of uncertainty. They accomplish this by creating an environment in which people are highly interactive and problem-solving groups are organized not to do away with uncertainty, but to find adaptive ways of dealing with the new problems and issues.

POLITICAL UNCERTAINTY

Political uncertainty arises when there is ambiguity: Who has the power to make decisions? Who will be rewarded with a promotion? Who will have the opportunity to influence the goals of the organization? In times of change these issues come to the fore. At General Motors the reorganization left thousands of people unsure about who would fill the new positions. GM managers could have reduced uncertainty dramatically by passing out new organizational charts with people's names in the boxes. Alex Cunningham chose instead to create problem-solving groups to develop a set of new criteria for advancement, as well as a process that would enhance the problem-solving capacity of the staffing function. Since the process was characterized by widespread participation it also ensured a greater commitment to the decisions. This approach was organic; passing out new organization charts would have been mechanistic.

Political uncertainty is triggered generally by differences around organizational goals, means for achieving the goals, and allocation of power, opportunity, and money. Figure 8.1 presents a range of responses for dealing with political uncertainty. On one end of the spectrum is the politically mechanistic system that provides little capacity for problem-solving in the organization. Extreme examples of politically mechanistic organizations are armies and oligopolies like the Communist Party in Russia. In these organizations power is highly concentrated and the social system does not easily evolve to meet changing circumstances. Change in the social structure frequently requires mutiny or revolution. On the other hand, an

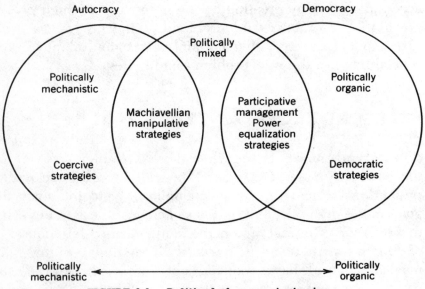

FIGURE 8.1. Political change strategies.

extreme organic system is a purely democratic system in which people can vote to change the rules, bargaining and exchange happen freely, leaders can be voted in and out, and the social system continues to absorb the uncertainty. While the democratic system is less efficient in the short run, it has the capacity for surviving a great deal of political uncertainty.

Two companies with politically organic managerial systems are the ICI internal board, which elects the chairman, and Volvo Corporation's heavy labor representation on its board and through multiple layers of the organization.

CULTURAL UNCERTAINTY

In diverse multibusiness organizations, cultures frequently vary because of differences in the life cycle stage of the business, geography, or type of business (i.e., service, high-tech or heavy manufacturing). As with the technical and political uncertainty, leaders can either try to reduce uncertainty or look for ways of absorbing it. IBM has served as an example of how to reduce cultural uncertainty by homogenizing the culture. They use a tight screening process to select new employees and reinforce their values through career-long developmental activities.

Organizations vary in the degree that they are able to handle diverse subcultures. Cultural uncertainty is triggered when the organization attempts to deal with a variety of values in one social system. Certainly the problem of decision-making at the national level in the United States, where the demands of pluralistic interest groups must be considered, gives us a sense of the difficulties that diversity can present. Mechanistic approaches to dealing with cultural uncertainty include the attempt to screen new members in the organization so as to minimize the difference in values between new entrants and the existing members, or to strongly socialize new members so that they buy into the values of the existing culture. Organic organizations tend to deal with cultural uncertainty by saying that it is all right. They create cosmopolitan organizations that take pride in their diversity. Universities and strong research oriented organizations tend to have these cultural characteristics.

A DYNAMIC JIGSAW PUZZLE

The TPC framework we presented in Chapter 4 provides transformational leaders with a planning template. It can be conceived of as a nine-piece dynamic jigsaw puzzle which at any point in time can have all or some of its pieces out of line. The transformational leaders must first decide which pieces need attention and then dynamically get the pieces to fit together. The problem is complex, since a change in the shape of any piece in the puzzle requires modification in some or all of the others if the puzzle is again to present us with a seamless whole. When the puzzle is solved, however, the organization achieves structural integrity. This static state is usually temporary and frequently is disrupted in a rapidly changing environment. The core dilemma is control and guidance of the organization in the face of various levels of uncertainty. Transformational leaders must identify the level of uncertainty in each of the systems and select the appropriate point along the mechanistic-organic continuum that will provide the problem-solving capacity the organization needs to deal with its environment. Once the systems have been designed, the final step is to integrate the three systems or complete the weaving of the strategic rope.

Since most organizations operate in an increasingly turbulent world, there is clear bias on our part toward organic structures. We feel, in the long run, that organic systems will outsurvive and outperform mechanistic systems in a fast-moving globally competitive environment.

Adjusting the Technical System

In the last 30 years, General Motors moved away from Alfred Sloan's original concept of a lean, decentralized organization to one with large, strong corporate staff groups. Power was increasingly consolidated in the corporate suite on the fourteenth floor. The overall General Motors system became mechanistic with bureaucratic committees and many hierarchical levels to guide the 760,000-person behemoth. The result was an organizational dinosaur. The rapidly increasing environmental uncertainty required a much more organic structure. Roger Smith recognized this and developed a decentralization strategy which he feels enhances the organization's capacity for absorbing uncertainty. The logic of creating more self-contained business units within General Motors is similar to the move from large centralized computer systems to distributive processing. Each unit has the capacity to make adjustments needed for its own unique environment. The reorganization of General Motors North American Auto Operation into two semi-autonomous units, each with its own structure, is part of Smith's strategy. GM still faces the challenge of streamlining its corporate staff and eliminating layers from the General Motors hierarchy. To compete globally, General Motors must reduce the size of staff groups and numbers of managers so that they are in line with those of their principal competitors—the Japanese.

Like General Motors, General Electric also developed large corporate staffs during the 1970s, especially in the strategic planning area. With the complex planning process centralized at corporate headquarters, it became increasingly difficult for individual businesses to rapidly respond to changes in their environment. Much time and energy was spent managing upward as opposed to managing outward. Jack Welch's technical solution was to create a much simpler organization at the corporate level and to decentralize decision-making authority to the business units. By dramatically cutting staff and eliminating layers of the hierarchy the overall organization becomes much more organic.

In contrast to General Motors and General Electric, both Honeywell and Burroughs are moving in the direction of centralizing certain aspects of managerial problem-solving and decision-making. This is because of the nature of the environmental challenges facing both organizations. Burroughs's strategy is to market a line of interrelated products. Centralization allows the company to drive this strategy out of a more responsive headquarters. He comments on one aspect of this shift:

> We had some product management people attached to the factories and engineering and manufacturing associations. We had some attached to planning organizations. We totally reorganized and brought it all together in one product management organization. With that kind of central organization we found we needed substantially fewer people, thus the centralization gave some economies of scale but it also brought problem-solving up at the top of the organization rather than distributed around the organization.

Honeywell needs to develop more problem-solving capability at the top of the organization to absorb the uncertainty arising from attempts to integrate its information systems and control systems businesses.

Adjusting the Political System

The political imperative for General Motors is to become much more organic. The uncertainty will continue to go up as they move through this transformation. Such issues as who stays and who goes, how rewards are distributed, and how decision-making power is allocated still need adjustment. While it is difficult to make the changes as quickly as they are required, Roger Smith is experimenting with systems that are politically organic. One of these organizations is the Chevrolet-Pontiac-Canada group headed by Lloyd Reuss.

While the Saturn Organization is being designed as one of the most organic in U.S. industry, it will be only a $5 billion part of a $96 billion giant. Before reviewing some of the plans for the Saturn Organization, it should be pointed out that it has many striking similarities to the strategy Volvo developed 15 years ago. Under the transformational leadership of Per Gyllenhammer, Volvo made a commitment to improve the work environment in order to deal with morale, absenteeism, turnover problems, and world competitiveness. The centerpiece in the early strategy at Volvo was the Kalmar assembly plant. It was created to provide an environment that encouraged teamwork. This was part of Gyllenhammer's strategy when he stated:

A way must be found to create a workplace which meets the needs of modern working man for a sense of purpose and satisfaction in his daily work. A way must be found of obtaining this goal without an adverse effect on productivity. The Volvo Kalmar plant is an illustration of the technically, politically, and culturally organic system. The work is organized between teams of 15 to 25 workers, each of whom has responsibility for a different work process, for example, electrical systems, brakes, wheels, and so on. There is no assembly line. Each team establishes its own work rhythm. The plant is designed so that there is no assembly line; there are buffer zones for storing work completed between teams so that they can work at their own pace. Cars are moved on electric trolleys enabling teams and individuals to control their own work speed. Teams control their inventories and decide whether to work on a stationary car or one that is moving on an assembly line.

The political system is one in which work teams have considerable say in the total management of the plant through a joint council. Teams are also responsible for a portion of the selection and training of new members, as well as for the management of problems related to productivity of its own members.

The Volvo design effort is based on the following set of cultural assumptions:

1. Participation in decision-making increases the commitment and motivation to carry out the decision.

2. People are motivated to work for many different reasons, including material rewards, social rewards, self-recognition rewards, and growth rewards.

3. The core unit for improving employee satisfaction and performance is the work group, not the manager or the individual worker.

4. A sense of completeness and satisfaction with a task accomplished is enhanced when individuals participate in a total task.

5. Tasks should be organized to give a team maximum control over them.

6. The physical environment is important in securing satisfaction and productivity.

There are many interesting parallels in the proposed new Saturn Organization where workers will be full partners.

Representatives of the United Auto Workers will sit in on all planning and operating committees. Work teams will operate without foremen. To emphasize the new equality, old job titles will be replaced with neutral ones. (See Figure 8.2.) And blue-collar workers will earn a salary just like managers. Both will earn bonuses based on performance, and although the UAW will keep the right to strike, it will try to agree on changes in pay by consensus with management instead of bargaining. The Union will have a say on managers' salaries too. . . . In exchange for its new voice in management, the UAW will give General Motors an initial 20 percent break on guaranteed wages plus less restrictive work rules.

Like Volvo, Saturn will use teams as the basic unit. They will elect a counselor from among their own ranks and control job assignments, maintain their equipment inventory, and deal with scheduling of vacations. They will control their own quality and variable costs and they are expected to continuously

Traditional GM Plant	The Saturn Plant
Plant manager	Strategic advisory committee Does long-term planning. Consists of Saturn president and his staff, plus top UAW adviser
Production manager	Manufacturing advisory committee Oversees Saturn complex. Includes company and elected union representatives, plus specialists in engineering, marketing, and so on.
General superintendent	Business unit Coordinates plant-level operations. Made up of company representatives and elected union adviser, plus specialists.
Production superintendent (5 per shift)	Work unit module Groups of three to six work units led by a company "work unit adviser"
General supervisor (15 per shift)	Work units Teams of 6 to 15 workers led by an elected UAW "counselor"
Supervisor/foreman (90 per shift)	

FIGURE 8.2.   Saturn Organization structure.

innovate. When new innovations are proposed, finance and purchasing departments will be required to come to consensus with the teams. There will be a joint labor–management work council.

The entire Saturn complex will be run by a fourth group, the manufacturing advisory committee. It will consist of top UAW and com-

pany officials from the business units plus the manager of the Saturn complex, an elected UAW official. This is the committee that is supposed to reach consensus decisions on changes in salaries and benefits. It will answer on this and other decisions to the highest committee in Saturn, the Strategic Advisory Committee made up of a top UAW official plus Saturn's president and his staff. The committee will handle long-term planning for the company.

At least 80 percent of the Saturn workforce will have job security for life. In addition, seniority rules will be eliminated and pay will be driven by performance.

The proposed Saturn Organization is radically different from traditional General Motors organizations. The fact that it won't come on line until 1989 means that the lessons from this organization will not have much impact on General Motors until the 1990s. Thus the question of how fast and how far General Motors will go in the direction of creating a politically organic system to meet the demands of uncertainty remains unanswered until the marketplace begins to provide the evidence.

At General Electric one can see a more extensive organizational drive on the part of Jack Welch to move toward a more politically organic system. He calls it ownership, getting the people in the businesses to act as if they owned the business. This means dealing with more of a "pushback theory of management," fighting for what one believes is right for the business, rushing decisions upward instead of waiting for top management to decide. This is coupled with a major effort to streamline the number of decision-making layers at General Electric. The company is also using internal boards similar to the one proposed for the Saturn Organization to provide ways of handling political uncertainty while the reorganization continues.

Adjusting the Cultural System

Unlike the other organizations we looked at, Drake Business Schools has filled its top management slots with women. Mary

Ann Lawlor says this was not done deliberately but as a matter of survival:

> They were the best. We could pay good women less than good men. Given the salaries that we could afford to pay in those days, the women who applied for the jobs were better qualified than the men. Now we take care to pay ourselves appropriately for the work we do, but back in the early 1970s we were paid less than a man would be paid in the same spot.
>
> Does it make a difference that we are all women? I think there are differences. I had an interesting observation earlier today. In day-to-day operations, I think we are more tolerant of a lot of emotional baggage. I think we're very tolerant of people having a bad day or having a bad time in their lives with personal problems or whatever. I think we also try to read through the emotions and hear what people are really saying. But whenever crises come, I think we approach the crises far more rationally and intellectually than men do. On a day-to-day basis they tend to operate on a rational level, but when a crisis comes they're much more likely to react emotionally.
>
> Another interesting difference is something I observed recently at a meeting of representatives from our national association. I thought the women's comments were much more issue oriented. They didn't seem to go through establishing their status and strutting around. I'm not saying that what they said was any better or worse, I'm not making a judgment on that, but even when I didn't agree with them, they seemed to be more focused on what they had to say than they were in jockeying for position in the group.

It will be interesting to see whether Drake continues to have a homogeneous culture or if growth will increase the degree of cultural heterogeneity over time.

Cultural uncertainty will continue to grow at General Motors, General Electric, and Honeywell over the remainder of the 1980s. General Motors will need to differentiate its once monolithic culture and allow for much greater cultural diversity. This is no easy challenge when one considers that corporate headquarters are located in Detroit, a one industry town dominated by GM. It is interesting to observe some of the actions being taken by Roger Smith to shake up the culture. One strategic shift with technical, political, and cultural implications is the EDS acquisition. Ross Perot's information system organization acquired by General Motors has brought a fast-moving entrepreneurial set of managers and workers into staid, conservative General Motors. The cultural clashes have led to significant political turmoil, but they have also provided an experience in dealing with alternative cultures. The Saturn Organization will provide another counterculture, as does the 1985 Hughes Aircraft acquisition.

General Electric will become much more culturally organic as the organization is decentralized, and career opportunities will occur primarily within the lines of business. The dilemma for GE will be to find the right balance point between centralization and decentralization so that there can be a strong set of company-wide GE shared values.

Honeywell is faced with the need to blend the Information Systems and the Control Systems cultures. The cultural and political uncertainty will be extremely high during this phase of strategic change.

TOOLS FOR CREATING ORGANIC SYSTEMS

Figure 8.3 illustrates the array of tools and techniques transformational leaders use to move the TPC systems toward the organic end of the spectrum. Starting in the strategy area, open systems planning is a participative planning process that asks groups of people to map environmental forces and identify organizational responses needed to deal with them. The process is as important as the output in this planning system. It is congruent with the normative planning process or visioning process outlined in the Clark Equipment example in Chapter 5. Individuals at all levels of the organization start with a definition of the core mission of the business. They then identify

	Strategy	Structure	Human resource management
Technical	Open systems planning	Matrix structure Subunit autonomous work teams	High tolerance for ambiguity Cognitively complex Flexible
Political	Fluid power system Contention system	Few players coupled with high level of delegation	Voting procedures for leader (ICI) Rewards divided via Scanlon plan Peer & subordinate evaluation
Cultural	Core value coupled with respect for deviance	Participative style Heterogeneous subculture Overarching core value	Heterogeneity not screened out/ core value maintained

FIGURE 8.3.   Tools for creating organic systems.

environmental forces that affect the organization's capacity for delivering on its mission both now and five years into the future. They identify the current organizational responses and the ones that will be required in the future. The result is a set of action steps to ensure that the organization effectively responds to market demands. The important point of the activity is that it sensitizes large numbers of organization members to the environmental changes and gets them to feel a sense of ownership for the needed strategic changes.

In the structure area, network and matrix structures are much more organic than hierarchical functional organizations. On the shop floor the autonomous work teams in the Volvo plant and in the proposed Saturn Organization can absorb more uncertainty than existing forms. In the human resource area, people who have high tolerance for ambiguity, cognitive complexity, and flexibility fit more consistently with an organic system.

In the political area, it is important to develop fluid power systems in the organization so that decisions can be made on the basis of expertise rather than position. IBM's management contention system is an example of an organic political strategy that provides for resolution of boss–subordinate conflict. In the structural area, fewer layers coupled with high levels of delegation certainly create a more organic system. In the human resource area, voting procedures such as those used at ICI to select the chairman are highly organic, as well as Scanlon plans where a portion of profits is divided up in a participatory fashion. Appraisal systems that collect data from peers and subordinates are another example of politically organic human resource systems.

Cultural tools for building organic systems depend on developing core values that drive business strategy while simultaneously dealing with the paradox of respect for individual differences. In the cultural structure area, there is a need for a participative management style that will support heterogeneous subcultures within a system of core values that tie the organization together. Finally, in the human resource area, the cultural screens done at the door somehow are subtle enough to capture some heterogeneity while at the same time maintaining homogeneity around core values in the organization. The tools listed in this figure are meant to be illustrative of the kinds of activities that transformational leaders can and should use. During this institutionalization phase we should keep in mind that the objective in times of scarce resources is to create architectural forms that can rapidly be adapted to new uses. By definition organic forms are constantly adapting to changing environmental conditions. Blumenthal talks about these issues at Burroughs:

> **I think we have created or recreated the company on the old
> foundation that can stand on its own two feet and that has**

achieved a certain amount of momentum—there is your famous architectural rendering. However, it is an architectural rendering of a very fine interim headquarters that everyone is happy to be in but that is not the permanent one. You know, people still ask the question, "Well, that's great, it's going to be good for the next three or four years but where are they going to be in 1992?" So we are in an interim stage because we still have to refine and fortify.

The returns are not in and there are still some fundamental questions to be answered. We have made one or two major acquisitions and we still have to strike out in some major new directions. There are still some major new product innovations ahead of us to really give us the 30 percent increase each year. Until we are clearly separated from the past, people will still wonder if this old Burroughs can make it. So clearly there is still a lot of work to be done. You build a permanent institution by creating new traditions, new habits, and I would think that at some point in the future, if we are to leave or retire, that simply by doing things for a while we will institutionalize a new way of thinking, a new way of acting. Everybody is now committed to teamwork and talking in groups. Everybody accepts the idea that training for responsibility is important. Everybody accepts the idea that Burroughs is okay, it is okay to speak out, to tell people what you think because no one is going to castigate you for thinking something different from what the boss thinks. Everybody understands you can be free to disagree and there is a certain amount of accountability that is required of people. I think that gets built into the organization.

There is one major tool that we used which I think is working extremely well, it is being institutionalized, and that is the employee survey. We are using very elaborate employee surveys where we publicize to all of our people what they have said and tell them what we have said . . . .

Jeff Campbell also talked about his social architectural problems. He described it to us.

First, I try to get them to sign on to the long-term goal. But then I give them a lot of freedom as to how they will do it. Part of institutionalizing what we've been doing is to get the guys to subscribe to a set of values once they have subscribed to the long-term goal. I believe that by giving them a lot of freedom as to how they will accomplish these goals will help establish a value system where they give freedom to their own people. I think the whole notion of venturing, risking, trying new things springs from giving people freedom.

I am starting our first venture. I think there may be an opportunity for mobile Burger King units. The problem was that this project was not a high priority for anyone. It was the eighth objective on one guy's list, the seventh on another, and the tenth on someone else's and it wasn't going anywhere. Then I started thinking, maybe what we need to do is take a group of zealots who think this is something they really can do and the number one zealot will be the person to run it.

Basically, I was looking for a champion for the mobile units—it turned out to be my director of government relations, who I always kidded did not have a real job. He's a very articulate, cynical guy but he really was bugging me about wanting to do something with these mobile units. Finally, he followed me out to the parking lot and I said, "Steve, if you really care so much about this project, why don't you do something about it? If I give you the people and the capital you need to run the business, what are you going to do?"

The next morning he was in my office and he said, "I didn't sleep last night. Are you serious about what you said?" I assured him I was and that he could give up the job he was doing and take on this new project. I gave him the folder and told him to pick some people and tell me what he needed. Well, a week from today his team is going to give me a proposal about what they need and what the return will be from this business over the next five years. He's excited as hell and if this thing works, I've got some other ideas I am going to try to get off the ground the same way . . . .

IMPLICATIONS THROUGHOUT THE ORGANIZATION

The value that encourages organizational adaptation to changing conditions should exist throughout the organization. The

Saturn Organization is illustrative of a trend that has been emerging since the late 1960s in Western Europe and the United States: the creation of more organic work team systems under the label of quality of work life. This trend will continue to accelerate in the 1980s and 1990s as the transformation of mature companies continues. This means that middle managers will be redesigning systems, and there will be an increased demand for transformational leadership all the way down to the shop floor.

The technical system will exhibit more expanded jobs, where people will be required to think as well as do, more teams will be used that demand flexibility about duties. Groups organized to accomplish a given task will dissolve and form again around new projects. There will be fewer hierarchical layers in the organization.

The political system will be marked by mutual influence systems in which information and not position determines power. Reward systems will be more flexible—in some cases groups rather than individuals will be evaluated and rewarded. Incentive systems such as profit-sharing and gain-sharing will be more widely used, and people will be paid for acquiring new skills rather than moving up the hierarchy. Finally, a great deal more emphasis will be placed on equality of sacrifice as all employees become partners in the organization's struggle to survive. Transformational leaders will find that the intellectual commitment to revitalization requires the elimination of status symbols and much broader dissemination of financial business data. Given the history of most organizations, these managerial prerogatives will not go quietly into the night, and only consistent examples will result in redesigning the organization.

THE LEADER AS SOCIAL ARCHITECT II: MOTIVATING PEOPLE

9

The way you do it is to hire the right people and have them hire the right people—you show them how you are running the company by encouraging them to speak up, by giving them responsibility, and you get them to function as a team by taking them along on retreats and talking things out and sharing your concerns with them and asking them their opinion—it is a very different atmosphere and you tell them to do that with their people and you start putting your money where your mouth is by investing in building training centers, putting money into R&D and doing all of those things and expecting them to do the same. So you do it by example, since you pick people in your own image chances are they will do it with their people.

MICHAEL BLUMENTHAL

241

Transformational leaders reinforce values and refocus organizational priorities through effective dealings with people. Selection and placement, appraisal, rewards, and development institutionalize culture by showing people what is and what is not important.

Human resource practices, from top-level succession down to the shop floor, have an effect on the culture of the organization. They are practical applications of the new vision and they institutionalize it. They also create the foundation for organizational flexibility and responsiveness in the future. Thus it is through the human resource systems that organizations develop the capacity for self-renewal.

CULTURAL SCREENING: SELECTION

A powerful way to shape and maintain a culture is by placing tight cultural controls both on those hired at the entry level and those placed in key leadership positions. Values, along with skills, become important screening criteria for hiring and promotion. Organizations with strong internal cultures like Exxon, Hewlett-Packard, IBM, and most of the Japanese companies spend a great deal of time screening and socializing new employees.

An example of entry-level cultural screening is the process used by the Honda Plant in Ohio. A blue-collar worker applying for a job at the plant must write an essay about his or her life goals and how working at Honda fits with this larger purpose. These essays are read by senior management and by representatives of the workers. Using this process, they screen out the 90 percent who cannot identify a place for Honda in their lives. Honda then focuses on the 10 percent who have passed the first screening. The plant's workers are involved in interviewing these people and in deciding who should work there. This is simply a cultural screen to determine how well these people will fit in with the Honda way of doing things. After people are hired, they go through an extensive training process—training that takes four to eight hours in an American automobile plant often takes three weeks at Honda. At an American plant, the newest employee on the assembly line gets the poorest job, next to the second most recent hire, whereas at Honda the best worker is selected to train the new employee so that the newcomer learns the best way of doing the work. Again, a strong cultural message. Why the three weeks? Obviously, what is occurring is cultural training. We often look on with amusement as the workers learn the Honda handshake and the Honda song and the Honda exercises and put on the Honda uniforms, but this is not different from the socialization that goes on in the Marine Corps. There, too, only a few are selected and they are subjected to intensive socialization. The rigor of the selection process increases employee self-esteem and fits with Jim Renier's idea that a person must feel that he or she is excellent before being able to do excellent work.

The caveat is that organizations must learn to walk a thin line in the way that they choose and socialize employees. Carried to an extreme, such cultural screening leads to a homogeneity that works against innovation and change. The transformational leader must help the organization to differentiate between a healthy challenge to existing methods and heresy.

TOP-LEVEL SUCCESSION

Most of us intuitively look for signals of continuity or change in organizations when a new CEO is selected. Ironically, strong cultures with a heavy emphasis on managerial "style" have greater difficulty installing CEOs with very different styles from their predecessors unless the company is in crisis. Among the companies we discussed, ICI, in all probability, would not have turned to John Harvey-Jones if the situation had been less critical.

General Electric and Citicorp provide an interesting study in contrasts in the way in which they handled their recent successions. At GE, Reginald Jones, the CEO prior to Jack Welch, had the task of selecting his successor plus two vice chairmen from among a field of about eight qualified candidates who had been groomed over a 10-year period. As with ICI, one of the keys to succession was getting teamwork at the top. By electing the leader at ICI the chances of commitment are greatly enhanced. Since democratic elections were not a feasible option at GE, Jones used the series of "airplane interviews" we previously described. The process resulted in four of the seven candidates leaving GE for other jobs, while the three remaining were selected because the chemistry was such that they could work together in spite of one being the winner.

At Citibank, the process seemed to be less consciously managed. Certainly the press treated it as a contest where winner takes all. The basis of their belief was the departure of key executives who had been considered as possible successors in the years immediately preceding Wriston's retirement. Walter Wriston's silence before the selection of Reed in the summer of 1984 added to the sense that the process was being undermanaged. Yet there has been no appreciable loss of key executives since Reed took office. The difference may well have been that Citibank did not have a strong management "style" characterizing its top management group. With no history that valued one management style above any other except as it was mirrored in the results that the manager achieved, Citibank was able to accommodate those who did not win the top spot. Certainly, Thomas Theobold's appointment to spearhead Citibank's assault on the traditional investment banks is a sign that he has Reed's confidence and support.

In all three cases, however, the process of succession is a reflection of central aspects of each organization's culture. The practice at ICI of democratically electing its chairman has a profound impact on the transformational leadership role the CEO plays. On the one hand, the group gave a mandate to John

Harvey-Jones, but as with all democratic processes there are checks and balances that limit his power: his term is restricted to one five-year period and the board that elected him has voting rights on all major policy issues. The election, however, provides a vehicle for strong internal commitment and sets a tone for the use of more democratic processes throughout ICI.

At Citibank, a long history of successful laissez-faire management enabled the organization to absorb the contention that surrounded the succession, and a commitment to decentralized responsibility seems to have provided sufficient autonomy to keep a talented contender like Theobold in the fold.

Finally, at GE, the message is that an orchestrated political process can be used to help sort out winners and losers, but that a price will be paid in terms of talent when a significant shift is made at the top of an organization where homogeneous management style plays a strong role in defining the culture.

The selection of an insider to lead an organization contrasts with the role that our "outsiders" played when they took over. Lee Iacocca and Mike Blumenthal came in and cleaned house at the top, bringing in their own teams. While the choice of an outsider certainly signals a shakeup, it also puts in motion the we–they dynamics that must be carefully managed if the change effort is to succeed.

Selection at the bottom and succession at the top are key filtering mechanisms, but they are merely the tip of the iceberg for the human resource management (HRM) systems. These systems ensure the continual reformulation and refocusing of the vision. At IBM, both Watsons, Tom Senior and Junior, knew this and built human resource policies and practices that enabled them to perpetuate their vision by remote control. This is also true of Hewlett-Packard, which has skillfully used the human resource systems to institutionalize important aspects of its vision. These companies go far beyond playing a gatekeeping role at entry level and at the top of the organization. They devote a great deal of time and attention to the middle. It is this attention to the middle levels of the organization that tends to sort out great companies from good companies.

The keystone to managing the middle is time and attention devoted to the performance appraisal system. Both IBM and Hewlett-Packard use the appraisal system to continue to reinforce the culture. Hewlett-Packard conducts a cultural audit of its managers once a year and hands out rewards, both cash and promotions, based on how well people are reinforcing the Hewlett-Packard culture.

HUMAN RESOURCE MANAGEMENT BASICS

A Human Resource System Should Have Internal Consistency. Many human resource systems resemble patchwork quilts; the procedures were developed piecemeal and rarely changed. There frequently is a built-in tension among the subfunctions of the system that makes it less effective than it could be. One of the principal areas of this tension is the lack of clarity that surrounds the appraisal system. Organizations often find it difficult to sort out the reason the system exists. Is it to distribute rewards based on merit or is it to counsel employees about how they can improve their performance?

The answer in most organizations is that the system is expected to serve both goals. It can do this as long as the organization is clear about its priorities. Is the most important goal to identify and reward performance or to minimize the competition between individuals? The answer to this question will help the company to identify the first priority of its human resource system. It will provide the philosophical underpinning on which the system exists. It will also then avoid the organizational schizophrenia we find when the reward system is clearly based on Skinnerian principles of reward and punishment, while the developmental system is sending out just as clear messages that are an outgrowth of Maslow's ideas that people work because they need accomplishments.

Select People with an Eye to the Job's Future Demands.
Few organizations look to their future when choosing someone
to fill a job. This is true even at the very top of the organization.
It is why most organizations do not look for leaders capable of
transforming organizations unless those organizations find
themselves in critical situations. It may also explain why succession planning systems usually identify and groom people to
fill existing jobs rather than asking what the organization will
look like if its long-range strategic direction is realized, and
then identifying and grooming people to fill the jobs that will
exist.

Design Appraisal Systems that Reward Being Right. The
purpose of standard operating procedures is to provide the answer for every possible question—a task that most would agree
is hopeless except in the simplest of all worlds. The result is a
human resource system that encourages people to avoid making
a mistake rather than to find a solution. The scale is weighted
heavily in favor of doing nothing rather than assuming a risk.
This method of managing people also places a disproportionate
burden on top management, since it violates the basic concept
that the solution to the problem lies with those who have the
most information about it.

People, Like Other Assets, Need To Be Maintained. Excellent organizations recognize that assets must be maintained if
the organization is investing in the future. Watson at IBM recognized the importance of his human assets and developed a
philosophy about them when he first assumed the reins at IBM:

*T. J. Watson didn't move in and shake up the organization. Instead he
set out to buff and polish the people who were already there and to
make a success of what he had. That decision in 1914 led to the IBM
policy of job security, that has meant a great deal to our employees
. . . and was adhered to during the Great Depression, when IBM produced parts for inventory and stored them. From it has come our
policy to build from within. We go to great lengths to develop our
people, to retrain them when job requirements change, and to give*

them another chance if we find them experiencing difficulties in the job they are in.

Organizations Faced with Diverse Problems Require Diverse Solutions. The social architectural problem for the large multiproduct and business corporation is to design a corporate human resource strategy that will parallel with the corporate strategy for the range of businesses. In companies with a portfolio of businesses at different stages of growth and/or decline, there should be a clearly articulated human resource policy that recognizes the diversity of each business's specific human resource needs.

Thus Jack Welch at General Electric has the most complex task of all of our transformational leaders. He has to design human resource systems that recognize the vast diversity of businesses in the General Electric portfolio. He feels that the systems are not sufficiently differentiated at the present time. The problem is complicated by his need to maintain some strong common cultural bonds in General Electric. This conflict between differentiation and integration is a major social architectural problem that is currently being tackled at GE.

COMPONENTS OF THE HUMAN RESOURCE SYSTEM

Selection and Placement

They all knew I was coming in to clean house, and each one was afraid he was going to be the target. They had no certainty in their lives. They were living in fear—and for good reason. Over a three-year period I had to fire thirty-three out of the thirty-five vice presidents.

In a few cases, I tried to resurrect some of the executives. But it didn't work—they just couldn't cut it. Charlie Beacham used to say that once a guy is over twenty-one, you'll never really change his style or his habits. You may think you can, but his self-image

> is locked in . . . . Unfortunately, Beacham was right—as usual.
> When Paul Bergmoser came in, I remember saying to him: "Try
> to save some of these guys." He worked with them for six
> months. "It's impossible," he then told me. "These people have
> learned the Chrysler way of running their own show. They will
> never adjust. It's too late."

Selection was a critical tool for transition management that
Iacocca used at Chrysler. Most of the top management team and
20,000 white-collar workers lost their jobs. The criteria for who
would stay and who would go was an evaluation of who could
succeed in the "new" Chrysler. Over time, it will be necessary
to develop a selection system that reinforces the culture. This
means thinking through the best way to screen employees culturally before they enter the company. The world will be waiting to see what Chrysler does during the next auto downturn. If
the leadership talent that exists at the top is not replicated
through the middle management ranks, the organization will
have precious little time to develop it.

Another selection issue for Chrysler is at the top. Not just the
horse race for Iacocca's position (which seems to be well defined), but the more complex process of developing a succession system for the top three layers below the office of the
chairman.

It is necessary to have a strong core of people, perhaps several hundred, to run a company the size of Chrysler effectively.
Yet with the turnaround and the leadership all coming from the
outside, there is a need to develop a credible internal succession system.

Another transformational leader who used selection as an in-
tegral part of making the change happen was Ed Thompson at
Schneider Transport. He described his change process:

> We worked hard to identify the people at all levels who were
> excited about being multiple "plate spinners." Managing change
> in accelerated time frames required people who could develop
> the personal energy and skill to juggle multiple projects and

goals. It's a little like spinning 10 plates on a big shiny table. You get the right 10 up there and keep them spinning. Get them going right and you can leave some alone while concentrating on a few. You start finding people who are good at this. That's where you start moving people to the sidelines who are single plate spinners. In normal times single plate spinners or specialists might be fine. In times of rapid change we looked to place and develop broader people—even if we had to bring some people in from the outside.

For Ed Thompson, his "plate" spinners, or people who were excited about handling multiple change agendas, must be selected and empowered early on in the change process.

Don MacKinnon at CIBA-GEIGY views succession as critical to the institutionalization of his vision. He states:

The next succession is vital. If we don't have the right people, progress as I want it will be diminished . . . it will take another generation . . . .

Mike Blumenthal also pays constant attention to succession at the top, because he does not want to leave Burroughs in the shape it was in when he inherited the job of chairman. He says:

There are very few speeches where I do not talk about the fact that I will be gone and that I have made a commitment to the board that we are building a bench, that we are building a team, that we are building a group of people. "You are going to be running this company long after I am gone and there will be enough of a team to do even better than I have done." This morning when I gave the speech, a lot of executives were there and I said I want to recognize the 25 people who are part of the Burroughs top team. "I want them to stand so you can see them. These are the people who are responsible for all of the things you heard about in connection with quality of service." Then they all stand up and receive the applause they deserve.

It may be a little corny but there is a reason that I do these things. It fits the description of what we have in mind, the vision of being a company that builds on the notion that we praise the old and demand the new. Sort of, as we say in German, "drag in by the hair examples of what is good and what is bad."

Don MacKinnon used staffing as a change tool, by selectively going outside to fill key positions. He had to take on the protectors of the status quo, since this was a significant departure from CIBA-GEIGY tradition. He said:

> My friends were furious with me. They said that's the one place you don't want to go—outside—because you'll hire someone who will come in, he'll do a strategic plan, and he'll leave you and go to another company and they will steal all our secrets. They'll know everything . . . where we are going and what we are going to do. And I had a real problem with it. This is the most confidential job in the company and we had traditionally filled it with an old-time trusted employee we could depend on. And I said, we don't have anybody who understands strategic planning so I can't accept what you are saying, and you're going to have to ride with the risk . . . . We brought in a real expert, one of the brightest people in the company.

Fred Hammer believes selection is the most important human resource activity because it can make the most difference in the organization:

> I'm not much into changing people. I can change the environment in the organization. I am a matcher so I try to position people in the places where they are likely to succeed. But I don't believe that I can change people. At Chase my solution was to bring in more outsiders . . . .

Appraisal

The problem is not a technical one, even though for years people keep redesigning the technical aspects without hitting the deeper cultural and political ones. Iacocca's review and appraisal process is marked by a technical simplicity and a political and cultural sophistication. He states:

> If our stockholders have a quarterly review system, why
> shouldn't our executives? . . . not only does it force each man-
> ager to consider his own goals, but it's also an effective way to
> remind people not to lose sight of their dreams.

The process that Iacocca describes and what he was involved
in in the early stages of his career is clearly not limited to the
evaluation of top management appraisals. It is a way to hold all
employees accountable, and his commitment to it has its roots
in the discipline imposed on a young Iacocca by Robert McNamara. It is essentially a mechanism that confers power on the
subordinate, since you cannot hold people responsible for
something they have no authority to influence. This philosophy
of management makes for regular reviews and builds into the
culture the ownership of the review process on the part of both
the boss and the subordinate, as opposed to the usual annual
appraisal ritual.

The challenge for the transformational leader is to use the
performance appraisal as the cornerstone of an effective human
resource system. It provides the information needed to make
fully informed strategic decisions by assessing the fit between
current human resource systems and those required by a
change in strategic direction. It also serves as a control in mea-
suring performance against strategic objectives once they have
been set.

In addition to the technical issues involved with effective
performance appraisal, the organization must also be concerned
with the *process* of appraisal. It is necessary to ensure equity
between evaluator and evaluatee by providing the system with
checks and balances to offset the imbalance of power that exists
in most appraisal situations. Organizations should also understand that they can move the organization on the centralized-
decentralized continuum by redistributing the power to ap-
praise performance of key staff personnel.

Finally, the politics that attend issues in appraisals, such as
managerial succession, are critical processes that must be man-

aged in effective organizations. Otherwise, you damage the ability of the organization to plan for its future, because it adds internal uncertainty to the environmental issues that the organization must face.

Rewards

The way in which rewards are administered affects the following organizational factors: (1) attraction and retention, (2) motivation, (3) culture, (4) reinforcement and definition of organization structure, and (5) cost. Thus our transformational leaders have a potentially powerful lever for change and for institutionalizing change. Mike Blumenthal had to make changes in the reward system soon after taking over at Burroughs. The issue resulted from the practices of his predecessor. As Blumenthal related the story, "McDonald's salary was not low when compared to CEOs in similar companies but there was a big gap between McDonald and everyone else. He was well paid but the others were not."

Thus the pay system merely represented the obvious status differential built into the McDonald style of management. In order to attract new talent, this system had to be totally revamped so that salaries among all the management levels were competitive with those in the rest of the industry.

As Edward Lawler summarizes:

The key, of course, is to ultimately come up with an integrated human resource management strategy that is consistent in the way it encourages people to behave, that attracts the kind of people that can support the business strategy, and that encourages them to behave appropriately.

Self-renewing organizations use rewards to encourage innovation. These will increasingly include phantom stock or some arrangement that provides for a percentage of the return on a new product or business. The trend is toward much more differentiated reward systems designed to encourage different types of behavior in different parts of the organization. Many transformational leaders are experimenting in this area. At CIBA-GEIGY Don MacKinnon describes how the bonus system is being used to drive new cultural values:

> **Roughly half of the bonus is financial and the other half is tied to other objectives. It covers progress on management development, safety, environment and other goals . . . I would reduce the financial goals to about 25 percent so that 75 percent would be against the personal objectives such as development of people and moves towards excellence, things we agree on and that we can measure . . . . Finally, we reserve the right under our bonus program to use subjective judgment. If we think he achieved the numbers in a way that he shouldn't have, that we don't think proper, for example, by firing 15 people he shouldn't have fired, we reserve the right to lower his bonus.**

The changes that General Electric is making in its reward systems may well be a harbinger of changes in many other organizations. In line with the notion that general managers should "own" their businesses and be given the freedom to fit compensation systems to their markets and competitive situations, there is increasing differentiation of the pay and reward systems within General Electric. This will range from top level compensation packages to wage agreements for rank and file employees. Revamping these reward systems will take place over several years. Similar signals are being sent out at General Motors, which had been characterized by a single reward system through the entire company.

Development

In organizations that strive to distribute power broadly so that each individual can be held accountable for his or her actions, the purpose of development is to

*Devise institutions that would draw from the best in human nature to
subdue the worst: to alter the social context of people's lives so that
the impulses of rationality and tolerance and generosity could overcome the thrust of unreason, cruelty, and selfishness . . . .*

There is extensive use of formal training by virtually all of our
transformational leaders. Jack Welch at GE personally visits
many of the management programs at Crotonville, the GE Management Development Center. He views this as an important
tool in shaping the new culture. At Honeywell, Jim Renier is a
strong advocate of workshop events for catalyzing change. Jack
Sparks launched new executive development programs at
Whirlpool, as have Mike Blumenthal at Burroughs and Don
MacKinnon at CIBA-GEIGY.

Don MacKinnon indicates that the two-week executive program that they ran was such an important vehicle for change
that he and the chairman split the two weeks. He claims

> Over a period of two weeks the members of the corporate man-
> agement committee spend a minimum of two days . . . we rotate.
> . . . They have the whole corporate management committee
> sitting in front of them and we break them into four groups—they
> give us what they think needs to be done, then we have an open
> discussion and we go back and forth and discuss points that they
> want and then we finally break up at lunch . . . .

Our protagonists spend a great deal of time thinking about
the socialization process in their organizations. As Mary Ann
Lawlor states:

> It's hard. It's mostly done informally although we do have in-
> service training. We call it "Drakeizing" and we talk shorthand
> to each other like "the ability to benefit the typical student,"
> which is our primary goal. When we have a member of the staff
> who's going off on his or her own agenda, we say they need to be
> Drakeized. When we hire people from other schools who don't
> understand how we do things, we put them through the formal

process of Drakeizing in that they have to go through training, but the informal process is the more important . . . .

There are many other tools for development that can be built into the ongoing process of the organization. These include restructuring the organization for learning. Small business units enable the organization to grow leaders.

The brand or product manager role at Procter & Gamble and General Foods is one where there is a great deal of responsibility but limited autonomy. These individuals learn a lot about themselves, interpersonal negotiation, and the total business as they integrate across manufacturing, sales, and to some extent, R&D.

A second way to enhance development is to turn almost every event into a learning event. At Hewlett-Packard the annual planning reviews for each of its 42 divisions are one-day affairs where they spend a good deal of time discussing what has been learned over the recent past. Specific work assignments often get used as developmental tools. At IBM positions of assistant to top executives are used as an important development experience.

Another growing trend and a very powerful tool is the design and use of management workshops. These are a blend of development activities (but built closely around organizational problems) and off-line problem solving sessions, one in which new conceptual frameworks are provided. For example, General Electric, because of the intense pressure to manage change, holds two-and-a-half-day workshops on leadership, vision, and change in conjunction with major business schools. Teams of human resource managers and line managers are brought together to focus on the issues of leadership, vision, and change. About 50 such teams of executives, staff, and line teams have worked together in acquiring some new concepts and tools for visioning, transition management, and change. The chairman, Jack Welch, uses the workshop to share his vision and challenges for General Electric. The workshop is an opportunity to keep underscoring his important cultural themes: the fact that the competition in the future will be more intense, that he does not want to see uniform change since each business has different needs. He stresses the need for honest communication to employees. There has never been a time in GE's history, he has said, when there was so much talk about competitive forces in the outside world, and he feels it is important to let every employee participate in facing the competitive threat. Finally, he has focused on the issue of culture.

> One culture for a company as diverse as ours doesn't make much sense, but there are a number of common threads like central research and the Management Education Center that can help us define certain shared values and be one company. The challenge we face is how to let each business find its own culture, to be different, to adapt to its marketplace, while at the same time keeping the best of the shared values that have made us as a total company so strong.

Such a workshop ended with the participants reexamining their own personal roles as leaders and focusing on the need to develop a vision to challenge the organization, to nurture debate, to increase the organization's analytic capacity, to depoliticize internal debate, to manage the motivation of managers, and to set the quality standards for change.

In some organizations there is a recognition that managers belong to a community and have a family. General Motors recently conducted a workshop that included spouses. Alex Cunningham describes this developmental experience:

> We had all the key players and their wives for a three-day off-site and I think at that time there was, again, a recognition of the need to work together. There was a common good. And, I think because we did include the wives, there was recognition of another dimension to people besides what we saw on a business basis. In this setting the people became more human . . . this event was very unusual at General Motors. When we got back we had a staff member say that we had settled some stuff down there

that would have taken a much longer time to resolve in a different setting.

INTEGRATION

The tough challenge is to make the human resource systems more integrated. This is never fully accomplished, but it should be a target. In organizations where there is a great deal of transformation the end point will feel even more elusive.

Continuous attention is needed to keep the core values in a culture alive and vital. The tools for doing this vary from symbolic, ritualistic events to very bureaucratic procedures built into the human resource system. Mary Ann Lawlor reflects on the ebb and flow of cultural values at Drake and underscores the importance of leaders constantly making adjustments in this area. She reflects on both her leadership role and the culture in the following terms:

> I get a fair amount of respect. They really do respect me but they certainly are not afraid to say, "You're wrong." Nobody is subservient. It was more hierarchical earlier. I think at the point when our skills were very unequal, it was very hierarchical. They had talent and they had brains but they had not yet acquired many skills. Now the skills are more equal. That does not mean that we all have the same skills but with the development that has occurred, the hierarchical situation would not work . . . .

> We now have a couple of levels. There's the middle management crew, whom we try to nurture with some personal links. For example, we took a group of those people out to dinner a couple of weeks ago to recognize the fact that we had a good year. Our behavior serves as a model for the next generation who try to keep personal links with their people. Even though we have gotten bigger, we do take care to gather the tribe and do tribal things. We have two meetings a year when every staff member must be present. When we celebrated our tenth anniversary together, we rented a sailboat and sailed around Manhattan . . . . In some ways Drake has been like a convent, we have religion. I

wrote this piece called "We Take Pride." I did it at a time when I was afraid that the religion was being lost. We gave it to the teachers and the students. This happened a couple of years ago when we were growing fast and we were into this thing to get the numbers, get the numbers, get the numbers. We started to have a lot of staff turnover. The schools looked dirty and maybe I felt a little alienated. I felt I had—I don't know—maybe it was guilt. I was making more money but I wasn't giving enough direction, and I really see my function as moral leadership because this is an educational business after all. And if you don't have some moral component, I think it is very difficult to succeed in this business. Teachers have to believe . . . . You have to balance the love of money with these other things. You really have to work at it to make sure you keep that other side alive.

We believe that most of our transformational leaders intellectually have accepted the need "to balance the love of money with the need to provide moral leadership." The challenge they face is to take these beliefs and implement them through human resource systems that give people responsibility, hold them accountable for its execution, reward them equitably based on the ability to do so, and provide the lifelong learning that enables an organization to renew itself constantly through the ideas and actions of its human resources.

EPILOGUE

HISTORY REPEATS ITSELF

Why did you do it?

It was fun. The problems were there and would not go away by themselves. It was more trouble to get out of it than to stay in it. People depended on me—our money was tied up in Drake—I used to picture myself in bankruptcy court and divorce court in the same week if I failed . . . .

Would you do it again?

Now? I might. It's not something I would seek to do but if I found myself in that situation I know I could do it again. I hope I don't have to do it again. There are other new challenges and exciting things I would like to accomplish. At this point in my life I'm interested in really getting involved more and more in public policy questions related to education . . . .

MARY ANN LAWLOR

These are the three acts of the transformational drama—each protagonist has played out part of his or her story. The epilogue is predictable: each organization will face the need for transformation again, and with the accelerating rate of change the drama will be repeated more frequently than in the past. In some cases the same leader will take an organization through several transformations as Walter Wriston did with Citibank. In others a new drama will be signaled by a change of the guard.

The only immutable fact seems to be that no company can insulate itself from the effects of this demanding environment. In the period from 1980 to 1985, IBM doubled its sales to become a $50 billion company with profits of more than $6.6 billion—more than any other Fortune 500 company. IBM is not about to become a boiled frog, but David Sanger's commentary in *The New York Times* points to the fact that the water is heating up:

In June of 1985, John Akers, the chairman of IBM, sent shock waves through the stock market when he stated, "Achieving the solid growth we expected for 1985 is now unlikely." The wire service reporters quietly slipped out of the room, breaking into a run once they were out of earshot. A half-hour later even as Akers was hustled into his limousine, IBM stock had started to plummet. By day's end it was down five points, taking the entire market with it. Bad news for IBM was bad news for the American economy: the next day the market dropped another 16 points.

Seldom has there been a more dramatic demonstration of the enormous power of the world's premier computer maker and of its current uncertainties.

Under the leadership of John Akers, IBM is exhibiting two of the characteristics of successful organizations that move through the epilogue of the transformational drama. First, the leaders at the top are sounding the alarm while things are healthy. The water is barely tepid and it will be many years before it comes to a boil. Nevertheless, there is a recognition that the environment will demand a new IBM in the future.

The second and more complex and subtle theme of this chapter is that different organizational cultures, structures, and management processes vary in their capacity for self-renewal. There are elements of the IBM culture that make it a more hospitable environment for self-renewal activities. Thus it is both the individual leaders found in complex organizations as well as the nature of the organization that determine the probability that they will adapt to changing circumstances before a crisis occurs.

Self-renewal is the real hallmark of the transformational leader. Sensing the right time to reinvest, initiating the creative-destructive forces necessary to transform an organization is an ability that few leaders and few institutions nurture.

Thinking about the process of self-renewal reminds one of an allegory in Plato's *The Cave*. Prisoners are chained in an underground cave, and the only view they have of the world is in the shadows reflected on the wall of the cave. The shadows are their reality. One of the prisoners escapes to the upper world and confronts the sun, the symbol of truth, for the first time. Initially, he is so dazzled that he turns away; but gradually he comes to understand the nature of truth and reality. He assumes the responsibility to share what he has learned with the prisoners chained in the cave. He discovers that the prisoners will not acknowledge or welcome the truth—they prefer their familiar illusions and shadows. When he persists in trying to tell the truth they laugh at him. They feel that he is the one who is at a disadvantage in their world because his exposure to the light made him blind in the cave—incapable of playing the game of interpreting the shadows. They vow that if another prisoner is liberated they will kill him. The allegory focuses on a number of concepts related to leadership and change.

First, when people are accustomed to a one point of view, they will reject another even if it makes more sense; and second, leadership that departs from familiar beliefs demands courage to see the truth and even greater courage to tell the truth. Third, unconscious assumptions and unquestioned beliefs are frequently a barrier to real progress. Fourth, leadership should not be confused with popularity. Truth is not always welcome to those who confuse illusion and reality.

This chapter examines two important aspects of self-renewal and courageous behavior in organizations: The organizational conditions in which management processes would tend to foster self-renewing activities and courageous acts, and the characteristics of transformational leaders that appear to give them capacity for self-renewal and courageous action.

It is in this second category that we will reflect on two questions: Why did they do it? And would they do it again? Mary Ann Lawlor answered these questions at the start of the chapter. We will look for patterns among the transformational leaders who are involved as protagonists in this book. In the process of doing so we find a pattern well represented by Lawlor's responses to our queries. "I did it because I was put in the situation." As Mike Blumenthal stated, he didn't realize conditions at Burroughs were as bad as they were, but once he was there he was intellectually committed and would not give up. Would they do it again? As Lee Iacocca repeatedly said, "If I knew how miserable and terrible it was going to be I probably wouldn't have signed up, but who the hell knows that before you sign up for the war?" Somehow transformational leaders tap into that part of human nature that stands up to the challenge, stays with it, keeps a sense of optimism and vision, and mobilizes others to do the same.

THE PARADOX OF RENEWAL: THE SELF-RENEWING ORGANIZATION

Paradox. An idea involving two opposing thoughts or propositions which, however contradictory, are equally necessary to convey a more imposing, illuminating, life-related or provocative insight into truth than either factor can muster in its own right. What the mind seemingly cannot think it must think; what reason is reluctant to express it must express.

Paradox, then, involves contradictory, mutually exclusive elements that are present and operate at the same time. One way to summarize a major theme of this book is that renewal is paradoxical for both organizations and individuals. As Arnold Toynbee in *The Study of History* stated:

Societies gain access to new energies and new directions only after times of growth initiate a process of disintegration wherein the old order comes apart. Withdrawal and return is needed.

Renewal involves creative destruction and disintegration. Fundamental change for people and organizations requires exchange. People have to unlearn and relearn, exchange power and status, and exchange old norms and values for new norms and values. These changes are often frightening and threatening, while at the same time potentially stimulating and provocative of new hope. One must recognize the nature of exchanges; there are costs and benefits which must ultimately be balanced in favor of the benefits side. Transformational leaders are able to empower others to endure the costs of change and be renewed with the new beginnings.

The paradox of renewal is captured in the cliché "no pain, no gain." There is a price paid in the short run to realize the longer term gain. The delicate balance in a transformation hinges on the need to see progress before people's psychological reserves are depleted. This is one of the major challenges facing several of the transformational leaders in this book. At GE, where Jack Welch has been driving the organization hard, there have been five years of cutting costs, rationalizing businesses, divestitures, downsizing, and more than 85,000 people in a workforce of 400,000 have left. Managers and employees are wondering when it will ease, where is the light at the end of the tunnel. One part of the answer from Welch is that if they think it is tough now it will only be tougher in the future—that is the painful side of renewal. On the other side, Welch answers that they are part of what is to become the most exciting, vibrant, challenging organization in the world, and that they will be winners. Getting people to feel this is one of the major leadership challenges facing GE in 1986.The acquisition of RCA with its 100,000 employees adds to the complexity.

Welch argues that there are two types of organizational issues. They are the hard issues: budget, manufacturing, marketing, distribution, head count; and the soft issues: values, culture, vision, leadership style, innovation. There are also two types of leadership: weak and strong. He believes that for several decades following World War II we were soft on both hard and soft issues. Since the early 1980s corporate leaders have been getting stronger on the hard issues. They have rationalized businesses, downsized their employee populations, and reduced the levels of management. GE, Welch claims, has been in the forefront here. These activities tend to take the fun out of the organization and they are not enough to renew the organization. The new frontier will be to provide strong leadership on the soft issues. Failure to do so leaves the organization drained, lacking the will to renew itself, and unable to effectively adapt to a changing environment.

At the core of self-renewing organizations is an implicit belief in the thesis that Joseph Schumpeter articulated in his book *The Theory of Economic Dynamics*. He postulated that the dynamic disequilibrium brought on by the innovating entrepreneur, rather than equilibrium and optimization, is the norm of a healthy economy and the central reality for economic theory and economic practice.

The entrepreneurial organization is one that values change as healthy. In this environment, entrepreneurial behavior seeks change, responds to it, exploits it as an opportunity, and is rewarded.

What Are the Characteristics of Self-Renewing Organizations?

In self-renewing organizations control is primarily self-control. There's less constraint, the emphasis is on learning with as few rules as possible. Errors are embraced. People admit mistakes, examine the causes, and learn from them. There's an emphasis on risk taking and innovation, and responsibility is realistically accepted and shared. Goals are set and constantly revised. Decision-making processes value intuition and creativity, and there is less emphasis on purely analytic approaches. People perceive power as a non-zero sum game; there is expansion in sharing. Uncertainty is confronted, not denied. Interpersonal relationships are open and there are high levels of trust.

Self-renewing organizations embrace paradox. They possess many attributes that are simultaneously contradictory, even mutually exclusive. It is these paradoxical attributes which provide the capacity for successfully surviving multiple unpredictable blows from the environment.

Kim Cameron identified a set of paradoxical attributes of organic organizations which we have further developed below.

1. *Loose–Tight Couplings.* To enhance creativity and innovation, transformational leaders need to give people throughout the organization power to initiate and sustain efforts based on the faith of an idea. Loose coupling fosters wide search and a creative perspective, and allows individual units a fair degree of latitude. This autonomy must be coupled with sustained financial support and with tight coupling for quick execution of the innovation. This is the antithesis of the mechanistic system that drives many organizations, which requires multilevel approval for new projects that must show quick returns. At GE one response to the loose–tight coupling paradox has been the creation of internal boards to govern a number of the businesses. They provide both latitude and control—loose–tight coupling.

2. *High Specialization and Generalization of Roles.* Innovation depends on professionals with a depth of expertise in their technical specialties. This frequently means they have been narrowly trained. At the same time they need to be flexible, broad-minded, and capable of working well with other pro-

fessionals. They must blend the talents of technical experts and business leaders. Mechanistic systems produce specialists and generalists, but rarely do they nurture these qualities in the same person.

3. *Continuity–Discontinuity of Leadership.* New leadership brings a fresh perspective to organizational problems, while old leadership enhances organizational stability and institutional memory. Both are needed. Change efforts require the sustained attention of a fairly stable group of highly committed leaders. Mechanistic organizations tend to miss this point and transfer managers in and out of units without regard to their commitment to a change mission.

4. *Productive Conflict.* Conflict is a dual edged sword. Unbridled it can bring out the worst in human nature resulting in violence and destruction. Properly channeled it is the source of energy for challenging people and renewing organizations. Organizations need both processes that encourage contention and processes that foster consensus. IBM has both elements. Its homogeneous culture provides the major support for consensus while its institutionalized contention system provides the major support for productive conflict.

5. *Expanded and Restricted Search for Information.* Organizations need to expand their ability to collect relevant information to enhance their problem-solving capacity. At the same time they must find ways to buffer decision-makers from information overload. Analytic frameworks enable decision-makers to reduce information and eliminate irrelevant data.

6. *The Paradox of Participation.* Democratic organizations are designed for long-term survival, not short-term gains. During the period of crisis Iacocca centralized power so that decisions could be made rapidly. However, Chrysler's ability to ensure its future survival depends on cooperation through involvement of its varied constituencies. Thus the current decentralization of power is meant to prepare the company for the

next decade, not the next year. Eliot Jaques makes the following point:

Participation has to do with the right to take part in the control of change by taking part in formulating and agreeing on new policies or modifications of existing ones. It is the control of the setting, the rules and the limits in which social relationships will be carried on [within which the social structure will function] that is so very important. It is important not so much for any immediate effect upon outcome or productivity; there is little evidence to support the notion that the introduction of opportunities to participate will act as a form of incentive system. Opportunity for participation is an essential element for the survival of democratic industrial society itself.

The self-renewing organization can planfully initiate the creative/destructive forces of change. This means taking on the paradox of the need for continuity and discontinuity in people. As we deal with the rapid transformation of the economy into a more competitive arena, the organization must develop a routine for waking up the organization, focusing it on a vision, institutionalizing the change, and remaining alert to the next call for transformation. We have identified some of the characteristics organizations need to permit this ongoing self-renewal to take place. The other condition is the quality of the people not only at the top but through the organization—the transformational leaders.

LEADERS WHO CAN INITIATE SELF-RENEWAL

An interesting question to ponder is the capacity of any individual to lead an organization through multiple transformations. It may be that the way in which this epilogue is played out in most organizations is by changing the leader when an era comes to an end and quantum change is required. For example,

Reginald Jones led General Electric for a decade. Perhaps his most significant leadership act was the recognition that General Electric's future success demanded a leader with qualities and skills very different from his own. At General Motors, the transformation did not begin until Roger Smith took the helm. At Citibank, Walter Wriston was certainly a transformational leader, one who not only made Citibank the largest and most respected banking institution in the United States, but who revolutionized the whole field of banking. At Chase Manhattan, Fred Hammer successfully took consumer banking, woke it up, provided a vision of a new set of market services, and started the institutionalization process. His successor won't be able to simply manage the processes that Hammer put in place. He must meet the new challenges that competitors like Citibank, Sears, and others are posing to Chase. Jeff Campbell at Burger King is in the midst of Act III. When the next wave of competitive pressure confronts the company he will have to decide whether he is excited by the prospect of leading another transformation at Burger King.

As we look at Whirlpool, Jack Sparks is preparing the organization for his retirement and will turn over the reins to the next leader who will have to face the challenge of keeping Whirlpool world competitive in the appliance business. Ed Thompson is still working through Act III at Schneider Transport. This is also true of Mike Blumenthal who in many ways is still working on Act II, attempting to work out a strategy, a vision for the long-term future of Burroughs. His competitor, Jim Renier, has moved on to a new challenge: the integration of Honeywell control and information businesses. Renier turned over the task of gaining commitment and institutionalizing the vision he forged for the information business to Bill Wray. Finally, Mary Ann Lawlor has made it through Act III and is making plans to lead Drake through another transformation. This effort will differ from the first because she is trying to alert the organization to a new vision in the absence of a crisis.

CHARACTERISTICS OF TRANSFORMATIONAL LEADERS

In this final section we stand back and share with you our observations of these transformational leaders. We feel that they share a number of common characteristics that differentiate them from transactional managers. These characteristics are:

1. *They Identify Themselves as Change Agents.* These leaders clearly identified themselves as change agents. Their professional and personal image was to make a difference and transform the organization that they had assumed responsibility for. None of the protagonists that we studied is a "professional turnaround artist"—someone who comes in, takes a mess, cleans it up, and leaves. By design or chance, each became responsible for leading an organization through a transformation. And they are able to articulate that they did assume the role of change agents, which is an interesting self-concept. It is not that of an entrepreneur trying to make a mark on the world by building a better mousetrap, and therefore building an organization to build the mousetrap. This is a group of people who have both the mousetrap (although not necessarily the mousetrap that customers are beating down the doors for) and the organization. Like athletic coaches who take over troubled teams with the goal of turning them into national champions, they must find a way to inspire the team while they rebuild the franchise. These are professional managers who have had to grow into transformational leaders.

2. *They Are Courageous Individuals.* Courage is not stupidity. These are prudent risk takers, individuals who take a stand. Don MacKinnon consistently fought for more autonomy for CIBA-GEIGY's U.S. operation. He has absorbed much of the resistance and concern from his own division presidents and corporate headquarters in Bern. The division presidents gripe that they had too much interference at the middle man-

agement level. On the other hand, the Swiss complain that it's important for them to have the proper knowledge to coordinate the businesses world-wide. MacKinnon said:

> [The Swiss] want to be kept informed on the important things. If we shift our advertising to promotion in pharmaceuticals without telling them they would have ten fits. Yet under our principles of organization, as long as we deliver our objectives which largely concern the bottom line, they don't have any say . . . .

Even though Don MacKinnon has been the outspoken, courageous advocate of this autonomy he's also a pragmatist. He tempers his position in the following way:

> But it doesn't work that way. So it's give and take. I think there's still too much interference but I'm a rather independent person. My boss thinks it's okay but the division presidents will say too much interference . . . . The Swiss monitor the monthly reporting on profits. They see what happens and they raise questions. Again, in theory they're not supposed to do that, but there's no way you can stop a parent company from raising questions. Our people have to take time out to answer what they think are basically stupid questions coming from overseas because of a lack of knowledge of our markets. I fight a constant battle with visitors who come over and say, "Look I want to investigate this and I want to understand this." I think that's a waste of time and against the principles of organization, which it is. But you'll never stop it . . . .

What does it mean to be courageous? In Harvey Hornstein's terms it means being able to take a stand, being able to take risks, being able to stand against the status quo in the larger interest of the organization.

There is both an intellectual and an emotional component to courageous behavior. Intellectually, one must get a perspective, being able to confront reality even if it is painful. Emotionally, one must be able to then reveal the truth to others who may not want to hear it. Social psychology and organization theory tell us that this is not an easy challenge. The pressures for conformity are great. Irving Janis has documented the power of group think as it influenced John F. Kennedy's Bay of Pigs fiasco and the work of many top management teams. Thus to be courageous means being willing to risk the ridicule and the social pressures of being a deviant. What makes our protagonists able to do this? These people had healthy egos—they knew who they were and did not need constant reinforcement to shore them up in difficult situations.

3. *They Believe in People.* These transformational leaders are not dictators. They are powerful yet sensitive of other people, and ultimately they work toward the empowerment of others.

One of the most articulate about the whole notion of empowerment is John Harvey-Jones. He talked about how his views on leadership developed:

> I suppose my belief in managing through motivating people is what we're talking about rather than through organizational controls. It derived from my naval service experience, particularly my submarining, which taught me that ordinary people have a lot more to offer than they are usually either allowed or encouraged to offer. This belief was honed by my experience as an industrial engineer. I spent my first two years in the company with a stopwatch in my hand, which teaches you a hell of a lot about how little you get out of people and how much they can do.

> I've always been interested in social science concepts and I suppose the next formative experience really was when I was given quite a different task from anything I had been given before. Our largest manufacturing site had a series of major industrial relations problems. I tried every sort of solution, every sort of approach . . . . My diagnosis of the problem, which I think was right, was that we're not a team. We're not working toward a common goal and we've gotten the shop to the point where they are working against us, They are really taking advantage of the lack of cohesiveness of management to seize the initiative . . . .

I was the deputy chairman responsible for the site. The site was a cooperative and I had no direct line control over these managers although I was senior official responsible for these managers. I suppose that it was that experience that taught me about everything. Industrial success is a matter of getting a commitment of people and the art is to get them involved and then you can sort of ratchet people up by continuously setting them or getting them to set themselves aims which are a little more achievable to them. Then every time they achieve, you can ratchet them a bit further and after a little while you can get a team which really believes it's a leading team . . . that corresponds very much to my service experience where I had learned over many years that there are really no bad troops, only bad officers.

Throughout this book we have framed the people issues in our own concepts and terms. These leaders were able to easily relate to the framework we used, although many of them used different terms and different concepts. But they all had a keen understanding and set of principles for dealing with motivation, emotion, pain, trust, and loyalty. Every one of them could articulate a set of principles that guided their actions as transformational leaders. In every case they dealt with the emotional side through use of humor, symbolism, rewards, and punishment. Ultimately each was a cheerleader, coach, counselor, and leader attempting to meld the team. Even those with the strongest and most visible power were clearly working toward empowerment of the organization. One of the most central concepts to Jack Welch's themes at General Electric is ownership of your business coupled with the pushback management philosophy. This means that people further down in General Electric are to be empowered to make things happen. They are the ones who need to make the decisions and carry them out, but stand up for them as well.

4. *They Are Value-Driven.* Each one of our transformational leaders was able to articulate a set of core values and exhibited behavior that was quite congruent with their value positions.

Harvey-Jones has thought long and hard about values in organizations and his philosophy about being value driven is captured in the following comments:

> Culture is about values and the values of the company congruent to those of the individual or vice versa . . . . My guys at every level know that I would like them to be a team and I believe that. If I believe that, there's a sporting chance that they may think they're lucky to have me leading them. The difficult part of this are the things you give. You give them and you may get them back—if you trust them, they'll trust you back . . . there are things you have to project and its terribly important that they are projected in the way that the company works, because people are very quick to see the difference between the words and the actions . . . .

He continued in his discussion to reflect on how to communicate, share and implement his cultural values.

> First the ten commandments, I'm not too happy about them. We've written the ten commandments at different times and I know the adjectives I want to apply to the company. I want the company to be caring, open, and a world leader but I don't think I'm going to achieve that by just saying it. I don't want you to hear in every speech that we're a caring, innovative, world leading company. But for God's sake don't do something which shows that you're not a caring company. Do things that show you can innovate. If there's one word that every one of us really tries to push through, it's caring. One thing that I really go bananas about is if I find cases where we had done something and didn't care enough . . . . Caring for everybody, customers included. If I get letters about people that have been treated in an uncaring way that's when I really go bananas. I answer every letter myself and I answer the day I get them and if I can't answer on the spot I say I'm deeply upset that you think that we've done something wrong and I'll contact Mr. X and get back to you. Or on occasion I'm overseas but that just gets passed on. The day I get back though, no matter how long it takes I dictate a letter that explains I was overseas and I'm sorry I couldn't get to you earlier. I see the mistakes that were made in your case . . . . Because the

company has got to be responsive and if you don't respond to
people you're never going to make it. The company can only
operate by the consent and the support not only of the people in
the company but all the communities in which we operate. You
try opening a chemical works in Bhopal next year or the year
after or the year after. I need the trust of the communities in
which I operate and that's strict business, that's not Sermon on
the Mount stuff . . . .

Jim Renier sums up the importance of values and being value
driven as follows:

A leader is more than a technician to me. If there's a need to
separate the two then I say leave the definition of leader to the
person who knows how to deal with the value system of the
organization and paint a picture of where we're going. The managers can take what the leader has done for a while as long as the
value system stays constant and the vision is valid. But if the
value system changes or the vision is no longer valid, the manager, the technical managers will take you right into oblivion.

5. *They Are Life Long Learners.* All of our transformational
leaders were able to talk about mistakes they had made. But as
with Warren Bennis's leaders, they did not view these as failures but as learning experiences. As a group, our protagonists
show an amazing appetite for continuous self-learning and development. Whether it be Mike Blumenthal learning the computer business after serving as Secretary of the Treasury, Ed
Thompson learning the trucking business after he left Procter &
Gamble, or Mary Ann Lawlor on a more personal note who,
after her successful career, added another career. She describes
it:

Now I've transformed myself, I've graduated from law school,
and I work in a law firm two days a week. I had to deal with the
feeling that I didn't know how to do anything right; it's sort of
funny. It turned out to be an interesting and liberating experi-

ence. Now I find that I'm interested in the Drake Business School again from a new perspective. I want to see what can be done in expanding into a new market. It's like I had to go out on a sabbatical.

There are other examples of self-transformation and self-renewal as we recall Jack Sparks's involvement with the Aspen Institute, which had a profound impact on his thinking. He came to a point in his career where standing back thinking about integrating and broadening perspectives provided an extremely useful experience that has influenced the way he has broadened the role of CEO at Whirlpool.

John Harvey-Jones talks about learning from mistakes, both personally and as an organization:

We did something a year ago which I wasn't too happy about but we did it. And I've been around to all sorts of places, been asked if there was a better way of dealing with it. I wish to God we hadn't done it. No question about it, it was a mistake. But oh well, you know, let's take three deep breaths and start again. If we can't learn from mistakes there's no hope for us . . . .

Bob Stempel and Lloyd Reuss at General Motors are going through a learning process. Bob Stempel talks about his learning in the following terms:

Sometimes it's like a cold shower but after you are in it for a while, it gets warmer. One realization is that when you really use the team process, you buy a group of people who are going to make it run, to reach that consensus decision and reach the idea that this is the way we want to do it. It might not be my first choice but I'm far better off to accept the fact that the team bought into it, took responsibility for it, and will go ahead and execute it. I think the lesson for me has been that it's a very powerful process and can be a very effective one in developing a strong organization.

Lloyd Reuss had a different lesson to learn. He said:

> One of the early realizations was that at Buick I managed about
> 17,000 people and you cannot use the same approach with
> 150,000 people. You still have to work with your strengths and
> weaknesses but you have to really take a look at how strengths
> and weaknesses apply to an organization that's ten times the size.
> It didn't take very long to realize that you're going to have to
> make some very significant changes in your style, to get the
> leverage you need with people in an organization that size. You
> look for ways to do that . . . but you don't change the basic
> philosophy. You change the way that you execute that philoso-
> phy. And that has been a growing process and I'm not through it
> yet. And looking back at one of the reasons why General Motors
> has traditionally been detail oriented is in fact because a lot of
> people did not change their management style as they went from
> a group of 10 people to 100,000 people and that's probably the
> biggest lesson I've learned. It's a continuing process because it
> happens deliberately. It's very easy every day to get up and do
> the same type of thing so you have to deliberately change the
> approach to get the same results . . . .

Perhaps one of the most intriguing parts of our protagonists is
their continuous commitment to learning. Their heads have not
become hard-wired. It would be interesting to study each in
more depth and to get a clearer view of what parts of their
personality and characters were deeply set in place early on
and what parts have been modified over time. Undoubtedly
their personalities are not that malleable. However, their attitudes, behaviors, approaches to managing and leading have
been very adaptable. They do spend time being self-reflective,
and many of them have made some rather dramatic shifts in
their style and approaches to management. Perhaps this is the
basic condition necessary for their own self-renewal that makes
them able to play a self-renewal leadership role.

We have defined transformational leaders as people who are
always in the business of renewal, the task never done. And
they consistently articulate this aspect of their leadership role.
They have no sense of being able to finish something before

they retire or pass the baton on to a successor, since they know that the dynamic forces in the marketplace will soon force changes in the organizations they lead.

Through this ability for self-analysis and personal commitment comes the energy for continual change. Jeff Campbell described the process:

> Okay, we're going to light the fire again. We've got to keep coming up with something to get their attention. And we have to continue to articulate often and in symbolic ways what the values are and what the goals are. Keep them simple, easy to articulate. But you also have to be willing to reach people emotionally and then give them the freedom to do what needs to be done.

6. *They Have the Ability to Deal with Complexity, Ambiguity, and Uncertainty.* Each of our transformational leaders was able to cope with and frame problems in a complex, changing world.

All of these protagonists were not only capable of dealing with the cultural and political side of the organization, but they were very sophisticated in dealing with the technical side. They don't argue for seat of the pants management, they don't argue for a nonconceptual approach to running the business. They are entranced by the world of ideas. Renier, Hammer, Welch, and Blumenthal all have Ph.D.s. Campbell recently completed a master's degree in history because "it was something that I got interested in after I got out of school." Jack Sparks, who claims little formal education, attributes much of his success in business to his own self-education, reading everything he could to enhance his Aspen Institute experience. All of them believe the disciplined thinking that went with formal education helped them to deal with complex problems that needed to be structured. These are individuals who build theory, articulate principles, examine assumptions. And this fits with the requirements of an increasingly complex world that demands complex problem-solving ability on the part of leaders. It is this balance of the emotional and the cognitive that is striking when we examine our transformational leaders.

7. *They Are Visionaries.* Our transformational leaders were able to dream, able to translate those dreams and images so that other people could share them. Mary Ann Lawlor describes her thought processes while she's in the midst of difficult problems as follows:

> When we're in any kind of problems, I always meditate and then I write and then I think some more and in the end I have a feeling in my gut and I trust it. I trust my instincts, my intuition. And eventually I just know what I have to do. I think of the organization as a kind of mystical body—you know the religious concept where the actions of each member of the body affect every other member. You need the ability to empathize if you want to lead . . . you need the ability to understand how your actions are going to affect others.

THE REMAINING CHALLENGES

As we stated in the beginning of the book, the transformational leaders we have been looking at "are in the race right now." We don't know who will win and we don't know who will lose, but we believe these people have a very good chance of making it. They are all keenly aware that the race is not over. As this book is completed the runners are passing various milestones with some challenges already met and some surprises waiting for them.

We shall take our leave by saluting their willingness to try to meet the revitalization challenges that mature companies and mature economies face. We would also like to extend an invitation to readers to join them in this race. The United States and many Western European companies have yet to work their way through Act I—they continue to bury their heads in the sand because they are not willing to face the truth. The truth is that there is no place to hide—individuals cannot insulate themselves from the consequences of continuing economic decline and at the same time safeguard their children's economic future. We have not yet come to grips with the reality: what has been can no longer be. We must deal with the endings so we can move on and create a vision consistent with the current reality—better if only because it is possible—and mobilize commitment to it.

Each of us must approach this issue on three levels: our personal dreams and aspirations, the organizations we work in and the society we live in.

At a personal level we must be willing to make the changes in our lifestyles that will enable the next generation to experience the joy of accomplishment that many of us have known. We need to develop the transformational leadership potential in ourselves and others since organizational and individual renewal are inextricably intertwined.

At an organizational level, we need to prepare our institutions to engage in the struggle for transformation. We must accept the challenge regardless of where we sit in the organization. Pockets of excellence tend to spread if the people who create them have the will to persevere. The reward comes from the sense of doing the right things rather than being rewarded for the things we do.

History contains powerful lessons about the fate of societies that lose their will to excel. Our founding fathers understood the lesson and they created a society able to deal with the aspirations of all people: one sharing and sacrifice as well as ambition. Our challenge is to transform ourselves and our institutions to meet the challenge of the new reality without losing the things that we value the most. We hope you will join our protagonists in this quest.

NOTES

Notes to Preface

PAGE	NOTE
xi	White, Theodore. *The New York Times Magazine*, July 28, 1985.
xii	Burns, James MacGregor. *Leadership*. New York: Harper & Row, 1978.
xii	Drucker, Peter. *Innovation and Entrepreneurship*. New York: Harper & Row, 1985.
xiii	Zaleznik, Abraham. "Managers and Leaders: Are They Different?" *Harvard Business Review*, Vol. 15, No. 5 (1977), pp. 67–80.
xiv	Levinson, Harry and Rosenthal, Stuart. *CEO*. New York: Basic Books, 1984.
xiv	Bass, Bernard. *Leadership and Performance Beyond Expectations*. New York: Free Press, 1985.
xiv	Bennis, Warren and Nanus, Burt. *Leaders*. New York: Harper & Row, 1985.
xiv	Maccoby, Michael. *The Leaders*. New York: Ballantine Books, 1981.
xiv	Kanter, Rosabeth. *The Change Masters*. New York: Simon and Schuster, 1983.

Notes to Chapter 1

PAGE	NOTE
4	The concept of transforming leadership was developed by James MacGregor Burns in his Pulitzer Prize winning book, *Leadership*. Burns's study focused primarily on political and religious leaders. His concepts provided the springboard for our thinking on organizational transformations. Burns, James MacGregor. *Leadership*. New York: Harper & Row, 1978.
9	"Burroughs," *The Detroit News*. August 11, 1985.

25   "General Electric," *Wall Street Journal.* July 12, 1981, p. 45.

28   The original framework for the transformational dynamic was developed with David Ulrich. Tichy, Noel and Ulrich, David. "The Leadership Challenge—A Call for the Transformational Leader." *Sloan Management Review,* Fall 1984.

31   William Bridges developed one of the most insightful analyses of the emotional dynamic that accompanies painful life transitions: the death of a loved one, divorce, being fired, and so on. We found this process described the emotion and personal trauma that individuals felt in organizations during periods of major revitalization.
Bridges, William. *Transitions: Making Sense of Life's Changes.* Reading, MA: Addison-Wesley, 1980.

Notes to Chapter 2

PAGE   NOTE

37   Schein, Edgar. *Organizational Culture and Leadership.* San Francisco: Jossey-Bass, 1985.

38   Lester Thurow's analysis of the causes of and cures for the United States' loss of economic competitiveness is convincing and painful. He argues that the trend in the United States toward a declining standard of living can only be reversed by equality of sacrifice in society.
Thurow, Lester. *The Zero Sum Solution.* New York: Simon and Schuster, 1985.

38   Robert Heilbroner presents a more troubling analysis of the challenges facing the industrial world: ". . . the long era of industrial expansion is now entering its final stages and we must anticipate the commencement of a new era of stationary total output and if population growth continues or an equitable sharing among nations has not yet been attained, declining output per head in the advanced nations . . . leading to convulsive change. . . .
Heilbroner, Robert. *An Inquiry into the Human Condition.* New York: Norton, 1973.

39   An extensive research inquiry into the effects of the recent reductions in force and subsequent organizational restructuring is being conducted at the Management Institute, Columbia University Graduate School of Business. Those interested in more detailed analyses of these issues can read:
Devanna, Mary Anne and Warren, E. Kirby. "Managing the Middle." *Human Resource Management,* Vol. 23, Nos. 1/2 (Spring/Summer 1983).
Ginzberg, Eli. *Resizing for Organizational Effectiveness: A Report of a Workshop.* Career Center Research Report, Columbia University Graduate School of Business, 1985.

41   For an analysis of the specific challenges facing U.S. manufacturers, see Hayes, Robert and Wheelwright, Steven. *Restoring Our Competitive Edge,* New York: Wiley, 1984.

42   "Japan's Service Sector." *The Los Angeles Times,* June 2, 1985.

43   Thurow, *Zero Sum.*

50   Readers who are interested in a more complete description can refer to Tichy, Noel. *Managing Strategic Change.* New York: Wiley, 1983.

Notes to Chapter 3

PAGE   NOTE

59   Paine, Thomas. *Common Sense and Other Political Writings.* Edited by Nelson F. Adkins. Indianapolis, IN: Bobbs-Merrill, 1976.

60   Toynbee, Arnold. *A Study of History.* London: Oxford University Press, 1972.

63   Bridges, William. *Transitions: Making Sense of Life's Changes.* Reading, MA: Addison-Wesley, 1980.

72   Tichy, Noel and Ulrich, David. "The Leadership Challenge: A Call for the Transformational Leader," *Sloan Management Review,* Fall 1984.

74   Tichy, Noel. *Managing Strategic Change.* New York: Wiley, 1983.

76   Hayes, Robert and Wheelwright, Steven. *Restoring Our Competitive Edge.* New York: Wiley, 1984.

77   Thurow, Lester. *The Zero Sum Solution.* New York: Simon and Schuster, 1985.

79   Schein, Edgar. *Organizational Culture and Leadership.* San Francisco: Jossey-Bass, 1985.

81   Rensis Likert and his colleagues at the Institute for Social Research at the University of Michigan present a systematic analysis of organizational climate and its relationship to change in the workplace.
         Likert, Rensis. *The Human Organization.* New York: McGraw-Hill, 1967.

85   Kaplan, Abraham. *The Conduct of Inquiry.* San Francisco: Chandler, 1964.

Notes to Chapter 4

PAGE   NOTE

91   Iacocca, Lee. *Iacocca.* New York: Harper & Row, 1985.

93   "Roosevelt was a Grand Improviser who frankly prided himself

on his ability to move one foot at a time, using every jot and tittle of his day to day power."
Burns, James MacGregor. *Leadership*. New York: Harper & Row, 1978, p. 394.

95   Schon, Donald. *Beyond the Stable State*. New York: Random House, 1971.

97   Tichy, Noel. *Managing Strategic Change*. New York: Wiley, 1983.

97   Iacocca, *Iacocca*.

100   A good analysis of the political dynamics of strategic decision making is the study of resource allocation done by Joseph Bower. Bower, Joseph. *Managing the Resource Allocation Process*. Boston: Harvard Business School, 1970.

103   Stewart Friedman studied over 230 companies to determine the relationship between succession practices and organizational performance. His research underscores the importance of approaching succession as a political issue.
Friedman, Stewart. *Leadership Succession Systems and Corporate Performance*, Career Center Research Report, Columbia University Graduate School of Business, New York, 1985.

106   Prokesh, Steven E. "Executive Pay: Who Made the Most." *BusinessWeek*, May 6, 1985, p. 78.

108   Galbraith, Jay. *Designing Complex Organizations*. Reading, MA: Addison-Wesley, 1973.

109   Multinational organizations that use movement of key managers as a design strategy for creating organizational networks were the focus of a study conducted by Galbraith and Edstrom.
Galbraith, Jay and Edstrom, A. "International Transfer of Managers: Some Important Policy Considerations." *The Columbia Journal of World Business*, Vol. 11, No. 2 (Summer 1976), pp. 100–113.

113   Iacocca, *Iacocca*.

114   Taylor, F. W. *The Principles of Scientific Management*. New York: Harper, 1923.

114   Blanchard, K. H. and Johnson, S. *The One Minute Manager*. New York: Berkeley, 1982.

114   Peters, Thomas and Waterman, Robert. *In Search of Excellence*. New York: Harper & Row, 1982.

115   Ouchi, William. *Theory Z*. Reading, MA: Addison-Wesley, 1981.

117   Iacocca, *Iacocca*.

Notes to Chapter 5

PAGE   NOTE

123   Levinson, H. and Rosenthal, S. *CEO: Corporate Leadership in Action.* New York: Basic Books, 1984.

124   Bass, Bernard. *Leadership and Performance Beyond Expectations.* New York: Free Press, 1985.

132   Schein discusses the role that culture plays in helping individuals and groups cope with problems.
          Schein, Edgar. *Organizational Culture and Leadership.* San Francisco: Jossey-Bass, 1985.

139   Levinson and Rosenthal, *CEO.*

Notes to Chapter 6

PAGE   NOTE

157   Flax, Steven. "The Toughest Bosses in America." *Fortune,* August 6, 1984, pp. 18–23.

163   McGill, Andrew and Tichy, Noel. "Transformational Change at Chase." University of Michigan Working Paper, 1985.

167   Iacocca, Lee. *Iacocca.* New York: Harper & Row, 1985.

172   Tichy, Noel, Dotlich, David, and Lake, Dale. "Revitalization: The Honeywell Information System Story." *Journal of Business Strategy,* Winter 1986.

180   Albert, Steven S. in J. Kimberly and Robert Quinn. *Managing Organizational Transitions.* San Francisco: Jossey-Bass, 1984.

Notes to Chapter 7

PAGE   NOTE

186   Burns, James MacGregor. *Leadership.* New York: Harper & Row, 1978, p. 394.

188   Tichy, Noel. "Networks in Organizations," in Paul Nystrom and William Starbuck (eds.), *Handbook of Organizational Design,* Vol. 2. London: Oxford University Press, 1981.

193   Durkheim, Emile. *Suicide.* Glencoe, IL: Free Press, 1951.

193   Iacocca, Lee. *Iacocca.* New York: Harper & Row, 1985.

195   Mintzberg, Henry. *The Nature of Managerial Work.* New York: Harper & Row, 1973.

195   Kotter, John. *The General Managers.* New York: Free Press, 1982.

196   Caro, R. A. *The Power Broker: Robert Moses and the Fall of New York.* New York: Knopf, 1974.

198   Tichy, "Networks."

212   Galbraith, Jay and Edstrom, A. "International transfer of managers: Some important policy considerations." *The Columbia Journal of World Business,* Vol. 11, No. 2, Summer 1976, pp. 100–113.

Notes to Chapter 8

PAGE   NOTE

215   Thurow, Lester. *The Zero-Sum Solution.* New York: Simon and Schuster, 1985.

216   Welch, John. "Competitiveness from Within—Beyond Incrementalism." Presented as the Hatfield Lecture, Cornell University, April 26, 1984.

216   Sanger, David. "The Changing Image of IBM." *The New York Times Magazine,* July 7, 1985, p. 12.

217   Drucker, Peter. *Concept of the Corporation.* New York: John Day, 1946.

217   Reich, Cary. "The Innovator: The Creative Mind of GM Chairman Roger Smith." *The New York Times Magazine,* April 26, 1985, p. 28.

218   March, James and Simon, Herbert. *Organizations.* New York: Wiley, 1958.

219   Peters, Thomas and Waterman, Robert. *In Search of Excellence.* New York: Harper & Row, 1982.

219   Merton, Robert. *Social Theory and Social Structure.* rev. ed, Glencoe, IL: Free Press, 1957.

229   Johnson, Bert and Lank, Alden. "Volvo: A Report on the Workshop on Production Technology and Quality of Working Life." *Human Resource Management,* Vol. 24, No. 4, Winter 1985.

229   Tichy, Noel. "Organizational Innovations in Sweden." *The Columbia Journal of World Business,* Summer 1974.

238   A more detailed discussion of these issues is found in work by Richard Walton, "From Control to Commitment: Transforming Work Force Management in the United States." Paper prepared for the 75th Anniversary Colloquium on Technology and Productivity, Harvard Business School, March 27–29, 1984.

Notes to Chapter 9

PAGE   NOTE

242   Ouchi, William. *Theory Z.* Reading, MA: Addison-Wesley, 1981.

245   Sobel, Robert. *IBM: Colossus in Transition.* New York: Times, 1981.

245   Harris, Stanley. "Hewlett-Packard: Shaping the Corporate Culture," in Charles Fombrun, Tichy, Noel and Devanna, Mary

Anne. *Strategic Human Resource Management*. New York: Wiley, 1984.

247   Watson, Thomas. *A Business and Its Beliefs: The Ideas that Helped Build IBM*. New York: McGraw-Hill, 1963.

248   Iacocca, Lee. *Iacocca*. New York: Harper & Row, 1985.

252   Iacocca, *Iacocca*.

253   Lawler, E., "Strategies Rewards," in Fombrun, C, Tichy, N., and Devanna, M. A. *Strategic Human Resources Management*. New York: Wiley, 1984.

255   Burns, J. McG, *Leadership*

258   Readers interested in a detailed analysis of the role that human resource management plays in both the formulation and implementation of organizational change agendas are referred to *Strategic Human Resource Management*. This book looks at the environment organizations are facing and discusses selection, appraisal, reward and development as managerial processes that can enhance organizational effectiveness. Fombrun, Charles, Tichy, Noel, and Devanna, Mary Anne. *Strategic Human Resource Management*. New York: Wiley, 1984.

Notes to Chapter 10

PAGE   NOTE

264   Sanger, David. "The Changing Image of IBM." *The New York Times Magazine*, July 7, 1985.

267   Toynbee, Arnold. *A Study of History*. London: Oxford University Press, 1972.

268   Schumpeter, Joseph. *Capitalism, Socialism and Democracy*. New York: Harper Torchbooks, 1950.

269   Cameron, Kim. "Organizational Paradoxes." University of Michigan Graduate School of Business Working Paper Series, 1985.

270   Peters, Thomas and Waterman, Robert. *In Search of Excellence*. New York: Harper & Row, 1982.

271   Jaques, Eliot. *A General Theory of Bureaucracy*. New York: Wiley, 1976.

274   Hornstein, Harvey. *Managerial Courage*. New York: Wiley, 1986.

278   Bennis, Warren and Nanus, Burt. *Leaders*. New York: Harper & Row, 1985.

279   Thurow, Lester. *The Zero Sum Solution*. New York: Simon and Schuster, 1985.

REFERENCES

Bass, Bernard. *Leadership and Performance Beyond Expectations*. New York: Free Press, 1985.

Bass, Bernard. In *Stodgill's Handbook of Leadership: A Survey of Theory and Research*. Revised and expanded edition, New York: Free Press, 1981.

Bennis, Warren, and Nanus, Burt. *Leaders*. New York: Harper & Row, 1985.

Blanchard, Kenneth, and Johnson, S. *The One-Minute Manager*. New York: William Morrow, 1982.

Bradford, D. L. and Cohen, A. R., *Managing Excellence*. New York: Wiley, 1984.

Bridges, William. *Transitions: Making Sense of Life's Changes*. Reading, MA: Addison-Wesley, 1980.

Burns, James MacGregor. *Leadership*. New York: Harper & Row, 1978.

Burns, T., and Stalker, G. M. *The Management of Innovation*. Chicago: Quadrangle Books, 1961.

Caro, R. A. *The Power Broker: Robert Moses and the Fall of New York*. New York: Knopf, 1974.

Devanna, Mary Anne, and Warren, E. Kirby. "Managing the Middle." *Human Resource Management*, Vol. 23, Nos. 1/2, Spring/Summer 1983.

Devanna, Mary Anne, Fombrun, Charles J., and Tichy, Noel M. "A Framework for Human Resource Management," in C. Fombrun, N. Tichy, and M. A. Devanna, *Strategic Human Resource Management*. New York: Wiley, 1984.

Dickson, J. W. "Top Managers' Beliefs and Rationales for Participation." *Human Relations*, 1982, 35.

Dow, T. "The Theory of Charisma." *Sociological Quarterly*, 1969, 10.

Drucker, Peter. *Innovation and Entrepreneurship*. New York: Harper & Row, 1985.

Drucker, Peter. *The Practice of Management*. New York: Harper, 1954.

Drucker, Peter. *Concept of the Corporation.* New York: John Day, 1946.

Etzioni, Amitai. *A Comparative Analysis of Complex Organizations.* Glencoe, IL: Free Press, 1961.

Fombrun, Charles, Tichy, Noel, and Devanna, Mary Anne. *Strategic Human Resource Management,* New York: Wiley, 1984.

Friedman, Stewart. *Leadership Succession Systems and Corporate Performance.* Career Center Research Report, Columbia University Graduate School of Business, 1985.

Galbraith, Jay. *Designing Complex Organizations.* Reading, MA: Addison-Wesley, 1973.

Galbraith, Jay, and Edstrom, Anders. "International Transfer of Managers: Some Important Policy Considerations." *The Columbia Journal of World Business,* Vol. XI, No. 2, Summer 1976.

Ginzberg, Eli. *Resizing for Organizational Effectiveness: A Report of a Workshop.* Career Center Research Report, Columbia University Graduate School of Business, 1985.

Hayes, Robert and Wheelwright, Steven. *Restoring Our Competitive Edge.* New York: Wiley, 1984.

Heilbroner, Robert. *An Inquiry into the Human Condition.* New York: Norton, 1973.

Hornstein, Harvey. *Managerial Courage.* New York: Wiley, 1986.

Iacocca, Lee. "Commencement Address," University of Michigan, Ann Arbor, April 30, 1983.

Jaques, Eliot. *A General Theory of Bureaucracy.* New York: Halsted Press, Wiley, 1976.

Kanter, Rosabeth. *The Change Masters.* New York: Simon & Schuster, 1983.

Levinson, Harry, and Rosenthal, Stuart. *CEO.* New York: Basic Books, 1984.

Likert, Rensis. *The Human Organization.* New York: McGraw-Hill, 1967.

Maccoby, Michael. *The Gamesman.* New York: Simon & Schuster, 1976.

Maccoby, Michael. *The Leader.* New York: Ballantine Books, 1981.

Machiavelli, N. *The Prince.* New York: Mentor Press, (Original work, 1513) 1962.

Martin, Joanne, and Tichy, Noel. "Corporate Culture as a Strategic Difference." Graduate School of Business, University of Michigan, Working Paper, August 1982.

Maslow, A. *Motivation and Personality.* New York: Harper, 1954.

McCall, M. W., Jr., *Leaders and Leadership: Of Substance and Shadow.* Technical Report No. 2. Center for Creative Leadership, Greensboro, NC, 1977.

McCall, M. W., Jr., and Lombardo, M. M. *Off the Track: Why and How Successful Executives Get Derailed.* Technical Report No. 21. Center for Creative Leadership, Greensboro, NC, 1983.

Merton, Robert. *Social Theory and Social Structure* (rev. ed.). Glencoe, IL: Free Press, 1957.

Mintzberg, Henry. *The Nature of Managerial Work*. New York: Harper & Row, 1973.

Ouchi, William. *Theory Z: How American Business Can Meet the Japanese Challenge*. Reading, MA: Addison-Wesley, 1981.

Peters, Thomas, and Waterman, Robert. *In Search of Excellence*. New York: Harper & Row, 1982.

Pettigrew, Andrew. *The Awakening Giant*. New York: Blackwell, 1985.

Prahalad, C. K., and Doz, Y. L. *Managing Managers: The Work of Top Management*. Seventh NATO Conference on Leadership, St. Catherine's Oxford, July 12–17, 1982.

Quinn, James Brian. *Strategies for Change*. Oxford, England: Irwin, 1980.

Romanelli, Elaine, and Tushman, Michael. "Executive Leadership and Organizational Outcomes: An Evolutionary Perspective." Strategy Research Center, Graduate School of Business, Columbia University, 1983.

Schein, Edgar. *Organizational Culture and Leadership*. San Francisco: Josey-Bass, 1985.

Schon, Donald. *Beyond the Stable State*. New York: Random House, 1978.

Schumpeter, Joseph. *Capitalism, Socialism and Democracy*. New York: Harper Torchbooks, 1950.

Simon, H. A. *The New Science of Management Decision*. New York: Harper, 1960.

Taylor, F. W. *The Principles of Scientific Management*. New York: Harper, 1923.

Thurow, Lester. *The Zero Sum Solution*. New York: Simon & Schuster, 1985.

Tichy, Noel. "Networks in Organizations," in Paul Nystrom and William Starbuck (eds.), *Handbook of Organizational Design*, Vol. 2. New York: Oxford University Press, 1981.

Tichy, Noel. *Managing Strategic Change*. New York: Wiley, 1983.

Tichy, Noel, and Ulrich, David. "The Leadership Challenge—A Call for the Transformational Leader." *Sloan Management Review*, Fall 1984.

Tuchman, Barbara. *The March of Folly*. New York: Knopf, 1984.

Vroom, V. H. *Work and Motivation*. New York: Wiley, 1964.

Watson, Thomas. *A Business and Its Beliefs: The Ideas that Helped Build IBM*. New York: McGraw-Hill, 1963.

Welch, John. F., "Competitiveness from Within—Beyond Incrementalism," Hatfield Fellow Lecture, Cornell University, April 26, 1984.

White, Theodore S., "The Danger from Japan." *The New York Times Magazine,* July 28, 1985.

Zaleznik, A., "Managers and Leaders: Are They Different?" *Harvard Business Review*, Vol. 55, No. 5, 1977.

Zaleznik, A., "The Leadership Gap," *Washington Quarterly*, Vol. 6, No. 1, 1983.

Zaleznik, A., and Kets de Vries, M., *Power and the Corporate Mind.* Boston: Houghton Mifflin, 1975.

INDEX